Human Sexuality

A PRELIMINARY STUDY

The United Church of Christ

United Church Press
New York • Philadelphia

Biblical quotations, unless otherwise indicated, are from the
Revised Standard Version of the Bible, copyright 1946, 1952, and
© 1971 by the Division of Christian Education, National Council
of Churches, and are used by permission. Scriptural excerpt
marked NEB is from *The New English Bible,* © The Delegates of
the Oxford University Press and the Syndics of the Cambridge
University Press, 1961, 1970. Reprinted by permission.

Excerpts from "Androgyny vs. the Tight Little Lives of Fluffy
Women and Chesty Men" by Sandra Lipsitz Bem (pages 132, 134)
and "How Nursery Schools Teach Girls to Shut Up" by Lisa A.
Serbin and K. Daniel O'Leary (pages 127-29) are reprinted from
Psychology Today magazine and are copyright © 1975 by the
Ziff-Davis Publishing Company. Used by permission.

Library of Congress Cataloging in Publication Data

United Church of Christ.
 Human sexuality.

 Bibliography: p. 255
 Includes index.
 1. Sex and religion. 2. Sex in the Bible.
3. Sexual ethics. 4. Sex instruction. I. Title.
HQ61.U54 261.8'34'17 77-25398
ISBN 0-8298-0341-6 pbk.

United Church Press, 287 Park Avenue South, New York, New York 10010

Contents

PREFACE   9

TOWARD A DEFINITION OF SEXUALITY   12

CHAPTER 1: A Collage—Some Facts and Perspectives   14
The Current Situation   17
Scientific and Medical Factors   18
Youth and Young Adult Data   20
Family Life and Marriage-related Data   22
Minority Perspectives on Sexuality   24
The Women's Movement   28
The Gay Movement   29

CHAPTER 2: Biblical Foundations   31
Some Principles of Biblical Interpretation   31
Biblical Culture and Religion: Patriarchalism
    and Androcentrism   35
    Legal Codes: Woman Disenfranchised   36
    Wisdom Literature: The Proverbial Woman   38
    Historical Writings: Emerging Real Women   39
    Summary: Woman In/Beyond Culture   42
Point and Counterpoint: Liberating Texts and
    Renewing Themes   44
    Human Images of Yahweh: Mixed Metaphors   45
    Muted Themes: Exodus, Ruth, Jeremiah 31:22   47
    Eve and Adam: Genesis 2—3 Reread   57
    Song of Songs: Sex Without Sin   64
    Man and Man: Genesis 19:1-11;
        Leviticus 18:22; 20:13   68
    The Sodom and Gomorrah Story   68
    The Levitical Holiness Code   72
    New Testament Perspectives on Human
        Sexuality   77

CHAPTER 3: Faith, Ethics, and Sexuality   **87**
     What Is the Meaning of Our Sexuality?   87
     How and Why Do We Experience Alienation
          from Our Sexuality?   89
     How Can We Experience Reconciliation
          with Our Sexuality?   92
     What Goes into a Decision About
          a Sex-related Issue?   96
     What Are Some Principles for Sexual Morality?   103

CHAPTER 4: Psychosexual Development   **106**
     Demythologizing Psychosexual Development
          Theories   106
     A Review of Variant Theories   109
     Toward a New Understanding   111
     The Old and the New   112
     Transcending the Status Quo   114
     Science Correcting Science   116
     Current Research in Psychosexual Development   116
     Sex-role Stereotyping   120
     Toward a New Definition of Mental Health   129
     Masculine, Feminine, or Both   131
     A Comparison of Old and New Perspectives   134
     Additional Questions for Consideration   135

CHAPTER 5: Sexuality and
          Public Policy—An Overview   **142**
     Sexuality and Women   144
          Sexual Self-determination   144
          The Economics of Female Sexuality   150
          Women's Sexuality and Violence   155
          Women and Economic Justice   164
     Sexuality and Men   166
     Young People and Sexuality   167
     Sexuality and Older Persons   170
     Sexuality and Single Persons   172
     Sexuality and the Gay Community   173

Handicapped Persons and Sexuality   177
Sexuality and Institutionalized Persons   179
    Prisons   179
    Institutions for the Mentally Ill and/or
        Mentally Retarded   180
    The Military   181
Issues Affecting Sexual Practice and
        Understanding   183
    Sexuality and the Mass Media   183
    Sexuality and New Birth Technologies   184
    Transsexuals   187
The Family and Human Sexuality   188
    The De Facto Family   188
    Pressures on the Family   189
    Toward Humane Public Policy   190

CHAPTER 6: Some Perspectives on Sex Education   192
    A Brief History of Sex Education   193
    The Need for Sex Education   195
    The Role of the Family   197
    The Role of the School   200
    What Is Sex Education?   201
    Approaches to Sex Education   204
    Implementing a Sex Education Program   206
    The Role of the Sex Educator   207
    Choosing Appropriate Resources   209
    Meeting the Needs of the Whole Person   210

CHAPTER 7: The Community of Faith and
        Human Sexuality   214
    Some United Church of Christ Yearnings   215
    The Bible and Our Common Life   216
    The Church—The Body   217
    The Covenanting People   219
    A Community of Love   220
    Rite and Sacrament   221
    The Civil Covenant   224

Congregational Life-style   225
Education   227
Leadership   230

APPENDIX: United Church of Christ Background   233

NOTES   243

BIBLIOGRAPHY   255

Preface

The United Church Board for Homeland Ministries was commissioned to do this study to fulfill the following vote of the 1975 General Synod of the United Church of Christ:

> The United Church of Christ has not faced in depth the issue of human sexuality. Changing morality and ethics within American society present both problems and challenges to the church.
>
> Therefore, the Tenth General Synod requests the Executive Council to commission a study concerning the dynamics of human sexuality and to recommend postures for the church.

One might ask, "What's a nice church like yours doing in an area like this?" Our history, our present concerns, and the pains and joys of people all direct us to see sexuality as a vital area of ministry.

The United Church of Christ traces its roots to
—the Reformation earthiness of Martin Luther;
—the concern for the common life of John Calvin;
—the authority-defying dissent and imprisonment of British Separatists in the sixteenth and seventeenth centuries;
—Pilgrims who sought a holy commonwealth in a new world;
—Anne Hutchinson who defended a woman's right to know and speak;
—Pennsylvania German men and women who covenanted to marry and to farm in mutuality;
—men and women who fought slavery and created schools for women and ministries where there were none, who fought for just laws, sexual equality, and the right of the young to know.

It is consistent with this denomination to see sexuality as part of the total human experience and to insist that questions of sexual justice are as important for Christians as matters of sexual expression. The United Church of Christ has a long history of concern for civil rights. It was the first denomination to ordain women. The Antoinette Brown Award is given in honor of the woman who, in 1853, broke the sex barrier in ministry.

This book is the product of a wide inquiry into the issues of human sexuality. In the early stages of the sexuality study, major efforts were given to definitional work. A variety of church groups offered their input. Minority caucuses, the Gay Caucus, and the Advisory Commission on Women in Church and Society of the United Church of Christ were invaluable.

A staff team worked in season and out to shape the study's directions and then its conclusions. They are a superb body of persons—insightful, dedicated, resourceful. The team consisted of Holly Henderson from the Office for Church Life and Leadership, Barry Lynn from the Office for Church in Society, and these members of the United Church Board for Homeland Ministries' staff: Mary Ellen Haines, Edward A. Powers, Susan Savell, Barbara Jones Weeks, and Ralph Weltge.

A team of consultants provided valuable insights into sexuality from the perspective of their several disciplines:

—Yoshio Fukuyama, head, Department of Religious Studies, Pennsylvania State University—sociological perspectives on sexuality and family life; Asian-American perspectives.

—Beverly Wildung Harrison, associate professor of Christian Ethics, Union Theological Seminary—ethical approaches, especially with regard to public policy.

—Eleanor Morrison, faculty, Department of Community Medicine, Michigan State University—psychosexual development and sex education.

—James B. Nelson, professor of Christian Ethics, United Theological Seminary—ethical approaches to sexuality.

—Richard L. Scheef, Jr., professor of New Testament, Eden Theological Seminary—New Testament perspectives on sexuality.

—Robert Staples, associate professor and chairman of Graduate Program in Sociology, University of California Medical School—minority perspectives on sexuality, sociological dimensions.

—Phyllis Trible, Samuel A. Hitchcock Professor of the Hebrew Language and Literature, Andover Newton Theological School—Old Testament perspectives on sexuality.

Some special people shared their perspectives and competence. They have influenced this book in ways known and unknown. The staff team is especially grateful to Samuel Acosta, Helen Barnhill, Barbara Bragonier, Robert Bragonier, Davida Foy Crabtree, John Deckenback, Barbara Gerlach, Norman Jackson, William

Johnson, Harold Jow, Chris Keff, Nancy Krody, William Longs-dorf, Robert V. Moss, Jr., Rey O'Day, Valerie Russell, Donna Schaper, Roger Shinn, Mary Terada, and Peggy Way. Alison McClure and Marjorie Winchester did major work in preparing the final manuscript.

The study team made some choices about where to put energies. These choices are reflected in the continuity and contents of this book. Our definition of sexuality is foundational. We begin with some of the contextual contours of sexuality today. Major concentration is given to biblical interpretation and some specific texts that provide guidance for an understanding of sexuality. Chapter 3, on ethics, points toward principles for ethical behavior. Chapter 4, on psychosexual development, is descriptive of scientific understandings, their flux and direction. The public policy chapter (Chapter 5) addresses sexual justice issues. Chapter 6 is direction-pointing, regarding sex education. The final chapter understands the church as a special community of grace in which our sexuality is acknowledged, judged, and celebrated.

While this book emerged from the widespread collaboration of the study process and the diverse insights this provided, some of us wrote particular chapters. We believe credit should be given where it is due. Ralph Weltge wrote Chapter 2, "Biblical Foundations," except for "Genesis 2—3 Reread," which was written by Phyllis Trible, and the New Testament section, which was drafted by Richard Scheef. James Nelson wrote Chapter 3, "Faith, Ethics, and Sexuality." The chapters on psycho-sexual development and sex education were written by Mary Ellen Haines. Barry Lynn and Susan Savell wrote the public policy chapter. The introductory chapter and the last chapter, "The Community of Faith and Human Sexuality," were prepared by Edward A. Powers. Holly Henderson and Edward A. Powers wrote a study guide, which is available separately.

The staff team is profoundly grateful to Howard E. Spragg, executive vice president, and to the board of directors of the United Church Board for Homeland Ministries for their faith in us and their strong support. We rejoice in the excellent response of the 1977 General Synod and hope this book will have wide use. We consider it a preliminary report and invite response to it through use of the feedback form in the study guide. We rejoice in our sexuality and in yours. A gracious, holy God has made that a special gift to the human community. We rejoice in our creation and in our Creator!

Edward A. Powers
Sexuality Study Administrator

Toward a Definition
of Sexuality

One's sexuality involves the total sense of self as male and female, man and woman, as well as perceptions of what it is for others to be female and male. It includes attitudes about one's body and others' bodies. It expresses one's definition of gender identity. Sexuality is emotional, physical, cognitive, value-laden, and spiritual. Its dimensions are both personal and social.

A distinction should be made at the outset between sex and sexuality. Sex refers to the physical act of making love, to genital expression. "Sex is, in fact, only a small part of sexuality. . . . Sexuality is, then, an integrated, individualized, unique expression of self."[1]

Sexuality is *emotional.* The infant person experiences what is later understood to be sexuality as it is fed and cuddled, in the sense of warmth or distance between bodies, in comfort or discomfort at wetness or dryness of body, in pleasurable sensations of one's own body. In the early years the child experiences bodily pleasure and discovers sensuality. With the coming of puberty boys and girls experience new awareness of their bodies, other persons, and related emotions. Throughout all of life sexuality deals with one's feelings about self and others, pain and pleasure, distance and closeness, love and hate, physical touching or restraint.

Sexuality is *physical.* It involves touching, physical closeness, and genital sexual expression. It is expressive of the desire for human contact and satisfaction of the need for closeness, intimacy, and physical pleasure. All five senses are involved in one's sexuality.

Sexuality is *cognitive.* Mental attitudes, self-understanding, analyses of human experience and relationships help express who and what persons are as sexual beings. One's understandings of genitalia, coitus, nakedness, other- and same-sex roles affect the body and its sexual expressions. Language is a key part of our sexuality both in naming bodily parts, physical acts, and our own experiences, and in communication with other persons.

Sexuality is *value-laden*. One's sense of the ought, the fitting, the possible, and the communal reflect value systems and ethical structures. Words and concepts such as justice, love, norm, should, and should not are ethical in character and central to a full understanding of sexuality. Values relate both to self-understanding and to expectations of others and of social structures. Values shape how and what persons communicate to one another. One's values determine approaches to honesty, fidelity, promise-keeping, truth-telling, and the purposes of sexual expression.

Sexuality is *spiritual*. The sexual act involves mutual self-giving. The spirit of one person relates deeply to the spirit of another. One chooses to relate to another and to oneself. There is a voluntary surrender of self to another through which a larger unity is achieved without the abridgement of freedom. Elements of transcendence, commitment, being in touch with another and with oneself are involved in one's sexuality and relationships to others as sexual beings. For Christians, sexuality is understood as the gift of God and as a dimension through which the love of God and neighbor is expressed.

Sexuality is *personal*. Each person is a sexual being on her or his own terms. In that sense one's sexuality is unique, one of a kind. "Our sexuality belongs first and foremost to us. It is pleasure we want to give and get. It is vital physical expression of attachments to other human beings. It is communication that is fun and playful, serious and passionate."[2]

Sexuality is *social*. It involves couples or partners. It has familial and community of caring contexts. Our sexuality has a bearing on the approach of such issues as war, economics, politics, or national priorities. It relates to such social policy questions as rape laws, equality of women and men in matters of employment, guidelines for genetic research, and abortion. It affects cultural understandings of socialization as male and female, the role of pornography, the meanings of marriage and community.

Sexuality is a central dimension of each person's selfhood, but it is not the whole of that selfhood. It is a critical component of each person's self-understanding and of how each relates to the world.

CHAPTER 1

A Collage—Some Facts and Perspectives

This chapter is impressionistic. It seeks to focus momentarily on those issues (historic and contemporary) that provide the cultural context in which ethical approaches must be developed. These staccato motifs are heard in the setting of the church's historic and long-term commitments to fidelity in human relationships, to the covenant of marriage and faithfulness, and to sexuality as one of the gifts of the good God.

The character of sexual practice, marriage, and family relationships has changed over time. This study cannot do full justice to the historical data of various eras of Christian history or to their perspectives on sexuality. But it can give a few impressions from which a fuller portrait may subsequently be drawn:

The people of God in Old Testament times found the commandment "be fruitful and multiply" to be a survival ethic. They lived in a patriarchal culture, with an extended family pattern in which women were understood to be property. This perspective is spelled out more fully in Chapter 2, "Biblical Foundations." The Jewish tradition emphasized the twin obligations to marry and to procreate. Marriage is seen as a religious duty. If a woman is widowed, it is the duty of the deceased husband's brother to marry her and provide offspring to carry on the lineage.

The sanctions regarding adultery, divorce, prostitution, polygamy, and concubinage were set in the context of enhancing marriage, assuring offspring, and sustaining the patriarchal scheme. Adultery was regarded as a violation of the husband's property rights. Polygamy and concubinage were allowed or encouraged when a marriage did not produce children. The prohibition against prostitution was primarily because of its association with primitive religions. It was seen as an act of idolatry. Under certain circumstances, a husband was permitted to divorce his wife; the wife had no such rights.

Greek and Roman patterns varied, but as Chapter 3, "Faith, Ethics, and Sexuality," notes, there is a strong component of spirit-body dualism. The ancient Greeks developed sexual ethics to refer to a variety of conditions not restricted alone to the marital state. In Roman civilization, marriage was the dominant motif. Over a period of time, laws regulating it developed that eventually applied to all citizens. As the Roman empire began to deteriorate, in the early centuries of the Christian era, its decline was blamed on sexual immorality and lack of respect for the marital state.

The development of sexual ethics in the Christian era relied heavily upon the biblical understandings noted above. Christian understandings developed in relation to three forces: the sexually licentious practices of much of the secular culture and some religious traditions, Gnostic and other views that were negative about sexual pleasure and saw the body as evil, and the growing importance of intentional celibacy as a life-style.

Augustine emphasized the procreative element in sexual expression. His writing furthered the development of the institution of marriage. His early experience with sexuality left him with a strong conviction of sin, and he saw sexual pleasure as a consequence of sin. Thomas Aquinas modified some of the earlier Augustinian views and saw sexual pleasure guided by reason as natural. During the Middle Ages, marriage came to be seen as a sacrament and as being under the regulatory power of the church. Most of the thinking concerning marriage and sexuality during this period was done by celibate persons in monasteries, thus leading to an exaltation of virginity.

Yoshio Fukuyama emphasizes the church's struggle through this period:

> Throughout the Middle Ages, the Church was engaged in constant battle with the open sexuality which prevailed, much of it carried over from pre-Christian times. As early as the eighth century the Church tried to popularize and establish monogamous marriages as unbreakable during the lives of the partners, but the actual practices of the people led to numerous accommodations.
>
> For example, a tenth century Anglo-Saxon ordinance allowed trial marriages for seven years; in Scotland, until the Reformation, trial marriage was permitted for one year.[1]

The Reformation focused in significant ways on sexuality-related issues. The issue of celibacy was addressed directly and the phenomenon of married clergy began to appear. Both Luther and Calvin emphasized the sanctity of marriage and affirmed the biblical notion of sex as God's gift. Yet, each was influenced by Augustine's notion of original sin as a complicating factor in sexuality.

As a sociologist, Yoshio Fukuyama reflects on the historical interplay of family and culture. He notes the interdependence of cultural perspectives and patterns of familial and sexual behavior. The Puritan family is a case in point:

According to Edmund Seares Morgan,[2] the Puritans believed that it was "a natural instinct" for parents to "Feed and Nourish, to take care of, and protect their young Ones." The "fundamental duties" of Puritan marriages were "Peaceable cohabitation, sexual union and faithfulness, and economic support of the wife by the husband." Upon marriage, the woman "gave up everything to her husband and devoted herself exclusively to managing the household." She was considered to be "the weaker vessel in both body and mind, and her husband ought not to expect too much from her." In arranging marriages, "the most important factor affecting the choice was the social rank of the persons involved."

For these Puritans, whose primary goal in life was "to love God and to glorify Him forever," the sole purpose of sexual union was to reproduce the human species, obeying the Biblical command "to be fruitful and multiply."

There sociological functions of the Puritan family were given theological and Biblical sanctions "by the usual metaphor by which the relation of Christ and the believer was designated."

Interestingly enough, the nurture of children was not completed within the Puritan family. At age 14, boys were generally sent out as apprentices, living with the master and learning a trade until they were able to be on their own; girls were often "put out" in the same way to learn housekeeping away from the parental roof.

The reason for these practices, suggested by Morgan, was that Puritan parents did not trust themselves with their own children, that they were afraid of spoiling them by too great affection.

The foregoing description of the Puritan family embodies the four basic functions usually ascribed to the family by sociologists: the family controls sexual access, it serves to nurture and socialize the young, it has an economic function, and the family is a means of ascribing social status.[3]

Christian thinkers through the generations before the present have sought ways to understand their sexuality and to determine norms and standards for sexual behavior. To do our historical homework means to be in touch with changing understandings of the nature of sexuality and with the attempts to bring to sexual expression adequate ethical standards and to develop cultural forms that nurture the fullness of human life. As we face almost staggering challenges and threats to American institutions in our time, it is important to know that the human race has faced changing patterns before and has found sustaining models for ethics and family life.

THE CURRENT SITUATION

In recent years enormous changes in American social patterns have taken place. Better statistics are now kept, of course, and debate continues about whether there is a sexual revolution or just a steady evolution bolstered by more accurate data. In either case, the demographic facts are startling:

In a report released on February 8, 1977, the Census Bureau reported that 1,320,000 unmarried Americans lived with a member of the opposite sex in a two-person household. This represents an increase from 654,000 in 1970. Of these persons 48 percent of the men and 43 percent of the women had never been married.

In the same report the bureau stated that the divorce rate had more than doubled between 1963 and 1975, rising from 2.3 per 1,000 population to 4.6 in 1975. In 1976 there were 2.8 million divorced men and 4.4 million divorced women who had not remarried.

According to a 1976 survey of the bureau, the number of persons between the ages of twenty-five and thirty-four who have never married has increased by almost 50 percent since 1970, from 2.8 million to 4.2 million persons. The number of persons in that age group heading their own households grew from 915,000 to 1.8 million, while the number living alone grew from 592,000 to 1.2 million during the same period. The median age at which people married climbed from 23.2 years to 23.8 years for men and from 20.3 years to 21.3 years for women.

From 1970 to 1976 the number of families with both husband and wife included declined from 81.2% to 76.9%. In 1976, 10% of US families had a female head, 2% had a male head, and 23% of all adults lived singly. In 1975 women constituted 40% of the labor force. Of women living with their husbands, 44.4% were employed. More than half the women with children age six to seventeen and a third of the women with children under six were employed.

Increased public attention is being given to patterns of sexual expression. The Kinsey reports of 1948 and 1953 have been followed by such studies as Morton Hunt's *Sexual Behavior in the '70's* (1974) and Shere Hite's *The Hite Report: A Nationwide Study of Female Sexuality* (1976). Hite discusses female experience with masturbation, orgasm, intercourse, and lesbianism. The questionnaire she is using for a study of male sexual experience will secure similar data, along with information about sadomasochism and rape.

Redbook sampled 100,000 women and reported the findings in its September 1975 issue. A summary of the findings covering marital sex is as follows:

> Sexual satisfaction is related significantly to religious belief. With notable consistency the greater the intensity of a woman's religious convictions, the likelier she is to be highly satisfied with the sexual pleasures of marriage.
>
> Regardless of how long they have been married, whether just one year or more than ten, a high and virtually constant percentage of wives (almost 7 out of 10) report sex with their husbands as "good" or "very good." . . .
>
> Oral-genital sex is an almost universal experience. . . .
>
> Regardless of age, education, income, and religious belief, the majority of women are active partners in sex.[4]

The best-seller lists have been dominated by books related to sexuality and sexual practice. The Boston Women's Health Collectives' book *Our Bodies, Ourselves,* first published in 1972, has sold a million and a half copies. Alex Comfort's *The Joy of Sex* has sold 3.5 million copies. Marabel Morgan's *Total Woman* has had sales of 3 million copies.

SCIENTIFIC AND MEDICAL FACTORS
A number of scientific and medical factors affect our understandings of sexuality today and our sexual practices.

Over the last generation a veritable revolution in birth control technology has taken place. The Pill has been in use for twenty years, and the number of American women using it is estimated at over 10 million. In the late 1960s the copper-bearing intra-uterine device became available, and it is now estimated that these are used by 3 to 5 million American women. Of course, condoms, diaphragms, and foam are still available and are widely used. The availability to women of reliable contraceptive devices has been an important factor in enhancing women's freedom and self-determination.

The rise in the incidence of abortions is great. Abortion became legal again with the January 22, 1973 decisions of the Supreme Court.[5] "Legal" means safer, since abortions are now done under adequate medical standards, and "legal" means more widely available to those who could not have abortions because of lack of money, transportation, or knowledge. "Since the court legalized abortions, 3.6 million of them have been performed in this country."[6]

Terri Schulz documents further the impact of legalization:

Now, since legalization, the number of abortions is more than twice as high for lower-income black women than for middle-income white women: 31 per 1,000 women of childbearing age compared with 14 per 1,000 of that age. These figures indicate that many poor, minority group women who want abortions are in fact now able to obtain them. One reason is that clinics often accept Medicaid payments, thus opening even private facilities to the poor.

Because abortion is more readily available, fewer women at all social levels are dying from self-induced or other unskilled abortions. Before the Supreme Court decision, there were 30 deaths for every 100,000 illegal operations. Today, as the most common non-diagnostic surgery, abortion is safer than tonsil-lectomy or even childbirth. There are 3.1 deaths per 100,000 legal abortions, compared with 15 for every 100,000 live births. In addition to reducing deaths, abortion saves taxpayers $550 million a year in welfare costs that the Department of Health, Education and Welfare estimates would have gone to support unwanted babies born to low-income women. Medicaid spends about $50 million a year in taxpayers' money to pay for abortions for these women, so the cost benefits are clear.[7]

The scientific and the medical communities have made some incredible strides forward in areas related to human sexuality. Over the past decade most medical schools have developed programs in human sexuality. The monthly magazine *Medical Aspects of Human Sexuality* is now a decade old. *Postgraduate Medicine, The Journal of Applied Medicine for Physicians Providing Primary Care* devoted its July 1975 issue to the topic "Removing the Plain Brown Wrapper from Sexuality and Sexual Health."

The World Health Organization held a meeting in 1975 on "Education and Treatment in Human Sexuality: The Training of Health Professionals." It was reported that

> a growing body of knowledge indicates that problems in human sexuality are more pervasive and more important to the well being and health of individuals in many cultures than has previously been recognized and that there are important relationships between sexual ignorance and misconceptions and diverse problems of health and the quality of life. While recognizing that it is difficult to arrive at a universally acceptable definition of the totality of human sexuality, the following definition of sexual health is presented as a step in this direction:
>
> Sexual health is the integration of the somatic, emotional, intellectual, and social aspects of sexual being, in ways that are positively enriching and that enhance personality, communication, and love.
>
> Fundamental to this concept are the right to sexual information and the right to pleasure.[8]

William H. Masters and Virginia E. Johnson have pioneered in research on what happens to bodily processes when sexual intercourse takes place. In the Reproductive Biology Research Foundation in St. Louis, which they codirect, Masters and Johnson have given major attention to how to overcome sexual dysfunction. The early work of Masters and Johnson was on the sexual dysfunction of heterosexual married couples. Of late their work has also included the problems of homosexual couples.

Additional developments in the scientific field are detailed in later sections of this report—research on human development (John Money and others, Chapter 4, "Psychosexual Development"), genetic developments (Chapter 5, "Sexuality and Public Policy: An Overview"), and sex-role development (Chapter 4).

YOUTH AND YOUNG ADULT DATA
In 1976 the Alan Guttmacher Institute published for the Planned Parenthood Federation of America a research summary called

11 Million Teenagers: What Can Be Done About the Epidemic of Adolescent Pregnancies in the United States.[9] The 11 million figure refers to the number of sexually active members of the US population of 21 million persons in the fifteen- to nineteen-year-old age group. The report contends that 20 percent of the 8 million thirteen- and fourteen-year-olds are sexually active. One fifth of all US births are to women in their teens; 247,000 of these are to those seventeen and younger.

The incidence of venereal disease, especially among teenagers, has reached epidemic proportions. Studies suggest that the majority of sexually active teenagers are unfamiliar with or do not use contraceptive devices. This heightens the spread of venereal disease as well as having the obvious effect upon teenage pregnancies that has been reported in the Guttmacher study.

In the case of teenage pregnancy the risks to the physical and mental health of mother and child are high, especially in the younger teen years. In 1974 the 1 million teenage pregnancies terminated as follows: 28% were marital births conceived following marriage; 10% were marital births conceived prior to marriage; 21% were out-of-wedlock births; 27% were terminated by induced abortion; 14% miscarried.

The Guttmacher study contends that

> very few of the 4.3 million sexually active 15–19-year-old women want to become mothers while they are so young. Even among the 1.1 million who are married, only about 275,000 are having a wanted pregnancy or seeking one in any given year. Of the 3.2 million who are unmarried, perhaps 80,000 may want to have children out of wedlock in a single year (assuming that responses of unmarried mothers to surveys *after* they have had their babies accurately reflect their wishes *before* conception).
>
> Thus, nearly four million sexually active 15–19-year-olds are at risk of having an unintended pregnancy during each year in the mid-1970's, and one in six of those at risk actually do get pregnant every year. In addition to the 15- to 19-year-olds, 420,000 to 630,000 13- and 14-year-old girls are at risk of having unintended pregnancies, of whom 30,000 become pregnant.[10]

These statistics reflect changing cultural patterns. Symptomatic of such changes is the rock music industry. *Human Behavior*, in its July 1976 issue, summarized the change: "A decade ago, the Rolling Stones found it almost impossible to get 'Let's Spend the Night Together' played on radio. But today, radio has become crammed with climactic groans." The Rev. Jesse L. Jackson, president of PUSH (People United to Save Humanity), has conducted a major campaign with record companies and radio stations on the grounds that his organization's effort among school children, "Push for Excellence," was being undermined by records that promoted promiscuity and drug use.

The Miami Valley Young Adult Ministry, Inc., which is primarily a campus ministry enterprise, did a survey of the young adult population in the Dayton, Ohio area. The results show a high degree of religious affinity, with 75% of the group surveyed reporting that they read the Bible, 80% saying they pray, and 90% saying they believe in God or a universal spirit. Their answers to three questions bear upon sexuality issues: Do you think it is wrong to have sexual relations before marriage? (78% no) Is it all right to use artificial methods of birth control? (86% yes) In your opinion are relations between consenting homosexuals morally wrong? (38% yes; 49% no)

FAMILY LIFE AND MARRIAGE-RELATED DATA
Sociologist Yoshio Fukuyama locates the beginnings of the present crisis in sexuality in the changing functions of the American family and the subsequent effect upon family members, especially as women's self-perceptions and roles change. He contends that

> the content of morality is in part determined by social forces and technological change. The pervasiveness of urbanization and industrialization has radically altered our interpersonal relationships; kinship relations have been weakened and urban life has been characterized by anonymity and segmented relationships. The growing mobility of our population—both geographical and social—has exposed us to alternative values and life styles; the rapidity of technological change, particularly in mass communications and the knowledge explosion, all impinge upon and challenge traditional ways of looking at ourselves and the world around us.[11]

Fukuyama describes the family in Western society as having five basic functions: (1) to control sexual access; (2) to provide an orderly context for the reproduction of the species; (3) to care for, nurture, and socialize the child; (4) to provide the context for economic activity and support; (5) to ascribe social status.

Currently, these functions have changed significantly or are shared with other institutions or social structures. If the Guttmacher statistics are any indication, control of sexual access is obviously not working.

Family types in the United States are extremely diverse. The breakdown is as follows:

Nuclear family (husband, wife, and offspring living in an intact common household)—37%

Couple (husband and wife alone—childless or no children living at home)—11%

Single-parent family (one head as a consequence of divorce, death, abandonment, or separation and usually including pre-school and/or school-age children)—12%

Remarried nuclear family (husband, wife, and offspring living in a common household)—11%

Kin network (three-generation households or extended families) —4%

Single without children—19%

Emerging experimental forms (commune-type family group-ings)—6%[12]

Studies done by the United Church Board for Homeland Ministries indicate the following demography in 1,000 United Church of Christ congregations: 71.6% of the members are presently married, 10.2% are widowed, 15.6% are single, 2.2% are divorced, and 0.5% are separated from their spouses.[13] (It should be noted that 8.4% of those included in the report are under age twenty.) Two pieces of age-related data are also perti-nent to the sexuality study. A relatively small proportion of United Church of Christ active members are in the twenty to thirty-four age group (17.1%), while a substantial proportion are in older age categories (fully 33.1% over sixty).

Since 29 percent of United Church of Christ members are not presently married, and since this segment in the culture represents an even larger percentage, it is clear that this is a major popula-tion group to which attention must be paid. Singles come in all shapes and sizes. They are the never-marrieds, the formerly-marrieds, the widowed, the divorced, those who live alone, and those who live together in various patterns of intimacy. Many single persons choose that status and the life-style they live as single persons. Many are forced into singleness through circumstances for which they are not at all or only partially responsible.

Single persons are sexual beings. They possess all the elements of the definition of sexuality found in this study. Their patterns of relationship as men and women are diverse. The forms of their sexual expression vary. Some are celibate. Others participate in a sustained primary relationship with a person of the same or other sex. Others are sexually and relationally pluralistic. Morton Hunt reports that 75 percent of single adult women have had sexual intercourse by age twenty-five.

Many single persons are heads of households, and they face the same problems of breadwinning, parenting, homemaking, friendship, and leisure-time activity that two-parent households face, except they face these alone.

MINORITY PERSPECTIVES ON SEXUALITY

The collage of facts and perspectives that this chapter represents can only hint at the diversity of human experience which enriches American cultural understanding. *Roots* has dramatized the radical differences between the experiences of Black and of white settlers in this country. The whites were immigrants, with a large measure of freedom of choice. The Blacks were stolen from their homes, families, and cultural setting. The new families that Black persons created in this country were under constant threat of separation as well as of indignities to their person. These experiences and those of racist dominance are part of the sexual history of both Black and white Americans. Robert Staples summarizes:

> It should be understood that Blacks arrived in this country from societies where the sexual impulse was under firm family and community controls. . . . It was under the experience of slavery that pronounced alterations of Black sexual behavior transpired. The practice of breeding slaves like animals, the coercive nature of sex relations between white men and Black women, the lack of a legal basis to marriage all tended to encourage permissive sexual behavior among America's Black population.[14]

Staples sees the myth of Black persons being sexually hyperactive as a form of racism and sexism that has deep roots in American culture. He contends that

24

any objective examination of Black sexual behavior would reveal that there are many variations in the type and frequency of sexual activity among this group; that the racial differences have their origin in cultural and class differences, not innate biological traits and that changes in time and space have brought about a convergence in the sexual attitudes and behavior of the two racial groups. Furthermore, it is instructive to note that the white fear of Black hypersexuality stems from a racism and sexism against which Blacks and women must constantly struggle. To be specific, the white group's resistance has been to Black male-white female sexual liaisons. Historically, white males had access to Black women, through force or economic inducement. In this transaction, Black women were often unwilling partners while white women and Black men violated the taboo on their sexual union at the risk of their freedom or lives.[15]

Black persons and families have developed unusual solidarity in resisting the demonic claims of racism and in building sustaining family relationships.

The Commission on Human Sexuality, created by the Pacific and Asian American Ministries of the United Church of Christ (PAAM), identified several parts of the Asian heritage that helped to shape patterns of human sexuality. In answer to the question "What aspects of our Asian culture and heritage assist us in developing a positive attitude toward human sexuality?" the PAAM study group concluded:

The importance of the family as the basic unit in society.
The family name is to be perpetuated through marriage.

The role of parents, children, and relatives is clearly spelled out:
Dominant role of the father as decision-maker;
Supportive role of mother;
Respect for elders;
Children trained to be obedient to elders and parents.
There is a specific name for each familial and social relationship, in contrast to occidental culture with names that are inclusive.

Chinese teachings and proverbs are moral in character in contrast to occidental proverbs, which are generally self-seeking.

High value is placed on education, reverence for scholars.

Respect for authority results in passive response to life, non-violent approach to problem-solving.

The marriage system is rigidly structured. Elements are matchmaking, dowry, genealogical research, family judgment on prospective couple, wife becoming part of the husband's family system.

Physical contact between the sexes is shunned in public, in socializing, and in sports.

Modesty is an Asian trait.

In Chinese culture, guilt feelings are absent.[16]

In a memorandum that was part of the study process, Yoshio Fukuyama describes changing patterns among Asian-Americans, especially those of Japanese descent. The extended family pattern is traditional, and the father is regarded as head of the household. Now, household chores are more fully shared and both parents often work outside the home. The *enryo* syndrome is a symbol of change.

The Japanese word *enryo* is perhaps best understood as "reticence" or "holding back," which means that there is a reluctance to be aggressive or outspoken in relation to whites. Real feelings often go unexpressed and aggressive behavior is frowned upon. Their children, the Sansei (third generation), are often characterized as being more aggressive and outspoken, and this is seen as another example of Japanese Americans becoming more like whites. The implication of this is that issues of sexuality which have traditionally been taboo, are becoming increasingly manifest in both discussion and behavior.[17]

Norman Jackson, speaking as chairperson of the Council for American Indian Ministry of the United Church of Christ, names two major elements in Native American experience that have important bearing on understandings of sexuality: First, Indian religion has both masculine and feminine elements that are strongly identified in defining the nature of God. There is a close interdependence of people and the earth, a wholistic view of man, woman, and nature. Second, Indian culture has clearly prescribed sex roles, but there is mutuality and equality of men and women.

The Hispanic Council gave attention to sexuality issues as part of the annual caucus convocation in November 1976. Samuel Acosta, council chairperson, summarized these views:

> Within our Latin heritage woman always has and will have a very important role. If we take, for example, the theological aspect, especially for those of us who come from a Roman Catholic tradition, the virgin always had and will continue to have an important place. The church, perhaps without being aware of it, gave woman an important place within the process of human creation.
>
> In music, poetry and literature in Latin America, the place of woman has been clearly marked.
>
> But despite these two dimensions, there has always been a lack of equality which is more apparent now that society is more aware of the elements which accentuate it. This inequality is reflected in the Latin *machismo* which gives the man total authority in the home, and outside it, leaving the woman a secondary role. This situation gives the man certain functions which are strictly his and the woman ones that are her own. Of course, the slow industrialization in Latin American countries and the means of communication which allow the women of the world to know what is happening in other parts of the earth, challenge this commonly accepted system.
>
> Machismo, taken into the sexual area has produced in Latin America and among the Latins a well-known double standard. Men require virginity of women, but they have the freedom to do whatever is convenient.
>
> All these things make us conscious that we are in a transition process. It is not possible to give a final verdict without first seeing the sociopolitical, economic and theological implications of these changes. But one thing the Latin Americans are conscious of is that whatever the status of women in the coming years, man will always look at woman with a romantic sense which has characterized Latin American songs, poetry and literature.[18]

The Hispanic convocation felt it important to discuss these issues to greater conclusion. With regard to homosexuality, it was thought important to press for civil rights and love and compassion for homosexual persons without sanctifying homosexuality. The church should promote this kind of dialogue having to do with the sexual life of Christians within the range of biblical-theological discussion of the church. This can help parents and children to have a sacred concept of sex and at the same time can help to open up the theme without the taboos that many times inhibit these matters.

THE WOMEN'S MOVEMENT

It is hard to remember that Betty Friedan's *The Feminine Mystique* was published as recently as 1964. Her analysis of the patterns of socialization for women in American society had the effect of shock, vision, liberation, confrontation. The contemporary women's movement has powerful predecessors, most notably the early nineteenth-century women's missionary societies, the cadre of women seeking abolition of slavery, and the suffrage movement near the beginning of this century. But the movement for full equality of women was an idea whose time had come.

The movement has taken many forms, each attempting to overcome the oppression of women, achieve solidarity, and affirm personhood. The movement is concerned with women's sexuality, but that is not its central dynamic. The movement is not about locating orgasms or claiming one's own body—critical as these may be. It is about sisterhood, self-definition, power, justice, elimination of sex-role stereotypes, overcoming sexism, and developing more humane patterns of community and leadership style.

The movement has brought to the forefront a new awareness of women's needs and capacities for sexual expression and understandings of sexuality. It has identified the forms of sexual oppression women face both personally and systemically. Women are confronted with the prospect of pregnancy in every act of intercourse. They are the victims of a system of sexism that has economic, psychological, legal, medical, and physical dimensions. Women are the primary victims of sexual violence. No wonder that sisterhood is so powerful or that solidarity is such a critical necessity.

As women seek to express their own sexuality and personhood, men encounter new options. They can be threatened by these developments and can reinforce patterns of dominance or sexism. Or they can respond in kind, reclaiming their bodies, reaching for the sexuality of mutuality, recovering emotions and attributes long identified as feminine. A men's movement is developing that seeks liberation and community similar to that sought by the women's movement.

THE GAY MOVEMENT

Members of the United Church of Christ Gay Caucus have made important contributions to the sexuality study. These persons— men and women, clergy and laity—have grown up in the denomination's churches, and they care about its life. Their insights into the nature of sexuality are profound, living as they have on the boundary of human acceptance and defining the nature of personhood, intimacy, masculinity, and femininity in the context of their own experience.

Several factors help to create the context in which issues of homosexuality are dealt with by the church at this time. The *action of the psychiatric community* is one of them. On December 15, 1973 the Trustees of the American Psychiatric Association voted to discontinue listing homosexuality in its official list of mental disorders. Homosexuality now appears in the category of "sexual orientation disturbance," which is "for individuals whose sexual interests are directed primarily toward people of the same sex and who are either disturbed by, in conflict with, or wish to change their sexual orientation." The action that identified this diagnostic category distinguished those who fell in this category from "homosexuality which by itself does not necessarily constitute a psychiatric disorder." The trustees' ruling was ratified by a majority vote of the APA membership on April 8, 1974.

A second factor is represented in the *studies of gender identity* conducted by John Money and others of the Johns Hopkins group and those psychologists who have assessed sex-role development. Their studies and those of others do not conclusively define the causal development (etiology) of homosexuality: Is it free choice? Is it the result of biology? Is it the effect of socialization processes? Or is it all the above? The answers to these questions remain open.

Alfred C. Kinsey identified a *scale of tendencies* toward homosexuality and demonstrated that individual orientations varied widely. Most persons fit in the continuum between the heterosexual and the homosexual orientations, with varying elements of both in their psychosexual composition. This third factor makes categorical compartmentalization impossible.

A fourth factor is the *varieties of life-styles and personalities* of persons who identify themselves as gay or bisexual. Chapter 5, which deals with public policy, identifies the issues gay persons face as they experience stereotypic and heterosexist oppression.

The civil rights issue addressed by the Tenth General Synod of the United Church of Christ continues to be critical for the gay and the bisexual community and for American society at large.

Selective enforcement of laws continues to exist in a variety of places. Legislatures and municipal governments consider or occasionally pass civil rights legislation in employment, but discrimination and actual physical violence directed against gay persons is widespread, especially among activists.

The gay rights movement has called attention to the concern for the dignity of all persons. The word gay, signifying joyfulness, delight, buoyancy, and aliveness, has been reclaimed as a word of positive self-affirmation for a significant number of Americans.

CHAPTER 2

Biblical Foundations

SOME PRINCIPLES OF BIBLICAL INTERPRETATION

One style of biblical interpretation has traditionally gone to great lengths to demonstrate the unity and continuity of the Bible. This, of course, can be done for the sake of teaching the Bible as literature and as theology, as story and as revelation. There are threads, themes, and theophanies that can be pulled together to help the biblical student comprehend the unfolding of God's revelation. A long and complex history becomes one story, and the diversity of biblical literature becomes a color spectrum emerging from the prism of interpretation. In seeking knowledge and understanding of the Bible, the mind seeks coherence and continuity. Teaching may provide it but not without a sacrifice.

The Bible is many books, and it speaks with many voices throughout a history that spans more than a millennium in time, several worlds in space, and countless generations of people. "The Bible says . . ." many different things with many different voices in many different ages. It is composed of diverse types of literature that yield many variant types of meaning, as might be expected. Taken as a whole, one finds in the Bible a multiplicity of viewpoints rather than a single perspective on human life.

The diversity of biblical history, literature, and viewpoints results in a plurality of interpretation within the Bible itself. Traditions live, move, and change; in the process of their history they often acquire new and sometimes even contradictory interpretations. The religious tradition of Israel was never absolutized once and for all time. The covenant history between Yahweh and Israel is dynamic and open.

This chapter emphasizes the importance of interpretation. *Hermeneutics,* which means *interpretation,* is used to describe a consistent pattern of interpretation rather than the way we understand a particular passage. The Greek word *hermeneia* involves three dimensions: translation, going from one language to another; interpretation, describing the meaning of something; and expression, putting into words our understanding.

The Bible contains a hermeneutic of multiple interpretations. This can be shown by the various internal relationships of the Bible. *Scripture builds on scripture.* A good example of this dependence, in terms of the man-woman relationship, can be seen by comparing Genesis 2 with Hosea 2 and the Song of Songs. *Scripture corrects scripture.* The covenant relationship between Yahweh and Israel is transformed by the various covenant traditions and their interpretations as found in Exodus, Deuteronomy, Amos, Genesis, and 1 Samuel 7. *Scripture sometimes contradicts scripture.* The meaning of Jerusalem in Isaiah is contradicted by the prophet Micah in the same period and also by Jeremiah at a later period. *Scripture reinterprets scripture* (cf. Deuteronomy 5:3 and 29:14-15).

Probably the most familiar examples of such interaction in scripture are those teachings of Jesus that follow this pattern: "You have heard that it was said. . . . But I say to you . . ." Jesus' conflict with the religious authorities, which proved fatal in the end, arose principally over the question of his authority to reinterpret, contradict, and even disobey the ancient scriptures. The context of the conflict was the hermeneutical issue or the principles of scriptural interpretation. And therefore, in the case of Jesus, it also became the issue of God's identity, authority, and revelation that was at stake. The religious revolution Jesus brought with his words and actions was, ironically, solidly based on scripture itself, claimed as the authority to transcend scripture when God speaks and acts anew in human life. Knowing the scripture far better than its defenders, he proclaimed himself to be fulfilling the law and the prophets, not abolishing them (Matthew 5:17-20). And he knew, also, the fate awaiting those who violate scripture for the sake of the weightier matters of the law (Matthew 23:23-24) or who presume to prophesy the imminent righteousness of God among those scribes and Pharisees engaged in building shrines to earlier prophets now safely dead (Matthew 23:29-36).

These various interactions of scripture with scripture happen in a living religious tradition where the literature produced continues to interact with subsequent human life and history, with all its contingencies, ambiguities, and developments. The Bible reflects this in terms of Israel and the early church; both testaments evince the changing internal struggles of scripture in successive historical epochs. It is to be celebrated not deplored or feared, for it is also a crucial sign of the faithfulness and renewal of the church in every age. Only a dead church can be either apathetic or unanimous about the meaning and use of scripture. The salient point is the fact that contemporary biblical scholars find a dynamic hermeneutic within the Bible. The biblical tradition is alive and changing not fixed and static. A biblical faith and a biblical church will reflect that dynamic tradition and never abandon its own struggle with scripture.

This dynamic hermeneutic within scripture is an important clue and norm for our own use and interpretation of the Bible. In the first place, no exegesis is exempt from the human experiences and cultural presuppositions of the person doing the interpreting. That means each will bring to the interpretive task a whole set of memories, experiences, values, claims, biases, investments, and assumptions which define that person and his or her world. It is not only inevitable but also serves to illuminate the text as well as to pervert it. The point is not to attempt the impossible, such as an absolutely true and eternal exegesis of scripture, but rather to approach the hermeneutical task with a modicum of discipline, a maximum of knowledge and scholarship, and a measure of humility. All are necessary if we are to hear what the Bible is saying.

Interpretation, therefore, is both necessary and inevitable. The person who claims to take the Bible "just as it is, at face value, according to what the words say" is actually engaging in one particular and rather popular type of interpretation. The result may be blind subjectivism and interpretive violence. Or again, when the Bible is claimed as the infallible word of God and then a string of quoted texts is offered as conclusive proof of the thesis being defended, diverse biblical literature is often being commanded to serve an ideological cause. (One is reminded of the observation that even the devil can quote scripture for certain purposes.) A sad fact is that the Bible has been used to support and condemn slavery, segregation, the subjugation of women, capital punishment, war, capitalism, and Marxism. And one can only suspect that the fallible is parading under the guise of the infallible.

In the second place, since no exegesis is exempt from the experience and presuppositions of the interpreter, our interpretations of the Bible cannot remain static if they are to have integrity. Human experience is also diverse, dynamic, and open to multiple interpretations. Individually and corporately, our human experiences are like the Bible: they build on one another, correct one another, contradict one another, and reinterpret one another. This points to "the double dynamic" where we find, both in the case of scripture and human experience, a living, changing tradition and history that requires reinterpretation in the given historical moment. This is recognized in the common aphorism that "there are different texts for different times." Who would recite a funeral text at a wedding feast? The contextual nature of interpretation is also witnessed in the common experience of having old familiar texts come alive with new and startling meanings.

This inevitability of interpretation requires informed and disciplined approaches that recognize the integrity and ambiguities of the Bible as well as the integrity and ambiguities of human experience. Our human interaction with the Bible will always be characterized by tensions, by new revelations of old truths, and by old judgments on new historical developments. Therefore, biblical interpretation always moves within the hermeneutical circle—the community of faith interprets scripture and, at the same time, scripture interprets the community of faith. In any given period of the church's life these interactions with the Bible may be harmonious, disparate, ambiguous. But the process itself must be constant and open-ended if the church is to hear the word of God anew and faithfully exercise its mission in contemporary society.

The open-ended nature of the interpretive task should not be confused with an open-ended god whom we seek to discover, because God is still working out the divine identity in history. Yahweh, the God of the Bible, has revealed the holy in the covenant history of Israel, has fully and definitely disclosed the identity of God in Jesus Christ. In this single person God has revealed the purpose and the end of human history, which is nothing less than the establishment of a new world. In Jesus Christ sinful humankind, sinful sexuality, sinful human history, and sinful creation have been redeemed and made new. God's Spirit is making all things new—new people, new sexuality, new families, new societies, new politics, new economics on the way to a new creation where death has been brought to life. The interpreter's task is, in the last instance, a confessional task in which faith seeks understanding and insight into God's renewing word and act.

There is a river in the Bible that carries us away, once we have entrusted our destiny to it—away from ourselves to the sea. The Holy Scriptures will interpret themselves in spite of all our human limitations. We need only dare to follow this drive, this spirit, this river, to grow out beyond ourselves toward the highest answer. This daring is faith; and we read the Bible rightly, not when we do so with false modesty, restraint, and attempted sobriety, for these are passive qualities, but when we read it in faith.[1]

BIBLICAL CULTURE AND RELIGION: PATRIARCHALISM AND ANDROCENTRISM

"The Old Testament is a man's 'book,' where women appear for the most part simply as adjuncts of men, significant only in the context of men's activities."[2]

If we believe that there is more truth yet to break forth from God's holy word, and that the Bible will speak with power to contemporary issues within the church when we search the scriptures with honesty, then we also need the courage to bear the judgment of the truth that sets us free. The truth is always a word of grace and promise that we hear first as judgment, because we do not know the truth or live within it. The truth is like the light that reveals the darkness and its true identity by contrast. In our sinful human situation in the church, grace comes as judgment and the light appears as darkness for as long as we refuse freedom and enjoy our captivity. Only on the other side of repentance, which is at the same time a confession of faith, do we understand the gracious source of judgment and the shadow cast by the light. Biblical truth can be a painful human experience on the way to God's liberation of woman and man for each other.

Such has been our experience within this sexuality study as we looked at biblical material on man and woman. For all persons who repudiate sexism in religion, reading the Bible is often embarrassing, sometimes painful, and here and there it is simply outrageous. The offense, as always, has its origin in the truth of the Bible itself or in certain truths that are now being rediscovered and biblically appropriated by the women's movement in the church. As has often happened in church history, certain traditions in the Bible are radically judged by competing traditions, and scripture rises up angrily to contradict and correct scripture. This process is ongoing and mandatory to Christian obedience in each age and is the lifeblood of the church's renewal and faithfulness.

Our study has rejected several common reactions to this truth breaking forth from God's holy word concerning the identity and relationship of man and woman: We refuse to support and defend the pervasive male supremacy of ancient Hebrew religion and culture recorded in the Bible. In our day it is a millstone around the church's neck and not a jewel in its crown. To attribute normative value to the patriarchalism of the Bible is a hermeneutical heresy, cultural obscurantism, and folly.

We refuse to jettison the whole Bible because "it is a handbook for the oppression of women," as some strident secular voices in the women's movement claim. The church purged of patriarchalism would be closer to the true church; but the church without the Bible is no church at all, because it has abandoned its distinctive source of revelation. (Why throw out the wine with the old wineskin?)

We refuse to reduce biblical *faith* to biblical *religion*, with all its historical, particular, and accidental forms. Neither the truth nor the power of biblical faith is refuted or established by the curious culture and sins of Israel. The God of the patriarchs will also reveal *herself* to be the God of all peoples, nations, races, and sexes. Patriarchs will be chastened by prophets.

With these preliminary comments and caveats, we turn now to the images of woman and man in the Old Testament. The focus is on *woman's* image, because it is subordinate and derivative, always in danger of being lost in the shadow of man. Ironically, the mere attempt to develop the profile of the biblical image of woman requires drawing man in bold strokes in order to establish the shape of his counterpart.

LEGAL CODES: WOMAN DISENFRANCHISED

The various legal codes of Israel reflect the ancient social and cultural milieu of the Near East, which included a thorough-going patriarchalism, the extended family, polygamy, concubinage, and slavery. A double standard of behavior for men and women was codified. The law addressed the whole community through the males and presupposed a society in which only males were full members and responsible persons, because "the father's house" was the basic social unit. The "people" Israel, or the religious congregation, was also composed exclusively of adult males. Therefore, discrimination against woman and the propagation of the image of the female as inferior were both a structure and a function of the system of socioreligious law. Woman was a legal nonperson.

Where woman does appear in the legal codes she has the role of a dependent (and normally an inferior) in an androcentric system. This is especially true in regard to laws dealing with human sexuality. The codes were especially protective of the integrity, stability, and economic viability of the family, and sexual transgressions were severely censured. Family legislation focused on the male, whose rights and duties with respect to other families were set down; the male's authority, honor, and property were protected against external threats.

The Hebrew woman's sexuality was her primary contribution to the family and society; she was to build up the husband's house by procreation. Her sexuality was the exclusive property of the male. Her adultery was a major crime that, along with murder and certain religious offenses, merited the death penalty. The issue, ironically, was not sexual infidelity but a violation of male property and authority and, consequently, the family itself. The adulterer violated the man's property and destroyed his honor, while the adulterous wife defied his authority and her sole sexual responsibility to him. The bride convicted of fornication was likewise sentenced to death, because the code required virginity of marriageable women.

In the case of the man, extramarital sex was dealt with quite differently. The man who violated an unwed virgin had only to marry her and pay her father, but he could not divorce her. Prostitution was a tolerated institution that served males and was demeaning to the women involved, who were social outcasts and prophetic metaphors for idolatry. While the sexual laws of Israel were intended to preserve the family and to confine sex to marriage, polygamy was a special concession to the male, along with the practice of concubinage. The husband's sexual infidelity was not ranked as a crime. Specific laws controlling divorce, which was practiced in Israel, are not clear, but it is known that it was an exclusively male prerogative.

Given Israel's pattern of patrilineal descent and inheritance laws, which were designed to preserve the patriarchal name and household, women were basically part of the family property rather than being property owners themselves. The management of family property, however, may have often devolved to the wife. With her total economic dependency on the man, the woman moved from support by her father to support by her husband after marriage. Consequently, the widow (especially one without a son to inherit the property she might manage but would never own) could be desperate, because her husband's property would pass to the nearest male relative, who apparently was not required by law to support her. Hence, the biblical injunctions to care for the widow and the orphan are the ethical norm defending women and children bereft of a man.

According to the religious law of Israel, woman was also uniquely disabled. Only males were eligible for the rite of passage into religious membership—circumcision. Only males were required by law to attend the thrice annual pilgrim feasts. Only males were allowed to serve as priests. Only women qualified for the ritual impurity of childbirth and menstruation. The birth of a male child entailed one week of uncleanness, and a female child merited two weeks of uncleanness.

In the legal codes, then, woman emerges as a dependent and largely derivative counterpart of man. She is covered by the code in cases that are exceptional or severely censured: (1) where the male is absent from an essential role (the female heir); (2) where she is defenseless and unsupported (the widow); (3) where she is a sexual offender; and (4) where sex-correlated roles or status are involved (slave, captive, mother, sorceress). In Hebrew culture only one role of woman is given the honor and status comparable to a man—the role of mother. The command to honor parents is the sole codification of her equality as woman, and her high value there is premised on the reproductive function and the place of progeny in the preservation of the family and society dominated by man.

WISDOM LITERATURE: THE PROVERBIAL WOMAN
The image of woman as it emerges from Proverbs is somewhat different from the picture given in the law. The wisdom instruction and its aphorisms comprise a type of literature that reflects the urban, monogamous, comfortable upper class of Israel. It is male folk wisdom in the sense that it addresses man exclusively and counsels him to heed parental counsel on choosing a wife, because his earthly fortunes will be significantly determined by woman. There are strong intimations of the power of woman to affect marital and familial life.

In Proverbs, woman is revealed as the teacher-mother, with emphasis placed on her instructional role in the family rather than on the reproductive function. As a teacher whom a wise son will heed, woman is ranked equally with man, and together they represent the parental teaching function. Both are to be honored and obeyed. As in the legal codes, the mother is highly honored but not primarily as womb-bearer. The valued role is the nurturant function wherein woman is the source of wisdom essential to life in addition to giving life through birth.

As a wife, in relation to husband rather than children, she is pictured with some ambivalence. The "woman of quality," who is also "the good wife," is described as being prudent, gracious, honorable, and a credit to her husband's reputation. Such a woman is the crown ("master") of her husband and is seen as a good gift from God. Where the specific skills and functions of the good wife are mentioned, we find her as household manager, provisioner of food and clothing, business manager, philanthropist, and wise teacher. Her husband trusts her, profits from her, and knows that "a good wife is far more precious than jewels." By contrast, "the bad wife" is characterized by one overriding personality trait—"contentiousness." Her metaphor is "a continual dripping on a rainy day." Her unforgivable sin is that she brings shame and disgrace upon her husband as well as herself.

The sexuality of woman in Proverbs is recognized only tangentially in cautionary counsel to man. The husband is advised to love, cherish, and enjoy only the wife of his youth and to avoid "loose women." This counsel of sexual fidelity is the counterpart of warnings about the seductions of "foreign women," the "adventuress," the adulteress, and the harlot. All such types portend disaster for the man who consorts with woman outside the confines and control of family and marriage. It is not erotic love that is condemned, but the power of woman's sexuality to destroy the life of the foolish philandering man.

It should be noted that in Proverbs woman is not chattel; nor is she simply a sex object. The power, mystery, and otherness of woman is recognized along with her intelligence, drive, and skill in managing domestic and economic pursuits. Presented with a trimodal typology of mother, wife, and foreign woman, the wise man is advised to choose and cleave to the woman of quality. That is the wisdom of the teacher-mother and the father, too.

HISTORICAL WRITINGS: EMERGING REAL WOMEN

It is only in the historical writings that woman becomes real—a flesh and blood person with name, biography, and individual character. We meet Deborah, Jezebel, the queen of Sheba, Rachel, Rizpah, Miriam, Huldah, Rahab, and Abigail. Variety and ambiguity emerge in the image and status of women; the portrayals are vivid and very human in comparison with law and wisdom literature.

We have summarized the types that are represented rather than individual biographies, because most of the women who are mentioned in the Bible serve the narrative dramas as types rather than as individuals. For

the roles played by women in these writings are almost exclusively subordinate and/or supporting roles. Women are adjuncts to the men: they are minor (occasionally major) characters necessary to a plot that revolves about males. They are the mothers and nurses and saviors of men; temptresses, seducers and destroyers of men; objects or recipients of miracles performed by and/or for men; confessors of the power, wisdom and divine designation of men. They are necessary to the drama, and may even steal the spotlight occasionally; but the story is rarely about them.[3]

Mother. Along with wife, the mother image is presented as a dominant type in the historical writings. The mothers of Israel are characterized by compassion, solicitousness, and jealousy for their children. They are the teachers who determine character and thus affect history and events through the lives of the primary actors, who are the males, their children.

No more poignant image of woman is given than the suffering mother experiencing the death of her child. There is Rachel weeping inconsolably for her dead children (Jeremiah 31:15) and Rizpah in vigil over the bodies of her sons (2 Samuel 21:8-14). Whether queen, heroine, harlot, or concubine, these mothers stand like Mary under the cross and share in common the desolation of woman's most profound loss—the death of the life that is her own flesh. In pain the child is born; woman in childbirth is a powerful image for the Hebrew poet and the prophet. It becomes a metaphor for great anguish and the fearful helplessness of all human extremity.

The barren woman emerges as a symbol of shame and reproach in Israel, a state of abandonment if not punishment by God. It is cause for derision by other women and reduces the status of the wife along with the whole household. The barren woman, by definition, is denied the principal honor of woman—motherhood. Lost is woman's sole source and arena of authority—the mother-child relationship—which alone among all her relationships would have granted her unchallenged power and independent authority over the lives of others.

Wife. The role of wife is the principal destiny of woman in Israel; yet her image as wife is elusive save as it figures exceptionally in narratives by altering or insuring the usual course of events and relationships. In patriarchal and other family stories the wife is necessary genealogy, but in political history also she often figures prominently (e.g., 2 Samuel 9—20) .

It is often said, with some justification, that the Hebrew wife is essentially chattel. A man's possessions consisted of wives, children, slaves, and livestock. Wives were an index of wealth, and women were part of the booty of war.

> Despite legal, economic and social subordination, however, wives were not simply property. They could not be bought and sold, and it is doubtful that they could be divorced without substantial cause. . . . But the rights of concubine and wife were not fixed by contract or by any surviving law. They were presumably customary and negotiated by agreements between the husband and wife's family. A wife's rights and freedom within marriage would depend in large measure on the ability of her family to support and defend her demands. . . . Her status as a wife would reflect the status of her family.[4]

Marriage was arranged between families, initiated by the man, but there are indications that the woman could refuse an "offer."

There are numerous instances in the historical writings where wives transcend their subordinate and mundane roles by virtue of some gift—beauty, intelligence, cleverness, or sheer drive. Especially noted are woman's gifts of persuasion derived from her sexuality or her intellect, which might save the husband to whom she is loyal or serve to undo the man she is opposing. The power of woman is recognized as both asset and threat to man, and this ambivalence is greatest where the man-woman relationship is most intimate, namely marriage. For in addition to inherent female powers, the wife is an engrafted member of the man's household, a "stranger" taken in who carries continuing ties and loyalties to her father's household and who might be used subversively by her kinspeople. Thus, "foreign wives" are eschewed for in-group marriages, because their loyalties are even more uncertain.

Harlot. She is the classic outcast in Israel; at the same time she symbolizes the sexual double standard. Throughout Hebrew history she is the woman of shame and disrepute, ostracized and even put to death for high crimes and misdemeanors but also tolerated by society and used by men, who bore no legal penalties for going into her house. Those stories of the harlot heroine (e.g., Rahab in Joshua 2:1-21) that are preserved gain their power from the unexpected virtues evinced by "women of no virtue," the faith and courage shown by the very person symbolizing unfaithfulness. Generally, the harlot serves as both a surrogate and a nemesis to the wifely image of woman. The harlot is woman loved and hated by man, the ambivalent creature.

41

Special roles. Although they were permitted to be only wives and mothers, some women in Israel managed to establish second vocations on the side. There were a few women prophets (Deborah, Hulda, and Noadiah), though little is known about them perhaps because they were outside the guilds, and their oracles were not preserved. But the prophetic charisma is no respecter of sex, and these women represent the recognition by Israel that Yahweh speaks through women and calls them to deliver revelations to God's people. In contrast to the cultus, where women were disallowed as religious functionaries, the prophetic role was open and inclusive, even though the majority of prophets were men.

Along with men, there were women who practiced the occult as mediums and sorceresses; both were banned. More common were the "wise women," town counselors who established reputations for reliable advice, which was a gift arising from astute insight, sage observations, and the efficacy of their words. Wisdom, like prophecy, was *not* strictly sex correlated. All other recorded specializations of women conform more closely to their primary female roles in that culture—midwives, singers, mourners. The servant and slave class of women in wealthy or royal households were allowed to cultivate certain aptitudes and to become specialists, such as perfumers, bakers, and cooks.

SUMMARY: WOMAN IN/BEYOND CULTURE

In summarizing the images of women in the legal, wisdom, and historical literature, a number of statements can be made that mitigate against facile or narrow generalizations about women in ancient Israel. "No single statement can be formulated concerning *the* image of woman in the Old Testament."[5]

First, although a woman's sexuality is the sine qua non of her life, her identity and role in that culture and religion, she is rarely reduced to the one-dimensional image of sex object. When a composite is made of woman's attributes, nonsexual characteristics predominate. Intelligence, prudence, wisdom, practicality, diplomacy, and religious insight displace or overshadow mere concern with her body. Woman is taken seriously as a person and is not considered inherently foolish, frivolous, or inane; there is a tacit recognition of her powers that cannot be contained by her subordinate status.

Second, in spite of the family locus and the roles of women, the personal powers and abilities of women are not restricted to the household nor contained by narrowly defined female work.

Special gifts and powers are recognized and utilized by the larger community, leading to instances of professional specialization as an avocation, along with the required wife/mother roles. Curiously, these usually involve the gift and practice of special knowledge: judging legal disputes (Deborah) ; common sense (the wise women of Tekoa, Abel); receiving divine revelations (Deborah, Miriam, Hulda); and the occult art of summoning the spirits of the dead (the medium of Endor).

Third, in terms of economic criteria and the necessity of perpetuating the family name and household, woman is generally considered to be inferior to man. Legally, she has few recognized and protected rights, and cultically, her participation is strictly limited. This is her given cultural situation and the social realities within which she lives. The real miracle is found in the numerous women who broke out of this cultural captivity and in the ingenious ways they devised to use the system against itself for personal or familial ends.

Fourth,

in many situations the woman was in fact and/or in theory an equal, despite manifold and combined pressures to treat her as an inferior. She was recognized as equal (or superior) in the possession and employment of certain kinds of knowledge and in religious sensibility and sensitivity. In love she might also be an equal, and could exploit (Judges 16:4-22) as well as suffer exploitation. She was in general charged with the same religious and moral obligations as man, and she was held responsible for her acts.[6]

Fifth, man still recognizes woman as a human being essentially like him: a partner in pleasure and work, one on whom he depends for essential roles and relationships, one who determines his fate in significant ways. Woman is his helper ('ezer, a relational and beneficial other or partner) and counterpart, whose wife/mother labor is essential to his life and fortune. Woman complements and completes man yet has her own independent integrity. She is equal and other.

Sixth, in the human and religious insights of Israel there are moments of cultural transcendence and intimations of divine revelation that radically judge the whole system, including the historic social realities of the man-woman relationship. In spite of its cultural setting, the biblical faith carries a counterculture and subdued motif which recognizes that woman is man's equal

43

and that he is her partner, both of them discreetly responsible to Yahweh for their cohumanity and their common life. It is to this counterpoint, to this minor theme which today will be heard as the major harmonic progression, to this hidden revelation that we now turn. "A prophet will arise in Israel. . . ."

POINT AND COUNTERPOINT:
LIBERATING TEXTS AND RENEWING THEMES

Every one who curses his [her] father or his [her] mother shall be put to death.

—Leviticus 20:9

So God created man in his own image, in the image of God he created him; male and female he created them. . . . And God saw everything that he had made, and behold it was very good.

—Genesis 1:27, 31

Oh, may your breasts be like clusters of the vine,
    and the scent of your breath like apples,
and your kisses like the best wine.

Song of Songs 7:8-9

For the Lord has created a new thing on the earth:
    a woman protects a man.

—Jeremiah 31:22

Many traditions of the Bible view human sexuality from a patriarchal perspective in which the male is dominant and superior while the female is subordinate and inferior. These traditions have been documented above, and one may laugh at them, cry over them, or merely take them as a witness to the culture of that place, time, and people. The question is: Is that all? Does the Bible have anything else to say about the man-woman relationship, some redeeming and liberating word? Must contemporary Christians bear the patriarchal tradition either as a platform or as a cross?

In spite of the fact that patriarchalism and androcentrism dominate the culture reflected in the Bible, the revelation also contains fundamental challenges to this patriarchal culture and religion. There are real biblical alternatives to both the blind propagation of sexism and simply suffering its continuing effects. There are suppressed texts for which the time has come, because they represent scripture contradicting and correcting scripture.

44

Also, there are familiar texts that can be reread and reinterpreted without the tunnel vision of many centuries of male exegesis. "The hermeneutical challenge is to translate biblical faith without sexism."[7]

We accept this basic premise and distinction: the purpose and norm of biblical *faith*, as distinguished from the cultural forms of biblical *religion*, is not the perpetuation of patriarchy but rather *the salvation of women and men together in their full and equal cohumanity.* There is sexism in sin, and there is sin in sexism; but there is no sexism in the salvation proclaimed by the biblical faith.

HUMAN IMAGES OF YAHWEH: MIXED METAPHORS

The God of Israel is unique and utterly distinct from the various fertility gods of the ancient Near East. All the gods of the surrounding cultures had a particular sex as male or female gods. Their worship involved a cult of sexuality wherein human sex acts were sacralized in the temple for the purposes of paying homage to the sexual identity of the gods and evoking their favor on all fertility and reproduction—human, animal, and planted crops. Sexual gods were worshiped, propitiated, and manipulated by sexual acts within a theology that offered human control of the gods and therefore also human destiny by means of correct ritual behavior. Canaanite religion was a fertility cult that employed sexual magic.

Hebrew religion reserved its strongest condemnations for Canaanite religion and the sexual cults of the baals. The holiness of the sex act was emphatically rejected by Israel; human sexuality belonged to the order of the profane, not to the order of the gods. The religion of Yahweh rejected the cult of sexuality because Yahweh is one, complete, whole and therefore exists beyond sexuality and the dimorphic sexual distinction between male and female. Israel also repudiated the sexuality of God, in contrast to the fertility baals, which means that *Yahweh is neither male nor female.* As the creator of human sexuality and the lord of human history, Yahweh embraces and transcends man and woman, who are sexual creatures. Yahweh is neither he nor she: not one sex that requires the other to be complete, not asexual, and not even an androgynous or bisexual god, according to some specious theory of a "higher sex," "third sex," or "composite sex." All theories and theologies that impute specific sexuality to God commit the primary and primordial human sin—confusing the Creator with the human creature, which can end only in the confusion of the creature with God, or idolatry. They derive from a Babylonian or Canaanite myth, not from biblical faith.

One finds abundant evidence in the Bible to contradict such assertions. Yahweh is frequently depicted as a man, and the male pronoun is normally used when referring to God. One should not be too surprised that a patriarchal culture would yield a largely patriarchal portrait of God; but what happens, then, to the theological claim that Yahweh is neither male nor female?

Two important realities of biblical faith must be stressed at this point. First, we confront the paradox that even though Yahweh is often depicted as a man, Hebrew faith repudiates both anthropomorphism and andromorphism. God is neither man nor male. At some points we are told that Yahweh repents; in other places that Yahweh "is not a man, that he should repent [Num. 23:19; 1 Sam. 15:29]." An illustration of this paradox can be found in Hosea's poem about the loving God and Israel, the faithless son (Hosea 11:1-11). Anthropomorphic language is used even while it is being denied by being transcended. Like the Hebrew mother, Yahweh teaches the child to walk, heals the son's wounds, and feeds the infant child. Like the human parent, Yahweh worries, works, and suffers over the wayward child. But the final verdict is mercy, in which love triumphs over wrath, because God refuses identification with the male: "for I am God ['el], and not man ['ish], the Holy One in your midst [Hos. 11:9]." The climax is God's transcendence of man as man and as male.

Second, one of the best kept secrets about the Old Testament is its use of feminine imagery for Yahweh, which sharpens the paradox by supplanting the male metaphors. In the traditions of the exodus and the wanderings, in response to the murmurings of the people, Yahweh provides those necessities that were always obtained through women's work—food and water, a spring in the desert and manna to eat. In Nehemiah 9, Yahweh is a seamstress, just as she also made garments to cover the naked couple in the Garden (Genesis 3:21). The prophet boldly uses gynomorphic speech for Yahweh, so that God speaks of her birth pangs: "Now I will cry out like a woman in travail, I will gasp and pant [Isa. 42:14]." Or again, we have the maternal God bringing forth children in labor: "Shall I bring to the birth and not cause to bring forth? says the Lord; shall I, who cause to bring forth, shut the womb? says your God [Isa. 66:9]"; and serving as the comforting mother—"As one whom his mother comforts, so I will comfort you [Isa. 66:13]." God's remembrance of Zion is compared to the love of a nursing mother (Isaiah 49:15) and the work of a midwife (Psalm 22:9-10; 71:6).

Although the patriarchal image of God dominates in the Old Testament, the crucial point for biblical interpretation is the astounding fact that Israel did not absolutize this patriarchal portrait into a theological assertion. If God as male had been a confessional statement, then the female imagery for God would have been taboo. It is this explicitly female imagery for Yahweh that corrects any tendency Israel may have shown to affirm God as male and that enhances its understanding of Yahweh in metaphors that involve both sexes.

Yahweh created male and female in the divine image (Genesis 1). Accordingly, both female and male function as symbols for God. These symbols participate in the reality to which they point, but they do not define, type, stereotype, or limit God. Female and male are metaphors for understanding and relating to God. Human sexuality witnesses to the creator of sexuality but does not characterize the identity of the creator except in poetic and metaphoric language. God is not a sexual creature, because he/she is not a creature but the creator. Israel would not say that God is a man any more than it would say God is a woman.

Therefore, contemporary theological assertions that God is masculine are thoroughly unbiblical and exceed the connotations of permissible sexual distinction in God. The theologian is always a creature of culture, grammar, and sexuality; but these human limitations cannot limit the theological understanding of God. The *imago dei* interpretation in the tradition has been one-sided, male-dominated, and chauvinistic. Yahweh, the God of the Bible, embraces and transcends both sexes as creator and lord. The God of Israel defies and prohibits theological sexism.

MUTED THEMES: EXODUS, RUTH, JEREMIAH 31:22

The story of the exodus and of Israel's deliverance from slavery has captured the imagination of the oppressed throughout history and has functioned consistently as a model of liberation. In our own day it has informed the civil rights movement, the women's movement, and many third-world Christians. The irresistible theme is the triumph of human freedom over the social, economic, and political structures that serve the rulers and subjugate various classes or races or one sex. Today women are reading the story with new eyes and are learning that women played important roles in that revolution. Moses, the liberator, is himself first saved by a conspiracy of Hebrew and Egyptian women.

Within their culturally and politically defined roles as mothers, midwives, daughters, and slaves, these women nurture the revolution and save the revolutionary (Exodus 1:15—2:10). With the oppressor's natural dread of the oppressed, the Pharaoh orders the Hebrew midwives to kill every male child delivered, but the women disobey him and prevent the pogrom. The succeeding general order that all Hebrew male children be drowned in the Nile is disobeyed by a woman from the house of Levi, who hides her infant in a basket among the rushes. Liberation begins in the house of the oppressor when Pharaoh's own daughter enters the conspiracy to preserve life. This Egyptian princess initiates a scheme in which she adopts the Hebrew child, names him Moses, and involves female slaves—mother and daughter—in the care and protection of the child. Women alone take the initiative and bear the risks that lead to the deliverance of Israel from bondage. That patriarchal religion can embody and preserve such feminist traditions is a sign of its capacity to transcend patriarchy for the sake of truth.

The book of Ruth has been largely ignored or, when treated in the popular tradition, has been interpreted as a love story in which two abandoned, poor women scheme to achieve protection and support through the seduction of Boaz and his subsequent marriage to Ruth. This classic male interpretation of the story supports patriarchal culture and enforces the stereotypes in which the strong male protector, who is essentially good, acts justly toward the weak and vulnerable female, who uses her sexual powers cleverly to achieve what she needs from him but at the price of her innocence. In other words, the story is turned into a midrash on Genesis 2—3 *misinterpreted*. This is untenable and obscures the truth and the beauty of the feminist theme in the book of Ruth.[8]

This narrative tells woman's story in man's world and is a genuine love story of two women who reveal the power of love transcending human sexuality. The aged Judahite widow, Naomi, and the young foreign widow, Ruth, together struggle for survival in a patriarchal culture where they have no identity, no rights, no powers as women without men. They face hardships, insecurity, dangers, and death. No god blesses them and no man takes up their cause. Together they take charge of their own destiny, risking initiatives and roles that are alien to their culture. And their triumph over patriarchalism, achieved by surviving death and sexual domination by males, ends not in a reversal of sexual roles but in a new beginning with men. It is the story of human love and faithfulness between women transforming the relationship between man and woman, redeeming love from sexual domination and redeeming society from sexual injustice.

48

There are four scenes in this story: The first begins with the women alone, without men, shaping their own destiny in a cultural situation that offers only despair. The scenes that follow record their struggle to survive economically and socially in interaction with a strong male, Boaz, who is the recipient of their initiatives and a benign reactor to their fate. The final scene begins with the threat that their future may be determined by men alone, in keeping with the patriarchal traditions on fertility, family name, and inheritance. Yet, the women do not allow this to occur; the story ends with shalom wherein the bold decisions of women evoke the blessings of God and new life for both man and woman.

Although the story plot is not discussed here in detail, there are several elements of the narrative that deserve emphasis:

First, Naomi speaks to her daughters-in-law after all three have become childless widows and their fortune has been only famine, dislocation, and death and evokes the blessing of Yahweh on them: "Go, return each of you to her mother's house. May the Lord deal kindly with you, as you have [already] dealt with the dead and with me [Ruth 1:8]." Curiously, the basis for Naomi's invocation is not the past blessings of God, which none has received, but the love and kindness of the two young women that Naomi and her now dead menfolk have received. These female foreigners are affirmed as human models for Yahweh, who is being shown a more excellent way. Human loyalty becomes a paradigm for God's future.

Second, Orpah returns to her people and her god, which represents the only reasonable and secure choice within the structures of that society; but Ruth makes the radical and precarious decision to remain with Naomi and the God of Israel. Ruth's disobedience for the sake of love is expressed in one of the most beautiful troths found in the Bible, *spoken by woman to woman*:

> Entreat me not to leave you or to return from following you; for where you go I will go, and where you lodge I will lodge; your people shall be my people, and your God my God; where you die I will die, and there will I be buried. May the Lord do so to me and more also if even death parts me from you.
>
> —Ruth 1:16-17

Ruth has disavowed the solidarity of family, has given up her national identity, and has renounced her religious faith for the

49

sake of love and loyalty to the beloved. In the history of Israel, Abraham alone confesses such radical faith when he moves family and household to a foreign land under the divine promise. By contrast, Ruth stands alone, without family, without possessions, without promise or divine blessing for her leap of faith. Furthermore, not only has she abandoned family, country, and faith, but also she has reversed the sexual allegiance of the culture. A young woman has chosen commitment to an old woman rather than to the search for a husband. Woman chooses woman when she is supposed to choose man in a world where life depends upon men. Naomi is silenced by this radical decision and awesome faith (Ruth 1:18).

Third, Boaz is a man of worth and means, a kinsman of Naomi. While he acts generously toward Ruth in the gleaning scene and at the threshing floor, even invoking a divine blessing on her for her loyalty to Naomi, he never takes the initiative in the story. As a kinsman who knows of their poverty, he has done nothing to help these women. He extends "the wings of Yahweh" over Ruth but not his own protection and care. As a male redeemer to his kinswoman, he has not extended the redemption of marriage which is within his power.

By contrast, it is Ruth who is portrayed as the defier of custom, the decision-maker, the one who works out the salvation of both women. She initiates the marriage by challenging Boaz to enact the blessing he himself invoked. In other words, it is a foreign woman who calls a Hebrew man to responsibility for his family, his wealth, his maleness, and his faith. Justice for women is achieved in a patriarchal situation not by means of paternalism from the man or seductiveness by the woman, but rather through the human and moral agency of an extraordinary woman, whose love and loyalty engenders her resistance to culture for the sake of transforming that culture.

Fourth, the story that begins under the threat of death and despair for woman works its way toward shalom for both woman and man. What begins in tragedy, ends in human wholeness and well-being through the agency of women who boldly act to embody and enact the blessing of God.

The closing celebration begins: "So Boaz took Ruth and she became his wife; and he went in to her [Ruth 4:13a]." But this human male initiative is limited by the intervention of Yahweh: "and the Lord gave her conception, and she bore a son [Ruth 4:13b]." Consistently in the faith of Israel, it is Yahweh who opens the womb and authors conception, for the gift of life is not the inherent power of either the male or the female; rather it is God's activity, power, and gift to the human couple. Sexual intercourse, in the context of shalom, is the activity of God, transforming the curse of sexuality into a blessing.

The closing celebration of the story belongs to women alone, closing the ring construction of the narrative that began with women alone under judgment. The women of Bethlehem speak as a chorus in the drama: "Blessed be the Lord, who has not left you this day without next of kin [Ruth 4:14]." The advent of the child turns death into life for "he shall be to you a restorer of life and a nourisher of your old age [Ruth 4:15a]," they assure Naomi. And, surprisingly, given the importance of a male child in the patriarchal tradition, the blessing reaches its climax in the exaltation of Ruth over child, male child, and the ideal number of sons: "for your daughter-in-law who loves you, *who is more to you than seven sons,* has borne him [Ruth 4:15b]." The blessing nullifies the patriarchal tradition by transcending it within the event of its principal religious ratification—the male child born—and through the agency of a foreign woman whose sacrificial love and loyalty to woman is identified as the mediation of life in the midst of death. Woman giving birth becomes a primordial parable of God's gift of new life and salvation; and woman's love becomes an incarnation of God's faithfulness to man and woman in their cohumanity. A more profound or moving affirmation of biblical feminism cannot be found. Woman emptied by judgment and by culture is henceforth woman fulfilled by faith, love, and hope.

"And the women of the neighborhood gave him a name, saying, 'A son has been born to Naomi.' They named him Obed; he was the father of Jesse, the father of David [Ruth 4:17]." In the lineage of biblical faith in Yahweh's redeeming action in the life of God's people, which can even celebrate as the advent of shalom in the human and commonplace event of woman birthing a child, this muted theme of Ruth will emerge generations later in the birth of another male child: "And Joseph also went up from Galilee, . . . to the city of David . . . with Mary, his betrothed, who was with child [Luke 2:4-5]." In that birth, patriarchalism will be overcome in principle and in reality by the coming of the new humanity promised to woman and man. The story of Ruth is a harbinger of that triumph.

Similar feminist themes emerge elsewhere in the Old Testament, even in the prophetic literature where, for example, one finds a larger measure of egalitarianism than is normally expected from a patriarchal culture's religious tradition. The distinctions, division, and alienation of man and woman are evident in the prophetic writings as well. However, if the historians of Israel glimpsed an original equality and peace in creation "preceding" the fallen state of human sexuality, the prophets vividly perceive the present realities of inequality and exploitation and respond with oracles of justice coming with Yahweh's judgment. The prophetic vision of justice foresees an act of God that will purge the world through retribution and rectification. The proud will be humiliated (Isaiah 2). Those of wealth and distinction will head the column of exiles (Amos 6:4-7). But she who is now the outcast (the harlot in man's eyes) will not be punished for her sin (Hosea 4:14). Tax collectors and whores will enter the kingdom of God before self-righteous and religious men (and women).

And the greatest among the prophets saw even more, saw beyond the present sinful scheme of things and the inevitable judgment this order would bring upon itself. They envisioned a new creation established by the power of God that would radically reorient human existence and finally abolish alienation and exploitation based on age, sex, race, and economic status. The lion will lie down with the lamb, the wild beasts and powerless children will live together in peace when hurting and destroying is ended in shalom (Isaiah 11:6-9). God's spirit will be poured out on young and old, man and woman, slave and free, who will all prophesy (Joel 2:28-29). God will make a new covenant with the people, who will know the Lord in their hearts, liberating them from sin and injustice and therefore also from the law, judgment, and death (Jeremiah 31:31-34).

One particular eschatological vision should be lifted up, because it is a unique oracle, reversing the traditional sexual roles and identities and thereby transforming the man-woman relationship ultimately. Again, it is found in Jeremiah, whose imagery, in this case, is so shocking that it has alternately confounded and abhorred biblical interpreters through the ages.[9] Jeremiah says Yahweh is about to do *two new things.* The one is the unique but very familiar oracle concerning the new covenant: "Behold, the days are coming, says the Lord, when I will make a *new covenant* with the house of Israel [Jer. 31:31]." The other prophecy of newness, which stands in a coordinate and complementary relationship to the new covenant, is this remarkable passage:

Set up waymarks for yourself,
  make yourself guideposts;
consider well the highway,
  the road by which you went.
Return, O virgin Israel,
  return to these your cities.
How long will you waver,
  O faithless daughter?
For the Lord has created a new thing on the earth:
  a woman protects a man.
                    —Jeremiah 31:21-22, italics added

Both of these oracles of newness are offering hope and restoration to Israel, which, in Jeremiah's time, was conquered as a nation, exiled in Babylon as a people, and broken as a faith in God's covenant. Using an ancient address, "virgin Israel," the prophet suggests marking the road to exile so that, like Hansel and Gretel, the people can find their way home again! They are lost, at the end of their historical identity without a king, a government, an army, or land and are scattered among the nations. In one of the hardest judgments ever uttered on a people, the prophet claims that Yahweh has done it all to a faithless and disobedient people, resulting in a destroyed covenant and nation. Israel is finished as a people and as a faith, and justly so.

Paradoxically, in the midst of historical death these oracles of newness proclaim that what is humanly impossible is possible with God. Yahweh will draw up a new covenant that cannot be vitiated by human sin, because God will fulfill the human responsibility as well as the divine. So outrageous is this vision that it will be immediately abandoned by the Hebrew tradition, only to be recovered much later by a maverick prophet, Jesus of Nazareth, and the writer of the epistle to the Hebrews. The new covenant of Jeremiah totally disappears until a new Jewish sect begins doing Christology.

But what then is the meaning and fate of the companion oracle about a "new thing on earth: a woman protects a man"? Can such a contradiction of human sexuality as we know it fare any better than the new covenant? Are we any better prepared to. receive the oracle that woman redeems man than we are to receive the revelation that God becomes human? In the tradition of Israel both forms of newness are equally absurd, marking Jeremiah as a prophet of the impossible, humanly speaking, which is always the way eschatological hope is received in human history and human sexuality as well. Or put somewhat cryptically in these days of the feminist movement, woman will encompass man when God encompasses humanity.

The enigma resides in the last line of the oracle—"a woman protects a man"—which holds the key to the mystery of this new thing Yahweh will create. The language context is sexual. The word for female (*negeba*) is not the common word for woman (*'ishsha*) but that used in the Priestly creation story where "male and *female* he created them [Gen. 1:27]." However, the Hebrew word for man used by Jeremiah is not *zakar* (the male counterpart to *negeba* in Genesis 1:27 and elsewhere) but *geber*, which connotes not so much male sexuality but man as warrior. Therefore, a literal translation of the line would read: "*the female embraces or encompasses a warrior.*" The enigma seems to deepen.

Jeremiah's language suggests that he is playing with two very different uses of the word female in this passage for the sake of contrast: irony and revelation. One use of female (Jeremiah 31:21-22a) has the familiar cultural associations of innocence and helplessness (virgin Israel, daughter), tenderness, and even silliness and irresponsibility (wavering and faithless daughter). The tone is something like saying, "My darling daughter Israel, you helpless people, stop meandering around in the desert of exile like a foolish girl child."

By strong contrast the second associational word that "female" carries is the word of the soldier and the curses of battle, moving from the tender to the brutal and the bloody. As with any army, there was a standard catalogue of military curses, sayings, and diatribes used by Semitic warriors. One went, "Your warriors are women!" So the Assyrian army was taunted, "Behold your troops are women in your midst [Nah. 3:13]" (see also Jeremiah 50:35-38; 30:5-7).

Military men have not changed essentially since the Babylonian exile, for armies have always sought ennoblement and encouragement for the killing role of the male through the metaphysics of religion and the dynamism of sex, requiring the crucial military functions of chaplain and woman. The chaplain symbolizes the moral righteousness of the war and the favor of the gods upon the day's battle.

Woman, by contrast, is a morally ambiguous symbol in the military world. She represents the myth of innocence (defenseless mother and defended fatherland) and, in the curious way that sexuality becomes a curse by inversion, also identifies those males who fail the military code of duty, honor, and country. In military symbolism woman is defended and derided (which is analogous to her cultural roles as mother and whore), depending upon her representational role—either as virginal female innocence or shameful male failure. Thus, the Roman army's practice of publicly sodomizing their prisoners of war, forcing defeated soldiers to enact a "woman's role." Thus, also, the continuing basic training rituals of the US armed forces, in which soldiers are created by a forced conversion process including brutally sexist references.

Now, Jeremiah is doing just what training sergeants do. He is applying the ancient military curse to his own army. He has said earlier, using the irony of "warriors with labor pains,"

> Thus says the Lord:
> We have heard a cry of panic,
>> of terror, and no peace.
> Ask now, and see,
>> can a man bear a child?
> Why then do I see every man [warrior]
>> with his hands on his loins like a woman in labor?
>> Why has every face turned pale?
> Alas! that day is so great
>> there is none like it;
> it is a time of distress for Jacob
>> [and out of *this* he shall be *saved*!]
>> —Jeremiah 30:5-7 (translation by William L. Holladay)

These two associations with femaleness seem then to have come together in Jeremiah's mind. . . . He seems to be saying, in effect, "You have traditionally been addressed with a tender, feminine reference—virgin, daughter—and this feminine reference has finally turned nightmarish as God's punishment on his people has turned our own warriors into women. Never fear: stop acting like a silly female, out there in the wilderness; God has withdrawn the curse, he is about to revise a creation, he will reverse sex roles so that the female will surmount the warrior! Take heart; come home!"[10]

Now we come to the essential point, which is bringing coherence to these parallel oracles about the new covenant and the new creation. Jeremiah is saying that Yahweh will make a new covenant with Israel by re-creating the whole relationship between them, beginning de novo and forming a faithful people ex nihilo—from the nothingness of exiles in the desert, from a people paralyzed and demoralized by the defeat of their nation and the demise of their society. That is the radicality of God and the absolute faithfulness of her love.

And this new creation will be a new sexual covenant between man and woman, symbolized by Jeremiah in a reversal of sexual roles: "a woman protects a man!" Yahweh will start all over again and even the Genesis stories will be rewritten. If "your warriors are women," it is a revelation from God, who is even capable of reversing sex roles—woman will take the lead and the soldier will be submissive. If Yahweh can transform man's heart to do God's will, then Yahweh can also renew and re-create the age-old pattern of the man-woman relationship. What is humanly impossible because of sinful human nature and the sinful nature of human sexuality, is possible with the faithful and loving Creator. "Behold, I make all things new [Rev. 21:5]," a new heaven and a new earth, and a new sexuality as well.

This muted feminist theme in Jeremiah is a liberating word in our day, because it says there is nothing eternal and inevitable about our culturally defined sex roles. This radical word of God spoken by Jeremiah cuts across and in fact destroys all those human fears, truths, myths, and fatalities that we honor and live out in terms of our sexuality—the sexual determinism of Freud, who said that "anatomy is destiny," as if gender and genes were the lords of life; the folk myth of sexual typologies, which ascribe opposite characteristics to each sex, as if the gifts of the Spirit were dimorphically bestowed or denied; the dogmatic conclusions of behavioral scientists, sex researchers, sex therapists, and sex ideologists, as if the norms for human sexuality were revealed by counting orgasms, curing hangups, or preaching the latest sexual life-style; the American image of who is a man, a virile man, a soldier man, big man, he-man, powerful man, real man, as if these cultural types had anything to do with God's creation of man and woman.

No! Yahweh is utterly free to create and to re-create human sexuality; it is this unconditional freedom of God that is the true source of human sexual freedom and the liberation from sex roles. Creation is grace, but our sex roles, with all their dehumanizing consequences for the relationship between the sexes, belong to the order of the fall and life under judgment just as their re-creation belongs to the order of redemption. The hope for human sexuality is the same hope we hold for all human life and history—the coming of the new age, the new creation, the new humanity. And this "new thing" in Jeremiah's vision will revolutionize the relationship; "a woman encompasses a man." Eve will protect Adam. And to this primordial couple we now turn for a glimpse of God's initial grace in creation.

EVE AND ADAM: GENESIS 2—3 REREAD

The Yahwist account of creation and fall in Genesis 2—3 has seemed to many feminists as overwhelming evidence of the hostility of the Bible to women.[11] If one accepts the centuries of male exegesis of this passage, it is hard to read it any other way than as legitimating male supremacy and female subordination. But read the text again with fresh eyes and a look to the Hebrew.[12]

Ambiguity characterizes the meaning of *'adham* in Genesis 2—3. On the one hand, man is the first creature formed (2:7). The Lord God puts him in the garden "to till it and keep it," a job identified with the male (cf. 3:17-19). On the other hand, *'adham* is a generic term for humankind. In commanding *'adham* not to eat of the tree of the knowledge of good and evil, the Deity is speaking to both the man and the woman (2:16-17). Until the differentiation of female and male (2:21-23), *'adham* is basically androgynous: one creature incorporating two sexes.

Concern for sexuality, specifically for the creation of woman, comes last in the story, after the making of the garden, the trees, and the animals. Some commentators allege female subordination based on this order of events.[13] They contrast it with Genesis 1:27 where God creates *'adham* as male and female in one act.[14] Thereby they infer that whereas the Priests recognized the equality of the sexes, the Yahwist made woman a second, subordinate, inferior sex.[15] But the last may be first, as both the biblical theologian and the literary critic know. Thus the Yahwist account moves to its climax, not its decline, in the creation of woman.[16] She is not an afterthought; she is the culmination. Genesis 1 itself supports this interpretation, for there male and female are indeed the last and truly the crown of all creatures. The last is also first where beginnings and endings are parallel. In Hebrew literature the central concerns of a unit often appear at the beginning and end as an *inclusio* device.[17] Genesis 2 evinces this structure. The creation of man first and of woman last constitutes a ring composition whereby the two creatures are parallel. In no way does the order disparage woman. Content and context augment this reading.

The context for the advent of woman is a divine judgment, "It is not good that 'adham should be alone; I will make him a helper fit for him" (2:18). The phrase needing explication is "helper fit for him." In the Old Testament the word helper ('ezer) has many usages. It can be a proper name for a male.[18] In our story it describes the animals and the woman. In some passages it characterizes Deity. God is the helper of Israel. As helper Yahweh creates and saves.[19] Thus 'ezer is a relational term; it designates a beneficial relationship; and it pertains to God, people, and animals. By itself the word does not specify positions within relationships; more particularly, it does not imply inferiority. Position results from additional content or from context. Accordingly, what kind of relationship does 'ezer entail in Genesis 2:18, 20? Our answer comes in two ways: 1) The word neged, which joins 'ezer, connotes equality: a helper who is a counterpart.[20] 2) The animals are helpers, but they fail to fit 'adham. There is physical, perhaps psychic, rapport between 'adham and the animals, for Yahweh forms (yasar) them both out of the ground ('adhamah). Yet their similarity is not equality. 'Adham names them and thereby exercises power over them. No fit helper is among them. And thus the narrative moves to woman. . . . God is the helper superior to man; the animals are helpers inferior to man; woman is the helper equal to man.

Let us pursue the issue by examining the account of the creation of woman ([verses] 21-22). This episode concludes the story even as the creation of man commences it. . . . The ring composition suggests an interpretation of woman and man as equals. To establish this meaning, structure and content must mesh. They do. In both episodes Yahweh alone creates. For the last creation the Lord God "caused a deep sleep (tardemah) to fall upon the man." Man has no part in making woman; he is out of it. He exercises no control over her existence. He is neither participant nor spectator nor consultant at her birth. Like man, woman owes her life solely to God. For both of them the origin of life is a divine mystery. Another parallel of equality is creation out of raw materials: dust for man and a rib for woman. Yahweh chooses these fragile materials and in both cases processes them before human beings happen. As Yahweh shapes dust and then breathes into it to form man, so Yahweh takes out the rib and then builds it into woman.[21] To call woman "Adam's rib" is to misread the text which states carefully and clearly that the extracted bone required divine labor to become female, a datum scarcely designed to bolster the male ego. Moreover, to claim that the rib means inferiority or subordination is to assign the man qualities over the woman which are not in the narrative itself. Superiority, strength, aggressiveness, dominance, and power do not characterize man in Genesis 2. By contrast he is formed from dirt; his life hangs by a breath which he does not control; and he himself remains silent and passive while the Deity plans and interprets his existence.

The rib means solidarity and equality. *'Adham* recognizes this meaning in a poem:[22]

> This at last is bone of my bones
>   and flesh of my flesh.
> She shall be called *'ishshah* (woman)
>   because she was taken out of *'ish* (man). (2:23)

The pun proclaims both the similarity and the differentiation of female and male. Before this episode the Yahwist has used only the generic term *'adham*. No exclusively male reference has appeared. Only with the specific creation of woman (*'ishshah*) occurs the first specific terms for man as male (*'ish*). In other words, sexuality is simultaneous for woman and man. The sexes are interrelated and interdependent. Man as male does not precede woman as female but happens concurrently with her. Hence, the first act in Genesis 2 is the creation of androgyny (2:7) and the last is the creation of sexuality (2:23).[23] Male embodies female and female embodies male. The two are neither dichotomies nor duplicates. The birth of woman corresponds to the birth of man but does not copy it. Only in responding to the female does the man discover himself as male. No longer a passive creature, *'ish* comes alive in meeting *'ishshah*.

Some read into the poem a naming motif. The man names the woman and thereby has power and authority over her.[24] But again . . . reread. Neither the verb nor the noun *name* is in the poem. We find instead the verb *gara'*, to call: "she shall be called woman." Now in the Yahwist primeval history this verb does not function as a synonym or parallel or substitute for *name*. The typical formula for naming is the verb *to call* plus the explicit object *name*. This formula applies to Deity, people, places, and animals. For example, in Genesis 4 we read:

Cain built a city and *called* the *name* of the city after the *name* of his son Enoch (v. 17).

And Adam knew his wife again, and she bore a son and *called* his *name* Seth (v. 25).

To Seth also a son was born and he *called* his *name* Enoch (v. 26a).

At that time men began to *call* upon the *name* of the Lord (v. 26b).

Genesis 2:23 has the verb *call* but does not have the object *name*. Its absence signifies the absence of a naming motif in the poem. The presence of both the verb *call* and the noun *name* in the episode of the animals strengthens the point:

So out of the ground the Lord God formed every beast of the field and every bird of the air, and brought them to the man to see what he would *call* them; and whatever the man *called* every living creature, that was its *name*. The man gave *names* to all cattle, and to the birds of the air, and to every beast of the field (2:19-20).

In calling the animals by name, *'adham* establishes supremacy over them and fails to find a fit helper. In calling woman, *'adham* does not name her and does find in her a counterpart. Female and male are equal sexes. Neither has authority over the other.[25]

A further observation secures the argument: *Woman* itself is not a name. It is a common noun; it is not a proper noun. It designates gender; it does not specify person. *'Adham* recognizes sexuality by the words *'ishshah* and *'ish*. This recognition is not an act of naming to assert the power of male over female. Quite the contrary. But the true skeptic is already asking: What about Genesis 3:20 where "the man called his wife's name Eve"? We must wait to consider that question. Meanwhile, the words of the ancient poem as well as their context proclaim sexuality originating in the unity of *'adham*. From this one (androgynous) creature come two (female and male). The two return to their original unity as *'ish* and *'ishshah* become one flesh (2:24):[26] another instance of the ring composition.

Next the differences which spell harmony and equality yield to the differences of disobedience and disaster. The serpent speaks to the woman. Why to the woman and not to the man? The simplest answer is that we do not know. The Yahwist does not tell us anymore than he explains why the tree of the knowledge of good and evil was in the garden. But the silence of the text stimulates speculations, many of which only confirm the patriarchal mentality which conceived them. Cassuto identifies serpent and woman, maintaining that the cunning of the serpent is "in reality" the cunning of the woman.[27] He impugns her further by declaring that "for the very reason that a woman's imagination surpasses a man's, it was the woman who was enticed first." Though more gentle in his assessment, von Rad avers that "in the history of Yahweh-religion it has always been the women who have shown an inclination for obscure astrological cults" (a claim which he does not document).[28] Consequently, he holds that the woman "confronts the obscure allurements and mysteries that beset our limited life more directly than the man does," and then he calls her a "temptress." Paul Ricoeur says that woman "represents the point of weakness," as the entire story "gives evidence of a very masculine resentment."[29] McKenzie links the "moral weakness" of the woman with her "sexual attraction" and holds that the latter ruined both the woman and the man.[30]

But the narrative does not say any of these things. It does not sustain the judgment that woman is weaker or more cunning or more sexual than man. Both have the same Creator, who explicitly uses the word "good" to introduce the creation of woman (2:18). Both are equal in birth. There is complete rapport, physical, psychological, sociological, and theological, between them: bone of bone and flesh of flesh. If there be moral frailty in one, it is moral frailty in two. Further, they are equal in responsibility and in judgment, in shame and in guilt, in redemption and in grace. What the narrative says about the nature of woman it also says about the nature of man.

Why does the serpent speak to the woman and not to the man? Let a female speculate. If the serpent is "more subtle" than its fellow creatures, the woman is more appealing than her husband. Throughout the myth she is the more intelligent one, the more aggressive one, and the one with greater sensibilities.[31] Perhaps the woman elevates the animal world by conversing theologically with the serpent. At any rate, she understands the hermeneutical task. In quoting God she interprets the prohibition ("neither shall you touch it"). The woman is both theologian and translator. She contemplates the tree, taking into account all the possibilities. The tree is good for food; it satisfies the physical drives. It pleases the eyes; it is aesthetically and emotionally desirable. Above all, it is coveted as the source of wisdom (*haskil*). Thus the woman is fully aware when she acts, her vision encompassing the gamut of life. She takes the fruit and she eats. The initiative and the decision are hers alone. There is no consultation with her husband. She seeks neither his advice nor his permission. She acts independently.

By contrast the man is a silent, passive, and bland recipient: "She also gave some to her husband and he ate." The narrator makes no attempt to depict the husband as reluctant or hesitating. The man does not theologize; he does not contemplate; he does not envision the full possibilities of the occasion. His one act is belly-oriented, and it is an act of quiescence, not of initiative. The man is not dominant; he is not aggressive; he is not a decision-maker. Even though the prohibition not to eat of the tree appears before the female was specifically created, she knows that it applies to her. She has interpreted it, and now she struggles with the temptation to disobey. But not the man, to whom the prohibition came directly (2:16). He follows his wife without question or comment, thereby denying his own individuality. If the woman be intelligent, sensitive, and ingenious, the man is passive, brutish, and inept. These character portrayals are truly extraordinary in a culture dominated by men. I stress their contrast not to promote female chauvinism but to undercut patriarchal interpretations alien to the text.

The contrast between woman and man fades after their acts of disobedience. They are one in the new knowledge of their nakedness (3:7). They are one in hearing and in hiding. They flee from the sound of the Lord God in the Garden (3:8). First to the man come questions of responsibility (3:9, 11), but the man fails to be responsible: "The woman whom Thou gavest to be with me, she gave me fruit of the tree, and I ate" (3:12). Here the man does not blame the woman; he does not say that the woman seduced him;[32] he blames the Deity. The verb which he uses for both the Deity and the woman is *ntn* (cf. 3:6). . . . This verb neither means nor implies seduction in this context or in the lexicon. Again, if the Yahwist intended to make woman the temptress, he missed a choice opportunity. The woman's response supports the point. "The serpent beguiled me and I ate" (3:13). Only here occurs the strong verb *nsh'*, meaning to deceive, to seduce. God accepts this subject-verb combination when, immediately following the woman's accusation, Yahweh says to the serpent, "Because you have done this, cursed are you above all animals" (3:14).

Though the tempter (the serpent) is cursed,[33] the woman and the man are not. But they are judged, and the judgments are commentaries on the disastrous effects of their shared disobedience. They show how terrible human life has become as it stands between creation and grace. We misread if we assume that these judgments are mandates. They describe; they do not prescribe. They protest; they do not condone. Of special concern are the words telling the woman that her husband shall rule over her (3:16). This statement is not license for male supremacy, but rather it is condemnation of that very pattern.[34] Subjugation and supremacy are perversions of creation. Through disobedience the woman has become slave. Her initiative and her freedom vanish. The man is corrupted also, for he has become master, ruling over the one who is his God-given equal. The subordination of female to male signifies their shared sin.[35] This sin vitiates all relationships: between animals and human beings (3:15); mothers and children (3:16); husbands and wives (3:16); people and the soil (3:17-18); humanity and its work (3:19). Whereas in creation man and woman know harmony and equality, in sin they know alienation and discord. Grace makes possible a new beginning.

A further observation about these judgments: They are culturally conditioned. Husband and work (childbearing) define the woman; wife and work (farming) define the man. A literal reading of the story limits both creatures and limits the story. To be faithful translators, we must recognize that women as well as men move beyond these culturally defined roles, even as the intentionality and function of the myth move beyond its original setting. Whatever forms stereotyping takes in our own culture, they are judgments upon our common sin and disobedience. The suffering and oppression we women and men know now are marks of our fall, not of our creation.

At this place of sin and judgment "the man calls his wife's name Eve" (3:20), thereby asserting his rule over her. The naming itself faults the man for corrupting a relationship of mutuality and equality. And so Yahweh evicts the primeval couple from the Garden, yet with signals of grace.[36] Interestingly, the conclusion of the story does not specify the sexes in flight. Instead the narrator resumes use of the generic and androgynous term 'adham with which the story began and thereby completes an overall ring composition (3:22-24).

Visiting the Garden of Eden in the days of the Women's Movement, we need no longer accept the traditional exegesis of Genesis 2—3. Rather than legitimating the patriarchal culture from which it comes, the myth places that culture under judgment. And thus it functions to liberate, not to enslave. This function we can recover and appropriate. The Yahwist narrative tells us who we are (creatures of equality and mutuality); it tells us who we have become (creatures of oppression); and so it opens possibilities for change, for a return to our true liberation under God. In other words, the story calls female and male to repent.

SONG OF SONGS: SEX WITHOUT SIN

The beauty and mystery of human sexuality are captured more often by poets and lovers than by those who analyze sex, whether scientists or theologians. Love poetry is a mode of human celebration springing from the soul like a song, expressing depths of feeling and understanding that break the bonds of language and invite the spirit to dance. Love poetry is carnal knowledge, a hymn to the beauty of the body and the goodness of creation, to the sheer joy of bodily existence and its pleasures. In love the body is a means of grace, and the graceful forms of the body are a means of love.

The Song of Songs is a biblical love poem celebrating the joys of erotic love between woman and man. It is unique among the genre of biblical literature and has served to stimulate, confound, and even offend interpreters through the ages. Unable to excise it from the canon, most theologians have ignored it and a few have turned it into a fantastic allegory of the spiritual life in a religion purged of carnal realities. These docetic interpretations of the Song suppress its meaning for human sexuality within the doctrine of creation and censor the Bible for including a vision of erotic love restored to paradise where it is enjoyed without shame, sin, or guilt. It is a song the church sings with an uncertain voice, if it is sung at all.

The Song poem shows curious parallels with the Yahwist creation story in Genesis 2—3, and one cannot resist comparing and contrasting these two gardens and the two couples. The paradise created in Genesis 2 and lost in Genesis 3 is, in a metaphorical sense, paradise regained in the Canticles. The prehistorical saga in which sexual love is created, blessed, and then deformed by defiance of the Creator is again restored to innocence in the eschatological vision of the Song. Canticles is a midrash on Genesis 2—3.[37]

In the Canticles, woman initiates love-making: "O that you would kiss me with the kisses of your mouth! For your love is better than wine [1:2]." The place where the lovers meet is a garden: "Let my beloved come to his garden, and eat its choicest fruit [4:16c]." This garden of sensuous delight is filled with trees that provide beauty and food, incense, fruits, plants, and flowers. Fountains of living water nourish this paradise like the rivers flowing out of Eden (Genesis 2:10-14). The place and the people are thoroughly sensual, and love is sweet to the taste like the fruit of the apple tree (2:3; 4:16; 5:1). The lovers embrace, delighting in their touching bodies (1:2; 2:3-6; 4:10-11), a glance of the eyes, and the sounds of the voice. The animals also inhabit the garden and become metaphors of love: "My beloved is like a gazelle, or a young stag [2:9]"; "Your two breasts are like two fawns, twins of a gazelle, that feed among the lilies [4:5]"; "His eyes are like doves beside springs of water [5:12]."

In the garden of creation man works and, by implication, woman also works. In the Song woman's work becomes explicit; she keeps vineyards (1:6) and flocks (1:8); her lover may also be a shepherd (1:7). In both gardens the joy of work is affirmed, and it is free from the sexual stereotypes of work roles. The Song celebrates nature and work as pleasures leading to love, as both were before the original couple disobeyed, causing the earth to bring forth thorns and thistles and labor to become sweat and toil (Genesis 2:15; 3:16-19).

Neither the primeval couple nor the historical couple bear names, but both are concerned with naming. When 'adham names the animals, it is an act of authority consonant with creation. When he names the woman, it is an act of perversion preceding expulsion. In the erotic garden roles reverse, authority vanishes, and perversion is unknown. The woman names the man: "Your name is oil poured out; therefore the maidens love you" (1:3). Her act is wholly fitting and good. Naming is ecstasy, not exercise; it is love, not control. And that love marks a new creation.[38]

The Song has a strong matriarchal cast that counterbalances the patriarchalism of the culture and makes possible an affirmation of the mutuality of woman and man in their cohumanity and in their love for each other. Woman brings her lover to the "house of [her] mother" (3:4; 8:2); the mother is mentioned seven times in the Song, the father not at all. This hymn to love is sung by woman and man, but its feminine themes recall the first man leaving his father and mother to cleave to his wife (Genesis 2:24) and Naomi's counsel to her daughters-in-law (Ruth 1:8).

In keeping with our earlier exegesis of Genesis 2, the Song reflects and affirms the mutuality of woman and man, overturning historical sex roles and myths about male domination and female subordination. In the erotic garden woman is man's equal as one who is independent, who works, takes initiative, has an identity of her own apart from man. In contrast to the first woman, she is not identified as wife and her sexuality is not defined by procreation. Throughout the poem the lovers alternate the initiatives of meeting, with woman moving openly and boldly to find her lover rather than passively waiting for his coming. Each exalts the body and beauty of the other; each treats the other with respect and tenderness, for they are lovers united in love. They are not ashamed of their nakedness but together embrace their sexuality and enjoy it without the guilt of sexual exploitation. This is seen in the use of the word desire, which only occurs three times in the Old Testament (twice in Genesis, 3:16 and 4:7, and once in Canticles). In Genesis woman's desire for her husband, who rules over her, is Yahweh's judgment upon woman, given in the context of human sin. In Canticles desire is transformed by human love, which itself transforms the whole relationship between man and woman. Desire becomes a joy instead of judgment when human sexuality is experienced as grace, not sin. The Song is a parable of sexual salvation offered man and woman together in the coming of shalom to human life.

It is a song for lovers in the ecstasy of love-making, in the joy of life together, and in those bittersweet moments of separation from the beloved. The interpreter can only wonder why the primeval couple and not the erotic couple has become the paradigm for man and woman in the Judeo-Christian tradition. Why has this cameo of innocent and nascent sexual love been ignored or, at most, been allowed to speak only at the wedding feast? Is idyllic love too pure a vision or too precarious a reality in human life to serve as a symbol and norm for the man-woman relationship?

The Song itself suggests the limits inherent in sexual love, introducing a muted and minor theme that is barely perceptible but nevertheless present in the erotic garden. Like the first garden, with its tree and serpent, there are potential threats in the erotic realm. Nature furnishes the metaphors of the sterile winter now past (2:11), "the little foxes, that spoil the vineyards [2:15]," and ultimately death, which haunts all creation in its beauty.

66

But it is human history that harbors the perils unknown to nature: the anger of brothers (1:6), a knowledge of jealousy (8:6), the anxiety of woman separated from her lover (3:1-4; 5:6-8; 6:1), and her suffering at the hands of the watchmen (5:7). It is the story of love in history that threatens naturalism by revealing the contradictions between nature and human nature. Nature is controlled by instincts and inevitabilities that determine the course of life for the plants and animals of the garden. But the human couple is a mere design and an open possibility awaiting moral decisions by the partners, who are responsible for their destiny in the garden. The human story is unnatural, because human freedom, which makes history possible in all its glory and tragedy and which enables erotic love to become fully human by transcending simple animality, is the same freedom that permits the betrayal of love and the use of sex for power, domination, and selfish pleasure.

Canticles is a midrash on the Genesis story, and when both are reinterpreted without sexism, they commonly speak of the equality, mutuality, and love between man and woman. And in a curious reversal of the mythic and the historical, the prehistorical Genesis saga gives a more profound and realistic portrayal of the human sexual story; while the Canticles, which is a real historical tale of two lovers, borders on sexual myth, with its celebration of eroticism that knows no sin, no prohibitions, no disobedience, no betrayal. If their commonality lies in Yahwist theology, which rejects all sexual chauvinism as a perversion of creation and a sign of God's judgment, their difference also derives from that same faith. In the love Song there is no God participating in the story. Yahweh is neither present nor absent. That silence portends the limits of erotic love as a mode of salvation and of the power of sex to engender natural myths of gods created in our image, whom we may serve with erotic delight. If we cannot return to the Garden of Eden before the fall, neither can we find salvation in the garden of eroticism.

However, the last word, like the first, is grace for man and woman who live and love somewhere east of Eden. The Song is also a sexual midrash on the Christian doctrine of salvation, where we live in the reality of God's reconciliation as well as the reality of human sin. Sexual shalom has come and is the promise in which we live by faith, hope, and love. The Song sings of that love in a bold and shameless way, knowing that love is the meaning of life and human sexuality is beautiful and good as an expression of that love. Our destiny is not a garden but grace, freely given by the God who first conceived and created us in love.

MAN AND MAN: GENESIS 19:1-11; LEVITICUS 18:22; 20:13

Up to this point we have been dealing with Old Testament perspectives on the relationship between woman and man. The patriarchal culture and religion of Israel establishes the order as being man first, and then woman, who finds her place in the light and service of man. Biblical faith, however, is the carrier of a Hebrew counterculture based on revelations that may be interpreted as fundamentally challenging the dominant patriarchal tradition. Like woman herself, this revelation is a muted theme awaiting the fullness of time, the new historical moment when it will speak with power and grace.

Within the given historic order of the sexes, it is still the man-woman relationship, in all its pain and promise, that shapes the paradigm for human sexuality in the Bible. Even patriarchalism, by definition, requires the presence of woman as the other partner and the helper. The principle of male superiority also carries within itself the boundary of its power, preventing the exclusion of woman from the sexual relationship. The absence of woman is the end of patriarchalism. The inclusion of woman as the subordinate sex is the essence of patriarchalism. The equality and partnership of the sexes is the final transcendence of sexism and the promise of cohumanity as woman and man created for each other.

There is another possibility—a sexual relationship between man and man. This variation on the theme is a minor and minority issue within the essential paradigm for sexuality in the Bible. Today it is also being considered anew, and there are several texts that speak specifically to the issue or that have been traditionally interpreted as doing so.

THE SODOM AND GOMORRAH STORY

This story, found in Genesis 19, deserves a careful reinterpretation in our day, because it has become a sexual symbol and a notorious name that is evoked in criminal statutes and in moral theology to condemn homosexuality summarily, without a fair trial in the courts of the church or state. Any interpretation of a biblical text, which for millennia since Philo and Josephus has become an ironclad tradition and which is canonized for the condemnation of a sexual minority in social policy and church practice, must at least stand the generally accepted tests of biblical criticism.

The larger question is whether the fate suffered by homosexuals over the centuries is biblically based and fully deserved, or whether it is a case where a questionable exegesis has led the

Western church and culture to an equally questionable tradition of persecution and moral censure. The more narrow hermeneutical questions are whether the sin of Sodom is really sodomy and whether this can be demonstrated as such beyond a reasonable doubt.

The ancient and traditional interpretation of the story is well known but merits repetition even for those who believe it is a valid interpretation. This view goes as follows, in summary form: The two persons who came to Sodom and were offered sanctuary and hospitality by Lot were male angels sent by God to destroy the cities of the plain. The male mob that surrounded Lot's house and demanded that he produce the two visitors "that we may know them" (Genesis 19:5) meant by "to know" the intent to commit public homosexual acts on them. Lot's offering instead his "two daughters who have not known man" (Genesis 19:8) demonstrates the desirable but rejected heterosexual alternative. The Lord's destruction of Sodom and Gomorrah by fire and brimstone is a seal of God's condemnation of homosexuality and other wickedness. Subsequent historical disasters may also be attributed, at least in part, to sexual licentiousness, including homosexuality.

This interpretation of the story has persisted to the present because it was and, in some denominations, still is church teaching and moral instruction on the issue of homosexuality. Yet, biblical scholars disagree on the interpretation above, indicating that the exegetical consensus has collapsed and that credible alternatives now exist. In fact, the recent reworking of the story by several biblical scholars and theologians presents the thesis that the sin of Sodom had nothing to do with homosexuality. Their approach is also worthy of summary.

Here we are dealing with a contested verb, to know, which is the Hebrew word *yādhá*. On this verb everyone is an expert, given innocent scatological jokes among the clergy about "knowing in the biblical sense" and the fact that veteran lay listeners of sermons and scripture have inevitably learned that "know" is sometimes used in the Bible as a euphemism for sexual intercourse.

In the Hebrew-English lexicon of the Old Testament the word *yādhá* is used 943 times and ordinarily means "to know" in the common sense of that word. Apart from this disputed Genesis 19:5 text (and its derivative in Judges 19:22), *yādhá* is used without qualification to mean engage in coitus only ten times out of 943. And in such cases, aside from the two exceptions just mentioned, it refers to heterosexual intercourse. The verb used

69

in those instances where the Old Testament refers to either homosexual intercourse or bestiality is *shākabh* (not found in this passage). Linguistically, it is only a rare and singular chance that the verb means homosexual intercourse in this story. Probably it simply means to know, to identify the strangers, to find out who they are.

The nonsexual denotation of *yādhá* would alter the interpretation of the story but not its essential meaning. Lot was himself an outsider, a resident alien in Sodom dependent on the city's hospitality and tolerance. ("This fellow came to sojourn, and he would play the judge [vs. 9]!") His taking in two other strangers could have exceeded his own alienable level of suspicion among the residents concerning foreigners. Sensing a plot, as the rumor of strangers got around, "the men of Sodom, both young and old, *all the people to the last man*, surrounded the house [vs. 4]" as a vigilante party acting on a perceived threat to their community by outsiders. (That actually makes more sense than the image of everybody, even little kids and old men, turning out for a late night homosexual gang rape arising from some sudden and unanimous tide of community lust.) They demanded that the strangers be produced for interrogation, inspection, and identification—perhaps their mission in relation to the impending doom of the city was perceived by the residents. Lot pleads with them.

Then, sensing the crowd's mood and the peril of the angels, Lot tries a diversionary tactic by offering his two virgin daughters to the mob, hoping thereby to annul violence with sex and being willing to sacrifice his own children to protect the strangers who "have come under the shelter of my roof [vs. 8]." But it does not work, and they turn on Lot: "Now we will deal worse with you than with them [i.e., the strangers] [vs. 9]," the men threaten. And Lot himself is saved by the angels through the miracle of the blinding of the mob. Lot's whole family is saved from destruction by the strangers they fed and sheltered (vss. 1-3). As in the case of Abraham and the angelic visitors (Genesis 18:1-5), the good and righteous man is marked by the gracious reception of strangers.

The question is: What was the sin and wickedness of the cities that brought about destruction? Within the story itself the iniquity is not explicitly identified; and elsewhere in the Old Testament, Sodom becomes a symbol only of destruction. In none of these references is Sodom specifically characterized by sodomy.

Taking the story at face value, one could as easily say that the sin was Lot's in presuming to offer his daughters without their consent for totally dehumanizing purposes. Why hasn't that interpretation taken its place alongside the others?

Ezekiel's interpretation is as follows: Behold, this was the sin of your sister Sodom: she and her daughters lived in pride, plenty, and thoughtless ease; they supported not the poor and needy; they grew haughty, and committed abomination before me; so I swept them away; as you have seen (Ezekiel 16:49-50).

Isaiah indicts the city with injustice (Isaiah 13:19), and Jeremiah claims that it is moral and ethical laxity that is wicked (Jeremiah 49:18; 50:40). And Ecclesiasticus points to pride: "He did not spare the people among whom Lot was living, whom he detested for their pride [16:8]."

In the New Testament there is a curious confirmation of the contention that the real sin of Sodom and Gomorrah is inhospitality—the rejection of the messengers who come as strangers bearing salvation. It is found in Jesus' instructions to the seventy who are being sent out in pairs to the towns to preach the gospel:

> Whenever you enter a town and they receive you, eat what is set before you; heal the sick in it and say to them, "The Kingdom of God has come near to you." But whenever you enter a town and they do not receive you, go into its streets and say, "Even the dust of your town that clings to our feet, we wipe off against you; nevertheless know this, that the kingdom of God has come near." I tell you, it shall be more tolerable on that day for Sodom than for that town.
>
> —Luke 10:8-12

It is only in the later New Testament literature (2 Peter 2:4-10 and Jude 6—7) that we find Sodom's sin identified with explicit sexual practices—ungodliness, licentiousness, immorality, and unnatural lust. However, the context in both cases has to do with "angels when they sinned" or "did not keep their own position but left their proper dwelling" and were therefore cast into hell. The meaning of both texts is rather murky, and neither has served as a theological cornerstone or inspired much lucid preaching. These texts seem to be related to an apocryphal work of Pharisaic origin, the Testaments of the Twelve Patriarchs, and refer to a violation of the orders of creation involved in sexual commerce between angelic beings and human beings.

Furthermore, it can be argued, if the sin of Sodom had been understood in biblical times clearly and primarily as homosexual acts, then those biblical texts that definitely do refer to homosexuality might be expected to refer to Sodom as the classic example of the divine judgment. This never happens. None of the biblical texts commonly understood as referring to homosexuality ever mentions that city and its wickedness. This omission lends increased support to the hypothesis that the sin involved was principally inhospitality, along with pride, injustice, and sensuality.

Very early in the postbiblical period the church interpreted the story as dealing with homosexual practices, and this view has dominated to the present time. Still, the above critique of the customary biblical basis for the historic condemnation of homosexuality shows that the tradition is at least open to serious question and at most may be a hermeneutically untenable point of view. The story may have little or nothing to do with homosexual practices. In the latter case, according to John J. McNeill, whose research on this text we have followed,

> if this interpretation of the true sin of Sodom is correct, then we are dealing here with one of the supremely ironic paradoxes of history. For thousands of years in the Christian West the homosexual has been the victim of inhospitable treatment. Condemned by the Church, he has been the victim of persecution, torture, and even death. In the name of a mistaken understanding of Sodom and Gomorrah, the true crime of Sodom and Gomorrah has been and continues to be repeated every day.[39]

THE LEVITICAL HOLINESS CODE

In the Mosaic law found in Leviticus there are two texts that condemn male homosexual acts:

> You shall not lie with a male as with a woman; it is an abomination.
>
> —Leviticus 18:22

> If a man lies with a male as with a woman, both of them have committed an abomination; they shall be put to death, their blood is upon them.
>
> —Leviticus 20:13

There was a legitimate and understandable reason for such proscriptions in the life of Israel. The condemnation of male homosexual acts must be seen in the context of the procreative ethic that it served. The command of God to "be fruitful and multiply" was the overriding principle in the ordering of human sexuality and was clearly necessary for survival in ancient culture. On those premises homosexuality had to be outlawed. If procreation is the desired fruit of intercourse, then any sexual act that does not serve that end is by its very nature forbidden. In other words, the ancient Hebrew stigma on homosexuality was both wise and necessary for Israel.

Today the procreative ethic has been largely abandoned by Christians in those churches in Western industrialized nations that do not recognize the Bishop of Rome. Indeed, our own situation may be more nearly the opposite, where an unbridled procreative ethic may now be a sin violating the command of God to husband the earth and its resources. The question naturally arises, then, about the continuing merit of the proscription of homosexuality when its original premise no longer obtains. What is the status of this Levitical law in the lives of contemporary Christians?

These texts are sometimes isolated from the complex body of law that comprises the Holiness Code and are given an authority that most Christians would not attribute to the Mosaic law as a whole and certainly not to most of the specific rules found in the code. As a hermeneutical rule, one should be required to read the whole code (Leviticus 17—26) before evoking these texts so that the whole code, in all its splendor, is the conscious context for the claims being made. It is ignorance of the law that often breeds passion for its defense. And only a highly selective enforcement of the law enables the lawkeepers to indulge in stoning the lawbreakers.

Only a reading of the whole law prepares one for the liberating word of a young prophet who, many centuries later, summarized all the law and the prophets in a double commandment. For the Holiness Code is an intricate system of rules calculated to establish the ritual, moral, and religious purity of Israel and to separate the people from the pagan cultures and religions that surrounded them. Like other legislation, codes, and covenants in the life of Israel, the Levitical law had a positive function in the organization and regulation of Israel's life in a particular historical period under specific circumstances. That represents its genius and its limitations, its continuing authority and its irrelevance.

Examples of its genius and continuing authority are readily found. In terms of ordering human sexuality, the Hebrew laws against adultery (Leviticus 20:10), incest (Leviticus 18:6-18), and forcing daughters into prostitution (Leviticus 19:20) are enduring principles of sexual morality in the Christian community today. The condemnation of offering live children as burnt sacrifices to the god Molech was a historic break with that grisly pagan practice. The laws calling for love and justice are as honored today (often in the breach) as they were in the time of Moses:

> You shall not steal, nor deal falsely, nor lie to one another.
> —Leviticus 19:11

> You shall not oppress your neighbor or rob him.
> —Leviticus 19:13

> You shall do no wrong in judgment, in measures of length or weight or quantity.
> —Leviticus 19:35

> You shall not hate your brother in your heart. . . . You shall not take vengeance or bear any grudge . . . but you shall love your neighbor as yourself.
> —Leviticus 19:17-18

Such laws represent the highest ethic codified in the ancient world; one that has neither been surpassed nor often honored by our contemporary world. The church itself might find its life and politics renewed by taking the fundamental precepts of the code to heart.

Such ethical pearls are found scattered among laws about cloven-hoofed beasts and purifying baths. The code contains many laws that regulate the cultus and rituals of religion—slaughtering animals, animal sacrifices, food preparation and forbidden foods, priestly regulations and performance of rituals, feasts and offerings, cleanliness and defilement. Even the ardent law-lover will not claim their validity for contemporary Christians. Many of these rules strike us as being superstitious remnants of primitive religion. Who would reject a candidate for ordination simply because the person is blind or lame; has a mutilated face or a limb too long; is a hunchback or dwarf; has defective sight, an itching disease, scabs, or crushed testicles (Leviticus 21:16-21)? Who will cut off from the people a German parishioner who enjoys blood sausage (Leviticus 17:10-11)? Who believes that touching the dead or having an emission of semen renders one unclean until evening and until after one has taken a ritual bath (Leviticus 22:4-5)? Confronted with such laws, even the hard-core legalist would blanch and retreat into a contextual hermeneutic to justify ignoring most of the Levitical Code.

Some laws prescribed the death penalty for certain offenses and therefore comprised the catalogue of mortal sins in the life of Israel. These capital religious offenses were child sacrifices, cursing your father or mother, adultery, male homosexual acts, bestiality, being a medium or a wizard, blaspheming the name of the Lord, and killing a person. In today's society these sins are variously forgotten, ignored, applauded, or legitimized. Only killing is once again being established as a capital offense by law in certain states and under certain conditions.

Killing furnishes a good example of how these laws have suffered disparate fates and also shows the impossibility of absorbing them into contemporary Christian ethics in a literal and uncritical way. The law against killing has been refined and reinterpreted with a convoluted casuistry that is one of the seven wonders in the history of church doctrine. Our latest national violation of the Levitical proscription of killing required the Constantinian church-state concordat, over 1,600 years of just-war theology, hermeneutical headstands, the institution of the military chaplaincy, the war powers of the United States Constitution, and several immoral administrations to result in our Christian children being sacrificed by fire in the Vietnam War on altars erected by the policies of the state. Such an impressive political and intellectual effort has never been mounted by church and state on behalf of blasphemers, adulterers, and homosexuals, which may explain why these particular offenders can be pilloried while other lawbreakers become national heroes. Literal law seems to cover them; whereas killing men, women, and children is an abomination so transformed by legal and theological wizardry that it has acquired the status of Christian realism and ethical responsibility. An educated Canaanite would have difficulty following the logic of that moral transformation, even though the conclusion ratifies the propitiatory sacrificial system in which he or she believed.

In case the point still escapes the person who would use the Holiness Code to enforce selectively the laws that condemn both sexual sinners and those who eat eagles, hawks, vultures, and ostriches (Leviticus 11:13-19), it is that no Christian ethicist today will defend the code *in toto* or interpret it literally. Even the staunchest defenders of Levitical morality ignore whole chapters of the law, thereby using some unadmitted and perhaps unconscious principle of selection. Those who claim divine authority for certain laws and who call for current ecclesiastical enforcement of them are obliged, as a matter of simple honesty and fairness, to explicate the principles of divination being used. Why is this particular law binding while many others are not? Mere inclusion in the Bible obviously fails as a rationale, since other inclusions are readily dismissed.

A few comments and questions that must be faced by anyone using the Levitical texts on homosexuality for the purpose of condemnation and contemporary enforcement are as follows:

First, the cultural and political context of the code was a religioethical separation from the past in Egypt and the present in Canaan (Leviticus 18:2-5; 20:22-24), especially practices associated with other religions. There is evidence that homosexual acts were involved in the temple prostitution that was part of baal worship. The question is whether the code forbade homosexual acts because they were wrong per se, because they violated the procreative ethic, or because they were involved with idolatry. What is the precise nature of the offense and the norm being violated? Who is the injured party?

Second, if the texts condemning male homosexual acts are to be exempted from the code's historical locus and purposes that no longer apply and are to be made ethically binding in contemporary church life, how shall the law be interpreted and enforced? Should the penalty be death? Does the law apply only to overt acts or should it encompass a homosexual self-identification as well? How will sexual discrimination be avoided, since the Holiness Code deals only with male homosexual acts? If scripture ignores female homosexuality, what is the origin and reason for this exception? If the lesbian is not condemned, why the man?

Third, earlier we discussed the patriarchal bias of many biblical traditions, and nowhere is this male dominance more obvious than in the legal codes. In patriarchal culture and religion it is the duty of women to bear children, procreation is the purpose of sexual intercourse, and homosexuality is taboo. Why does the patriarchal principle, based as it is on male superiority, involve both the subordination of women and the fear of homosexuality? Why is there a disparity between the severity of judgments passed on heterosexual moral offenses and homosexual moral offenses?

Fourth, how shall the church, which is the new Israel or "Israel with a difference" because of its confession of Jesus Christ, deal with the ancient law codes of Israel? What is the role of the law when it is written on the hearts of those who love God (Jeremiah 31:31-34; Romans 5:5; 2 Corinthians 3:3)? What is Christian legalism? What does it mean, as Paul says, that "we are not under law but under grace [Rom. 6:15]"? Or consider Paul again: "For the whole law is fulfilled in one word, 'You shall love your neighbor as yourself [Gal. 5:14]' " (cf. Matthew 22:36-40; Leviticus 19:18).

Such questions merit serious discussion across the church today, when the traditional assessment of homosexuality is being challenged from several quarters within the church and our society. We do not presume the authority to answer these questions, only the obligation to raise them pointedly as the church makes moral decisions on these issues.

NEW TESTAMENT PERSPECTIVES ON HUMAN SEXUALITY

"God is love" is the central affirmation of biblical faith that forms the context in which all scripture must be interpreted. In expressing love, God creates, liberates, saves, and works through human history for the good and welfare of all people. One of the most characteristic biblical expressions of God's love is "God's reign," which is seen as stretching all the way from creation to the Christ event and its ultimate consummation at the end of history (Isaiah 40:9-11; Mark 1:15). Creation and history, therefore, are in God's gracious power. This is good news, because God offers life to people and encourages them to choose life (Deuteronomy 30:19-20). The biblical theme is reiterated in the United Church of Christ Statement of Faith—"God sets before people the ways of life and death." God seeks to save from aimlessness and sin all people in their pursuit of the life that God offers.

God has entered into covenant relationship with people as stipulated in the Torah, the way of life. The people, in turn, bind themselves to God in covenantal relationships that lead to life for them and the whole human community. Much of the biblical record reveals the failure of God's people in that relationship and their inclination to follow the ways of death rather than the ways of life. In the face of this recurring failure of people and the persistent faithfulness of God, the prophet Jeremiah foresaw a new covenant (Jeremiah 31:31-34) that was essentially inward and dynamic to empower people to life in new ways. The record of God's work in history toward the salvation of all is briefly stated in Romans 9—11. The failure of Israel, as seen in this passage, consists in Israel's insistence upon its own righteousness, its own way of doing things. In the self-concern and insistence upon its own righteousness, Israel neglected the opportunities that God had held before it and resisted the righteousness that comes from God (Romans 9:30—10:4). Thus, Israel had become bound up and imprisoned in its own history so that it lacked the necessary openness to new revelations and opportunities that God held out before it.

In the fullness of time (Galatians 4:4) God sent forth Jesus, born in human condition so that he might redeem his people from the very ways of death that their history created and made real. God's son, Jesus, came as one who reasserted God's reign as good news: "The time is fulfilled, and the kingdom of God is at hand; repent, and believe in the gospel [Mark 1:15]."

The nearness of the kingdom as proclaimed by Jesus calls people to repent (change and be open to God's way) and to trust in the good news of God's reign. The reign of God as seen in the work and teaching of Jesus calls into question all human institutions and ways and liberates people for new ways of life.

The Jesus portrayed by the gospels is one who could and did cut through a confusing and sometimes conflicting mass of rules to the spirit of the law. With reference to sabbath regulations, for example, he taught that "the sabbath was made for man, not man for the sabbath [Mark 2:27]" (cf. Matthew 12:1-14; Luke 6:1-11). Sabbath regulations are to serve the welfare of people, not merely to preserve the sanctity of the sabbath for its own sake. Jesus actually broke some laws in other areas of life in order to reveal their inadequacy or harmful effects. For example, he apparently disregarded laws pertaining to fasting (Mark 2:18-22; cf. Matthew 9:14-17; Luke 5:33-39), working in the grainfields (Mark 2:23-28; cf. Matthew 12:1-8; Luke 6:1-5), healing on the sabbath (Mark 3:1-6; cf. Matthew 12:9-14; Luke 6:6-11). The basic principle Jesus' teachings and actions show is that laws exist to serve human welfare and to enhance life.

Jesus' teachings contain few explicit statements regarding human sexuality. Many of his actions, however, show that he crossed over the boundaries of sex, national origin, and status in order to minister to people. He disregarded national and sexual barriers when he affirmed a Syrophoenician woman and healed her daughter (Mark 7:24-30; cf. Matthew 15:21-28). He crossed over accepted boundaries to speak with a Samaritan woman and to help her find the way to fullness of life (John 4:1-42). He ignored customary barriers in permitting a woman of questionable character to anoint him with expensive ointment and praised her sign of devotion to him (Luke 7:37-50; cf. Matthew 26:6-13; Mark 14:3-9). In his purpose of affirming the worth of persons, Jesus broke with many customs and regulations that tended to dehumanize people. No wonder he was accused of befriending tax collectors and sinners (Mark 2:16-17; cf. Matthew 9:9-13; Luke 5:30-32) and of being a glutton and a drunkard

(Matthew 11:19; cf. Luke 7:34). Thus, the gospels portray Jesus as one who affirmed persons at the risk and cost of breaking existing customs that tended to dehumanize persons and relationships among them.

Does all this mean that Jesus affirmed all forms of life or that he encouraged moral anarchy in sexual relationships? The answer is, "no." While he did not spell out many specific regulations in the area of sexual behavior, it is clear that he emphasized the primacy of neighbor love in making moral and ethical decisions (Mark 12:31; cf. Matthew 22:39; Luke 10:27). Moreover, his teachings make clear that Jesus used the word neighbor in its broadest possible sense to cover human relations ranging from a chance meeting of strangers on the Jericho road to intimate relations with a spouse. The dominant motif of this teaching is that attitudes, actions, and relationships are good when they affirm love for other persons.

The teachings of Jesus on divorce may be understood in this light. Divorce is wrong because it violates and destroys love between persons (Matthew 5:31-32; cf. Matthew 19:9; Mark 10:11-12; Luke 16:18). Even this teaching of Jesus, however, is not to be hardened into universal law for all times and in all situations. In our own day it would also be a violation of neighbor love to stigmatize persons who are divorced, to estrange them from the Christian community, and to deprive them of the resources of the gospel in reaching a new life.[40] Hence, the teachings of Jesus on divorce and similar areas of life need to be examined and reevaluated in light of the affirmation of persons in love.

Jesus also taught that adultery is wrong not only as an overt act but also wrong in the beginning of lustful desires that might lead to adultery (Matthew 5:27-28). This teaching is not to be understood as a condemnation of healthy sexual relationships or desires, for Jesus does not condemn sexual relationships as such. They are wrong only when they do violence to neighbor love and tend to degrade or dehumanize another person. On the positive side, it is entirely in keeping with the spirit of Jesus' teaching that healthy sexual relations, like all of life, are to be affirmed.

In adopting, developing, and maintaining the doctrine of the incarnation, the church through the ages has affirmed the reality of the Word made flesh (John 1:14). Among its many meanings, the incarnation affirms the goodness of human life as God created it to be, including the goodness and beauty of human sexuality and sexual relations in the context of love. Moreover, the incarnation means that the church affirms life as Jesus did. In cutting through and across regulations and customs that dehumanize persons, the gospel empowers people to fullness of life.

Because the world could not stand this radical critique, the power of darkness conspired to crucify Jesus. Early Christian churches that experienced that crucifixion saw in it a victory over the powers of this age and the offer of life to all who participated in Christ's resurrection. Hence, the death and resurrection of Jesus, along with his life, work, and teaching, are seen as the saving event.

Early Christian interpretations of the Christ event were influenced by apocalyptic and eschatological ideas. Basically, this meant that primitive Christians assumed a modified dualism in which reality was perceived in terms of overlapping ages, one manifesting the powers of evil and the other the powers of good. "The resurrection is God's mighty and sovereign penetration of the man-made fabric of earthly history, the breaking in of the eschaton, God's epiphany, and, in consequence, the establishment of the facts concerning Christ as saving event."[41]

A major representative of the apocalyptic/eschatological interpretation of the Christ event is the apostle Paul, who said, "The old has passed away, behold, the new has come [2 Cor. 5:17]." The Christ event ends the old aeon. It strikes at the very roots of all existing societies and calls into question all human institutions and values. Paul sometimes characterizes the old in terms of the "old self," which dies to sin and death with Christ (Romans 6). Elsewhere Paul describes the old in terms of idolatry, which leads to the wrath of God and consequent perversion in human life (Romans 1:18-32). Similarly, other catalogues of vices appear here and there in Paul's writings and throughout the New Testament as characteristics of the old aeon (e.g., Romans 13:11-14; Galatians 5:19-21; Ephesians 4:17-32).

For Paul, an important dimension of the old aeon is the complex of law-sin-death, which was built on righteousness based on works and symbolized by the practice of circumcision. Paul's polemic in the letter to the Romans concerns itself with the end of this works/righteousness dimension of the old aeon, which has now ended with Christ. In sum, Paul's critique of human society and value systems strikes at their very roots and foundations. In this respect Paul's critical insights for his day have been compared to the work of Norman O. Brown and Herbert Marcuse in the twentieth-century world.[42]

On the positive side, the fact that the new aeon has come calls for a new creation (2 Corinthians 5:17), new values, new life-styles, and new institutions. This new creation is operative as a power in individual persons as well as in society and particularly in the church. Paul expressed the power of the new aeon in a variety of ways, such as life in Christ (Galatians 2:20; cf. Romans 5—8), the coming of a new Adam with the consequent reign of righteousness (Romans 5:12-21; 1 Corinthians 15:47-50), and the power of God for salvation (Romans 1:15-16).

In the course of Paul's ministry in the gentile churches we can see the apostle working out some of the specifics of life under the new aeon. The best example of this is in Galatians, where he argues against circumcision and the law, which he believes represent the old aeon and which militate against life in Jesus Christ through faith. Paul insisted that circumcision must be eliminated as an institution, because through it the powers of the old aeon controlled people and prevented them from finding new life in Christ. One consequence of the new life in Christ that Paul eloquently expressed is: "For as many of you as were baptized into Christ have put on Christ. There is neither Jew nor Greek, there is neither male nor female; for you are all one in Christ Jesus [Gal. 3:27-28]." Here, members of the church are viewed as participants in the eschatological community of those who belong to Christ and for whom the old unequal distinctions of male/female, slave/free no longer apply. In this respect Robbin Scroggs is quite correct in pointing out that Paul is the great liberationist who witnessed to the liberating power of Christ in human life.[43] In other words, Paul took a fundamental principle of the new aeon and applied it radically to the institution of circumcision and the life of enslavement under the law that circumcision represented.

It is both interesting and significant to note that whereas Paul applied the critique of the new aeon radically to the institution of circumcision, he did not apply the same critique to other areas of life, such as the institution of slavery and the status of women. Hence, Elaine H. Pagels offers an important corrective to the above mentioned assertion of Scroggs by pointing out that Paul was not quite the liberationist in *all* of life, particularly in reference to the status of women.[44] However, Pagels does point out that in the modern world we are in a situation quite different from that of Paul, and we may now be in a position to push the principles of liberation that Paul enunciated to other areas of life, such as the status of women and human sexuality.

It should be obvious that the situation in which we live differs entirely from Paul's—economically, socially, and politically.

Certain conditions that Paul thought could be realized only eschatologically, like the social equality of slaves . . . we recognize can and must be realized now. What he considered the conditions of the eschaton may have become necessary forms of social, economic, and psychological transformation—for us.[45]

In asserting his doctrine of freedom in Christ, Paul states without equivocation, "For freedom Christ has set us free; stand fast therefore, and do not submit again to a yoke of slavery [Gal. 5:1]."

Galatians indicates that Paul means freedom from all the enslaving legalistic systems that circumcision represented. It is equally clear that he regarded circumcision as a manifestation of the yoke of slavery, which would deny the freedom of the gospel. The question before the church today (as in every age) is: What, in our experience, corresponds to the enslaving legal system that leads to sin and death? The positive side of the same question is: What are the appropriate life-styles and value systems for life in Christ Jesus? Paul provides some guidelines in Galatians 5. On the other hand, the life of freedom in Christ is empowered by the Spirit to bring forth the "fruit of the Spirit [vss. 22-23]." Paul underscores the fundamental ethical principle: "For the whole law is fulfilled in one word, 'You shall love your neighbor as yourself [vs. 14].'"

Paul is decisive about the issue of circumcision and the necessity of eliminating it and all the legalistic enslavements that it represents. He is uncompromising in his assertion of Christian freedom. Moreover, his examples of works of the flesh as contrasted with the fruit of the Spirit are obvious and general. In the specific questions that arose among the Christians of Corinth, however, Paul is less clear and less decisive. Throughout the Corinthian correspondence, and particularly in 1 Corinthians 7, we see Paul answering specific and immediate questions arising from daily life. He does not lay aside his major concern for life under the new aeon of Christ expressed so clearly in Galatians. Rather, in the context of that new aeon, he gathers whatever wisdom he can from whatever source and gives his counsel in specific situations having to do with sexual behavior, marriage, divorce, the status of women, the handling of daily household affairs, the status of slaves, and the like.

In short, Paul engages in a form of casuistry to guide the Christians of Corinth in their daily affairs for life in the new aeon until its consummation, which Paul expects to come soon

(1 Corinthians 7:29ff.). Neither here nor elsewhere in his letters was Paul conscious of writing "scripture" with the canonical status that the church later gave to his writings. Rather, he was giving his counsel to the Christians of Corinth in their situation and for their time. On some points it is clear that Paul's advice to the Corinthians does not apply in other situations, for example, that slaves should remain in their status as slaves (1 Corinthians 7:20ff.).

On the basis of this chapter Paul is often regarded as holding basic negative views about sexual relationships as such. He is negative about sex and marriage only as they, like other human activities such as holding property or doing business, may stand in the way of complete devotion to Christ (1 Corinthians 7:29-31). Because sexual involvement and marriage may detract persons from unswerving devotion to Christ, it is good for single persons to remain single and uninvolved in worldly concerns. At the same time, Paul recognizes the reality of healthy sexual desires and counsels persons to make orderly provisions for these desires lest they be tempted to immorality or irresponsible behavior (1 Corinthians 7:1-9).

In some respects, Paul is quite affirmative about sexual relationships, because he encourages husbands and wives to give each other their conjugal rights. They are not to deny each other except by mutual consent for the purpose of prayer (1 Corinthians 7:3-5). Even then, however, they are to come together again soon lest they be tempted to immorality (1 Corinthians 7:5). In summary, Paul recognizes the legitimacy of sexual relations. He only asserts that they, like all human concerns, must be subordinated to primary devotion to Christ. That loyalty to Christ, Paul claims, has a liberating and purposeful effect in all human relationships and concerns (1 Corinthians 7:17-24).

Hence, Paul's counsel is provisional and not to be understood in his specific life situation alone. He becomes a model for the church, not in the specific answers that he gives as counsel on immediate questions, but rather in the process of interpreting and applying the basic principles of life in Christ Jesus to specific situations. Paul, above all, would set us free today to work at applying the principles of life in the new aeon to our situation in our day.

In the course of writing letters to help Christians find their way to appropriate Christian life-styles, Paul and his contemporary leaders in the early church touch upon certain problematic aspects of human sexuality. The passages cited most frequently in this connection are Romans 1:18-32; 1 Corinthians

6:9-11; and 1 Timothy 1:8-11. Since these passages have often been drawn out of context and quoted in connection with current concerns about homosexuality, they merit serious attention. Each passage, like all portions of scripture, should be considered within its particular context as well as in the larger context of the whole biblical literature and its life setting.

In none of these passages is it the author's purpose to define particular sins. Rather, the purpose of each passage is to cite patterns of undesirable attitudes and behavior in the surrounding societies where Christians found themselves. In none of the passages is homosexuality as such singled out as a special kind of sin. Like any other form of sexuality, it is to be considered in its contemporary context and in light of responsible human relations, not in terms of the ancient world in which the New Testament letters are written.[46]

The context of Romans 1:18-32 stretches all the way to 3:20. Paul's purpose here is to demonstrate that all human beings are subject to the power of sin, a power from which they cannot liberate themselves by meritorious works of the law (Romans 3:20). His real point emerges in Romans 2:1, where he declares that anyone who judges persons like those mentioned in 1:18-32 is no better off. In fact, those who pass judgment upon others condemn themselves, because they stand under the same power of sin. In the passage as a whole it is the idolatrous distortions, which lead to immorality, as well as distorted religious piety based on works of the law that are condemned.

In 1 Corinthians 6, Paul is in the midst of discussing a variety of problems that confront the Corinthian congregation. In verses 1-7, he exhorts the Corinthians not to take one another to court, because they should have resources of faith among themselves to settle disputes. In verses 9-11, Paul speaks of other forms of unrighteousness, like legal disputes in court, that will stand in the way of inheriting the kingdom of God. While homosexuality is mentioned, it is not singled out as unique. Rather, what is wrong is the libertine view, which sets no limits or controls on any human behavior and consequently leads to a wide variety of irresponsible action as well as to abuse of a person's own body. In verse 12, Paul enunciates one of his own moral teachings—that all things may be lawful, but not all things are helpful. Paul suggests an open approach to problems of human relations, using the criterion of their mutual helpful effects upon the persons involved. Human relations, including sexual relations, are to be compared to the high spiritual relationships with Christ.

Consideration of the context of 1 Timothy 1:8-11 yields similar results. Again, the author does not single out or condemn homosexuality as such. Rather, he speaks against several forms of lawlessness and disobedience or whatever else is contrary to "sound doctrine." Here, as elsewhere in the Pauline literature, the basic criterion for judging the worth of attitudes and actions in the Christian community is "the glorious gospel," which among other things means the love of God shown in Christ and the welfare and good of all persons in the quest for fullness of life.

What, then, may be said about ways in which Paul and his contemporaries would address the problem and potentialities of human sexuality in the twentieth-century world? It would be a mistake merely to transplant in the modern world isolated statements out of the context of the New Testament and thus twist their meanings to fit situations quite different from those to which they were originally addressed. Christians can and should take basic biblical convictions and use them as resources for discovering and cultivating those human relationships that affirm life and love, support persons, and edify wholesome human relationships. Among the principles that may be so used is Paul's statement that what really matters is "faith working through love [Gal. 5:6]." The word faith may be understood to indicate all kinds of human relationships in which people are faithful to one another and responsible for the common good. Such faithfulness works through love, which here, as elsewhere in the New Testament, is understood in terms of God's love for the good and welfare of all human beings.

What are some of the guidelines that can be drawn from the resources of New Testament faith, particularly as Paul saw it? The following list cannot pretend to be complete, but it is offered as a way to help the church start on its pilgrimage:

First, in understanding, interpreting, and appropriating biblical faith we need to stand fast in the freedom with which Christ has set us free. This means to take the principles and power of the new aeon and to work out new life-styles and value systems, taking into account all wisdom and knowledge available to us. Among other things, this means to let ourselves be liberated from some of the statements that Paul made in a casuistic way (e.g., 1 Corinthians 7) and to reinterpret them for our day as Paul did for his. In other words, in its present task the church should seek to be free from any righteousness based upon mere history or dogma and should be open to any new righteousness that may come through faith in God (Romans 9:30—10:4).[47]

Second, the primary data needed for working out values and

life-styles is God's love as revealed in the covenantal history of God's faithfulness to all people and the good news that God wants people to choose life (Deuteronomy 30:19-20).

Third, the fundamental ethical principle is neighbor love. Paul, echoing the teaching of Jesus, says, "For the whole law is fulfilled in one word, 'You shall love your neighbor as yourself [Gal. 5:14]'" (cf. Romans 13:9-10). Coupled with this is another Pauline principle based upon faith working through love (Galatians 5:6). The word faith, as Paul uses it, is a rich and varied concept. Among other things, it means covenant faithfulness in human relations. This may mean that the church should increasingly discover and work out ways of covenantal life together among people.

Fourth, the church needs to deal anew with the problem of scriptural authority. On the one side, this means to reexamine, redefine, and redevelop the "canon within the canon."[48] Luther offers an instructive example in this process when he declares that the epistle of James is an epistle of straw. He does that on the basic conviction that James did not "preach Christ." Similarly, the church today needs to reexamine its own canon and find ways of separating "strawy" statements embedded in casuistry from essential theological principles related to God's faithfulness and love. On the other side, the church needs to enlarge its wisdom and to take into consideration whatever truth God may reveal from whatever source, for example, theology, sociology, the natural sciences, philosophy, history, or art.

Finally, the church needs to function as a covenantal community in the context of the *koinonia* of Christ. This means to engage in the task of defining and redefining the principles and applications of faith in the community of people toward the life and salvation of all.[49]

CHAPTER 3

Faith, Ethics, and Sexuality

Psychologist Carl Jung said that when sexual questions were brought to him, they invariably turned out to be religious questions; religious questions that were brought to him always turned out to be sexual. The religious and sexual dimensions of our lives are deeply intertwined, whether we are conscious of that or not.

This chapter addresses five basic questions from a Christian perspective:
—What is the meaning of our sexuality?
—How and why do we experience alienation from our sexuality?
—How can we experience reconciliation with our sexuality?
—What goes into a decision about a sex-related issue?
—What are some principles for sexual morality?

WHAT IS THE MEANING OF OUR SEXUALITY?

Sexuality, while not the whole of our personhood, is very basic and permeates and affects our feelings, thoughts, and actions. Sexuality is our self-understanding and our way of being in the world as female and male. It includes attitudes about our own bodies and those of others. Because we are body-selves, sexuality constantly reminds us of our uniqueness and particularity: we look different and feel differently from any other person. Sexuality also is a sign and a symbol of our call to communication and communion with others. The mystery of our sexuality is the mystery of our need to reach out and embrace others, physically and spiritually. Sexuality expresses God's intention that we find our authentic humanness in relatedness to others.

Sexuality, then, involves much more than what we *do* with our genital organs. It is *who we are* as body-persons who experience the emotional, cognitive, and physical need for intimate communion with others. All persons are sexual beings. No matter if we happen to be children or aged, divorced or widowed, unmarried and/or celibate, physically handicapped or mentally retarded, we are still sexual (even if others find that fact difficult to understand).

Our religious beliefs are interwoven with the ways we experience ourselves and others sexually. What we as particular Christians believe about such basic religious beliefs as God's purpose in creating us as sexual beings, what we believe about human nature and destiny, about sin and salvation, about love and community will condition our sexual self-understanding. How we experience ourselves and others sexually will also affect what we believe in our Christian faith.

A summary of three basic themes from the Bible concerning sexuality is important at the beginning of our theological reflection. First, the Bible expresses the unity of the person and the goodness of our sexuality. God creates us as whole beings, not as divided beings or spirits to whom bodies are accidentally or temporarily attached. God creates us sexual and deems this an important dimension of the goodness of creation. ("Male and female [God] created them. . . . And God saw everything that [had been] made, and behold, it was very good [Gen. 1:27, 31].")

Second, sexual expression is intended to be both personal and social in its effects. Although they are that, sex acts are more than biological functions or release from tension. When biblical writers used the verb to know as a synonym for sexual intercourse ("Adam knew Eve his wife, and she conceived and bore Cain [Gen. 4:1]"), they understood that coitus can be a deeply personal way of knowing and communicating with another person. And if sexual expression can be deeply personal, by that very fact it also has social implications. Like all others, both early Hebrew and Christian communities found it necessary to regulate the forms of approved sexual expression, knowing that sexual acts have results for the wider community whether for good or ill.

Third, in our own lives we experience profound ambiguity and the Bible knows this. We know alienation as well as communion, bondage as well as freedom, death in the midst of life as well as unbounded life, brokenness as well as health. As an intrinsic dimension of personhood, sexuality participates in such ambiguity. The Bible reflects this ambiguity of human sexual experience. Its pages describe sexual oppression, rape, impersonal sex, and infidelity as well as accounts of joyous human fulfillment in wholesome sex.

The following statements could summarize the divinely intended *purposes* of human sexuality:

First, sexuality is a basic dimension of every human life and is intrinsic to who we are and who we are becoming. At times it may distort one's personality in profound ways, and yet sexuality is intended for our fulfillment and joyous human wholeness.

Second, sexuality expresses the human need and desire for communion. We are destined for communion with God and with one another. As an important form of communication, giving and receiving, sexuality is intended to enhance that communion.

Third, this communion can be described through Christian understandings of love. The basic moral issue surrounding any form of sexual expression, then, is to what degree and in what manner this act nurtures and sustains love-communion or in what way such expression inhibits or destroys it.

Our experience as sexual beings is mixed. Thus, we must look more closely at the experience of our sexuality in terms of Christian understandings of sin, judgment, and salvation.

HOW AND WHY DO WE EXPERIENCE ALIENATION FROM OUR SEXUALITY?

Associations of sexuality with "sin" reflect common experience. Indeed, the very notion of sin has a distinctly sexual suggestion in the popular mind. The phrase "living in sin," for example, more quickly suggests one who has an improper sexual relationship than one who exploits the powerless or the poor. To be sure, there are numerous forms of sexual sin, such as the denial of women's full equality, impersonal and irresponsible genital sex, selfish and cruel sex acts. The sex-drenched appearance of our present culture is not so much an affirmation of full human sexuality as a flight from it through the quest for sexual sensation or performance technique. However, the basic form of sexual sin lies precisely in our alienation from our sexuality. Every dehumanizing sex act is linked with this more fundamental alienation.

At its root, sin always involves alienation in three directions: *separation from self, from neighbor* (meaning all creaturely companions), and *from God.* All three forms of separation are interwoven, but for the sake of understanding they will be considered one by one.

First, we experience alienation from the sexual dimension of our own selfhood. In such alienation we feel separated from our bodies. The body is experienced as "something I *have*" rather than as "something I *am*." Sexuality is experienced as focused on the genitals more than diffused throughout selfhood and relationships. Sexuality becomes depersonalized, losing its character as the will-to-communion and becoming instead the anxious quest for pleasurable reassurance of worth as embodied self.

89

The experience of the alien body, however, takes its toll on the emotions and on the mind's patterns. The loss of being in touch (quite literally) with the body produces loss of touch with emotions. The results are fear of bodily feelings and inability to recognize many of them, the sense of shame about emotional expression, and perhaps the gnawing sense that in some deep but little understood way "I" am unacceptable.

Even conscious thought patterns are not immune from the influences of sexual self-alienation. Particularly for men in our society, this is often evidenced in competitive styles of thinking and communication that make hearing one another difficult, in the overemphasis upon rationality at the expense of feeling, in discomfort with cognitive ambiguity, which presses us to over-simplify things in terms of rigid categories.

Second, sexual alienation finds expression in our relationships with other people. We distance ourselves from others, fearful of letting in too much emotional and physical expression. Centuries of male sexism infect the interpersonal relations of both sexes. Men and women struggle with one another, often unconsciously, in patterns of dominance and submission. Women frequently relate to other women with a competitiveness for male attention, which society has taught them is essential for their self-worth. Fear of sexual violence controls women's lives. Men find emotional intimacy and tenderness with other men a threat to the vigorous masculine, heterosexual self-image. Spouses find it difficult to talk honestly with each other about sexual needs and anxieties, and performance fears invade their love-making. Spouses become jealous and possessive of each other's bodies and selves, making affirmation difficult.

Sin is experienced as the betrayal of a covenant, the rupture of a vital relationship, the violation of an intimate bond. This brokenness brings with it a deep sense of guilt, which focuses upon the misuse of freedom, the freely chosen separation of persons from patterns of fidelity. Our alienation from others often results from the misuse of power that dehumanizes.

Sexual alienation is also expressed in the larger patterns of society and in the way humans relate to nature. We cannot adequately understand much of the world's organized violence without seeing its links to machismo, that hypermasculine image of power and toughness. We fail to understand white racism unless we recognize the history of the sexual exploitation of minority persons. We cannot fathom our ecological crisis unless we see how our alienated bodies are cut off from the organic sense of connectedness with nature and all that is earthy in God's creation.

Third, and most fundamentally, sinful alienation is separation from God. Some of our distorted religious and cultural influences have, sadly enough, convinced us that sexuality is a regrettable necessity in God's eyes and that our sexuality is an obstacle to our relationship with the divine. Believing this, we experience guilt for being sexual and having sexual desires. Moreover, we experience hostility toward God (then possibly guilt over the hostility) for God's alleged rejection of what is so much part of us. In our sexual alienation we fail to experience the divine immanence—God's presence infusing our embodied, creaturely world. Without a sense of God's presence in the flesh, we seek God only where it is "proper"—in transcendence, in aboveness and beyondness. Without immanence we lose touch with divine transcendence. (One wonders to what degree the accelerated flight of youth from our churches is linked to all of this. The God for whom our bodies are either evil or unreal is experienced as alienating and out of reach from our own intimate reality.)

How and why has all this happened? The individual histories of our alienation are as complex and varied as each person is unique. Nevertheless, there are some important and common threads within our experience. One thread goes back to the body-spirit dualism expressed in Greek philosophy and culture at the beginning of the Christian era. This dualism infected Christian understandings of the human self in ways that distorted the more wholistic view of the Old Testament (the body-spirit unity, the psychosomatic oneness of each person). For many Greeks, the immortal spirit was the temporary prisoner of a corruptible, mortal body. The good life consisted of escape from "the flesh" into the larger life of the spirit. Such a view was tempting for the early church, which was trying to cope with its surrounding culture—absorbing elements of Greek thought in order to interpret the new Christian message to the non-Jew, but also resisting the sexual distortions found among many non-Christians. Furthermore, the early church was waiting expectantly for the sudden coming of the new age. In this atmosphere the embodied and fleshly life of earth seemed insignificant or an impediment. Thus, the body-spirit dualism impacted Christian life and thought in lasting ways throughout the intervening centuries.

A second impetus to dualism was at least as important as the Greek influence. This was present within the Old Testament communities and in the early Christian church. The *subordination of women* was systematically present in the institutions, interpersonal relations, and religious life of patriarchal cultures. The alienation of mind from body, of reason from emotions, of nature from history, of the sacred from the secular, of higher life from fleshly life found cause and expression in the subordination of women to men. Men assumed their superiority in reason and spirit; hence, they assumed they were destined to lead the civil and the religious community. Women were identified with the traits of emotion, body, and sensuality. Their menstruation was labeled religiously unclean and a source of emotional instability. While men retained undisputed control, the life of the body, the emotions, and human sensuality became suspect (except for times of pleasurable escape), relegated to a lower order of existence and suppressed by those who aspired to the spiritual life.

The writings of the early church leaders were saturated with this dualism. The Greek type was there (Origen believed that original creation was entirely spiritual and sexless) as was the dualism inspired by male dominance (Tertullian called woman "the gate of perdition"). For a variety of reasons the greatest theologian of the early centuries, Augustine, was suspicious of human sexuality. He linked original sin causally with the lustful sex act that conceived the child. The development of the monastic movement in the medieval church fostered the cult of virginity, with its conviction that celibacy was a higher form of spiritual life than marriage. The Protestant Reformation and the subsequent puritan movement denied the special virtue of celibacy and brought new dignity to marriage. Yet, even there the deeply rooted suspicion of sexuality lingered. There was little recognition of the male sexism which sustained that suspicion and treated women unjustly, while depriving both sexes of their fullest personal development.

Since our histories are part of us, both for good and for ill, these influences of past centuries are far more than quaint relics of the past. They have become part of who we are.

HOW CAN WE EXPERIENCE RECONCILIATION WITH OUR SEXUALITY?

At the root of our alienation is *fear*. Thus, a simple intellectual understanding of the problem and its history cannot release us into fuller life. But the Christian gospel does not announce "salvation by correct understanding." Rather, it announces reconciliation by the gracious power of God, experienced through Jesus Christ and received by human openness and trust. Life's renewal is given many different Christian terms: salvation, redemption, reconciliation, and resurrection. But by whatever name it is called, this renewal experience, like that of estrangement, separation, and sin, is three-dimensional. *God, neighbor,* and *self* are all experienced in mysterious interdependency and harmony.

Resurrection of the body-self is always a miracle, although it is usually experienced through the common and everyday stuff of human relationship and event. We recognize that the source of power is beyond ours. It is the mysterious creativity of life itself, God's power in our midst. We experience the miracle that in God's incarnation in Jesus Christ our own bodies are affirmed. The miracle of recognition occurs in the midst of our disunity. In the midst of our sexual self-rejection we are totally accepted. We are accepted in all dimensions of our sexuality—in our masculinity and in our femininity, in our heterosexuality and in our homosexuality.

Frequently, we are conscious that this experience of bodily acceptance is God's gift through human relationships. With the assistance of modern psychology in the psychosexual development of the child, we are aware of the importance of physical holding, breast feeding, sensitive toilet training, comfortable and appropriate sex education. The child who is given a sense of the trustworthiness and goodness of her or his own body, rather than a legacy of shame and bodily rejection, receives a gift of grace. The same gift can be received by adults when one person is loved into a new self-acceptance by another. And we can experience grace through human agency in the pain of struggle and judgment. In our own time the women's movement has made it possible for many women to experience a new life of self-respect and intellect and a sense of power born of openness to their own pain and possibilities. Likewise, the movement has been a gift of grace to many men, who, through women's judgment upon their stereotyped masculinity and through their own self-awareness, have experienced new depths of self-acceptance in body and emotion.

So the self experiences resurrection of the body in the realization of unity. The "I" really is one person. Body and mind are more united. My body is me, just as my mind is me. At the same time I discover that I belong intimately to others and to the world.

To be sure, the experience of such acceptance is never once-and-for-all. Nor is it experienced completely. Yet, it is real, and such moments of grace are often followed by periods of growth in this newness. Four terms might illustrate such growth: *freedom, sensuousness, love,* and *androgyny.*

Psychologists studying the sexual lives of persons who display healthy self-acceptance and who know they are loved, point to a variety of ways these persons experience *freedom.* Such persons enjoy genital acts with greater intensity than the average person, and yet specific sex acts are not central to their philosophies of life. They can experience sex acts with a freer and broader range of emotions—from sheer playfulness and eroticism to mystical ecstasy. There is a freer acceptance of their own sexuality and that of others, and yet there is greater faithfulness and integrity in marriage. There is an unusual degree of affirmation of the partner's individuality, an eagerness for the freeing growth of the other.

Two important Christian insights concerning the nature of freedom in Christ are suggested by these descriptions. One is the freedom from works righteousness—freedom from the belief that our basic worth is in what we do and is our release into the freedom of being what we *are*. Indeed, the sexual relationship is always trivialized when it becomes a performance or an expression of technique devised to prove the expertise of the lover. Furthermore, true freedom is experienced in the paradox of commitment, which means that genuine sexual freedom is found in the creative tensions between spontaneity and discipline, between responsiveness and responsibility.

Sensuousness, another mark of growth, should be distinguished from sensuality. Sensuality, in fact, is a rejection of the body, for here the body is understood as an object, a tool, driven by ego needs to seek pleasures. Ironically, the libertine, who is driven to an increasingly varied diet of sex experiences, is similar to the ascetic, who renounces sexuality: both are alienated from the body, which they treat as an object. In authentic sensuousness we experience the rhythms of the body. We are in full tune with it. We are open to its joys and pains, its stresses and delights. In short, the body mediates the spirit.

The possibility of increased sensuousness seems to lie in the possibility of "letting go," and the capacity to let go, to relax, and to trust seems, in turn, to be linked to the experience of grace. Our bodies are, in some sense, the temple of God. If I really sense that I am totally accepted, then I can let go and trust my body-self in a new way. Just as the highest states of physical pleasure and emotional delight are possible only when we can let go, so also sensuousness, in general, is the experience of those who can trust—in grace, acceptance, and mutuality. And in this experience our sexuality seems to expand beyond a narrow genital focus, infusing the entire body with feeling and pleasure and thus giving a new warmth to all our relationships. Such might be the experience of new sensuousness.

The integration of *love* with sex is another indication of

growth in the resurrection of the body. Such integration is never automatic. Some persons still see sexual intercourse primarily as the means of procreation. Others see it primarily as a means of pleasure. Both procreation and pleasure are important considerations but should not be seen in isolation. Personal communication and intimate communion result from the fullest self-giving of one to another as sex becomes a dimension of love.

This possibility is not simply a matter of romance, of being in love—grand as this is. It is more basically a capacity of self-giving that rests upon one's security in having been and being loved. One who is fundamentally unsure of his or her own worth and thus is anxious about receiving the partner's approval can never be free enough to really love in and through sexual activity. But once again, such security, such assurance of self-worth is a gift of grace, bringing the real possibility of that psychic intimacy, which is loving sex.

Androgyny is the fourth theme that illustrates the resurrection of our body-selves. Literally, the word means the union of the male (*andro*) and the female (*gyne*) in one human personality. More accurately, however, the term means the blending of those personality characteristics that traditionally have been thought of as masculine with those traditionally labeled feminine. Characteristics such as autonomous and dependent, rational and emotional, initiating and nurturing, cognitive and intuitive, assertive and receptive are thought to be gender-related. While contemporary research has cast immense doubt on the notion that such traits are biologically determined or are only appropriate to one gender, and while such qualities seem to a large extent to be culturally shaped, stereotypes like these persist. But for each individual's personality to achieve full development requires both sets of traits.

In addition to the possibility of fuller development of our own unique personalities beyond the confines of gender stereotypes, there are numerous benefits that can occur as a fuller humanity is more widely experienced. Greater justice for women certainly is one. Another is the release of men from their harmfully exaggerated masculine stereotypes for social relationships, resulting in less violence and exploitation in institutional life. Interpersonally, androgyny offers the promise of closer friendships with persons of the same sex, since women's competing with one another for masculine approval and men's shielding their deepest needs from one another are both diminished. And, surprisingly enough, the capacity for heterosexual love seems richer between androgynous women and men. When dominance and submission are removed from a couple's relationship, when aggression subsides, each partner is able to discover in the other an intimate friend. (Isn't it surprising and saddening how many husbands and wives do not know each other as genuine friends?) Beyond stereotyped sex roles, each partner is able to identify more fully with the other and thus is able to discover the other as a sexual person.

An increase in androgyny depends in considerable measure upon institutional change: changes in sex-role images conveyed by the mass media, changes in the ways major institutions treat the two sexes, changes in laws and public policies. Yet, change within the self is not totally dependent upon what happens "out there." Basically, we do not have to *become* androgynous, for we already *are*. We simply need to accept the power to be what we essentially are—unique individuals, female and male, each with the capacity to be firm and tender, receiving and giving, rational and intuitive, like a skillful duet in which two instruments blend into a harmonious oneness. In Christian faith the power of God's grace frees us to be what we essentially are. And this makes sense in daily experience: the capacity to be an authentic individual and to move beyond conventional gender stereotypes is the capacity only of those who truly know their own self-worth, who accept their acceptance.

WHAT GOES INTO A DECISION ABOUT A SEX-RELATED ISSUE?

When we come to moral decision-making, we discover that it is never simply a matter of having our theology all worked out and then being automatically furnished with correct decisions. A variety of factors impinge upon us. It may be useful to look at some of the more important ones. This may make us more aware of why we decide the things we do about sex matters. It may also clarify why sincere Christians often disagree with one another on these issues. Consider these factors.

1. *Ourselves as the decision-makers.* We bring our unique personalities into decisional situations. We bring our family backgrounds, our formative sexual experiences, our sex education, and the influences of peer groups, church, and culture. We bring our self-images as women and men, our affectional orientations, our psychic and relational needs. We bring whatever consciousness of God we have in the midst of our relationships. In short, we bring ourselves—character, conscience, personal identity; "who I am" at a given moment will profoundly affect what I do.

2. *Our basic religious beliefs.* Intimately linked with our identities are what we most deeply believe and in what or in whom we deeply trust. Our articulated Christian beliefs may not consistently reflect our actual and operating faiths. Even so, in our better moments we strive to make our patterns of daily trust more honestly those of Christian definition. However, it is obvious that among Christians there are seemingly endless varieties of faith definitions. Two examples that concern God and human nature suggest how varying Christian beliefs may shape sexual decisions in different directions: I may believe that God has established eternally valid and binding rules of correct sexual acts. Or, on the other hand, I may believe that while God's nature is always unchanging love, God is intimately involved in the changing processes of history, which means that the divine will as expressed in sexually loving acts may vary with time and circumstances.

I may believe that the image of God in which all persons are created is clearly heterosexual, and hence, any homosexual expression violates divinely created human nature. Or I may believe that the image of God is essentially a divinely given capacity for loving communion between persons and that questions of sexual-affectional preference are not relevant to the fulfillment of our human nature.

These examples of differences in interpretations of basic Christian beliefs could be multiplied. Perhaps the point is obvious: What we believe about the realities of God and human relationships with God will give important shape to our sexual decisions. Our own theological views will give us a context out of which to make choices. Principles, rules, norms flow from (as well as help shape) the valuing center that represents our self-understanding regarding our sexuality.

3. *Our styles of decision-making.* There is no one correct style for Christian decision-making. Rather, there are several major patterns and combinations by which we propose to go about deciding. Consider these three.

One method is *the life of obedience.* Here God is experienced principally as ruler, governor, and judge of our lives, as the one to whom we are called to be faithfully obedient. Sexual acts in this pattern are usually seen as either right or wrong, depending upon whether or not they reflect our fidelity to the commands of the faithful God.

Another style is *the life of aspiration.* In this system our moral decisions take shape as they fit into a larger pattern of our aspiring toward or moving toward a great goal in life. God is experienced primarily as the one who sets the goal before us and empowers us to move toward it. The goals may be seen differently by different Christians: the kingdom of God, liberation from bondage, the realization of our authentic humanity, Christian perfection. However, the great goal of Christian life is visualized so that specific sexual acts are judged good or bad, constructive or harmful, insofar as they contribute to or detract from that aspiring life.

In a third pattern the Christian moral life is perceived mainly as *the life of response.* This view sees a dynamic interrelationship between persons and God. We are called to respond to the presence and activity of God in the midst of our varied and changing contexts. We are called to a life of responsible initiative and response. Sexual acts are judged to be responsible or irresponsible in terms of their fittingness to what God is doing and intending in the midst of our human relationships.

We may not be consistent in *how* we make our decisions. Perhaps some combination of the above patterns is our style. In any event, the patterns by which we decide will suggest the amount of emphasis that we give to each of the several elements of a decision:

—the *motive: why* should I (or why shouldn't I) do this?

—the *intention: what* am I aiming at in this act?

—the nature of *the act* itself: *how* will I implement my aims? Are certain sexual acts intrinsically right or wrong, or does it all depend upon the circumstances?

—the *consequences: in what way* will I be accountable for results and effects of acts and relationships?

Each of these elements of a moral decision is important, but most likely we will give more weight to some than to others. Equally sincere Christians will arrive at different sexual decisions not only because of individual uniqueness but also because basic Christian beliefs have varied intepretations. We might differ, too, because of the style and emphasis of our decision-making process.

4. *The facts and how we interpret them.* Our decisions concerning sexual morality are always made in the midst of a welter of concrete data—data about our own personal relationships, bits of medical and psychological information, images of what others are doing sexually. Several things should be said about the way we use this data in our decisions.

Facts are never pure. They are always filtered through our interpretations. And our interpretations are colored not only by the amount and kind of information we have, but also by our personalities, our needs and experiences, and our faith beliefs. In assessing attitudes about homosexuality, for example, one may have the impression that male gays are more prone to sexually molest children than are male heterosexuals. But then one reads that current research demonstrates the opposite, that heterosexual men are the more likely offenders. What then? One can adjust perceptions according to this new data or refuse to admit this information into decisional processes. In either case, interpretation of facts will influence attitudes and decisions about gay persons.

We ought to let *our best understanding of the facts* enter into the decision-making. "My mind is made up—don't confuse me with the facts" is hardly appropriate for any thoughtful person, much less for the Christian who believes that God enters into the tangled webs of human circumstance and who takes concrete facts seriously. For example, some Christians assume that sexual intercourse outside of marriage is always wrong and that intercourse between married partners is always moral. While there is basic truth in that statement, such a sweeping judgment appears to be made with considerable disregard of concrete facts. The evidence is clear: rape *does* occur between marriage partners; often the weapons are psychic ones, but sometimes there is physical force as well. Other evidence is clear: loving intercourse *does* occur for some engaged couples who are deeply committed and yet prevented by circumstances from marrying for a considerable time. The specific factual circumstances surrounding any specific sexual act do enter into the fabric of its morality, and we ought to take such concreteness seriously.

Facts and values are different. As important as facts are, they can never be sufficient grounds for a decision about moral values or actions. It is true, for example, that properly used contraception is much more reliable today than ever before. It also appears to be true, according to the best studies, that premarital intercourse is now experienced by a majority of both sexes by the time of their early twenties. Yet, we cannot appropriately conclude that premarital intercourse is right and good simply because of the facts that contraception can be dependable and that most people are doing it. These truths will influence our decisions, but they must be grounded in something more.

We should be open to *insights from a wide variety of sources* as we make decisions about sexual morality. In particular, those human sciences that deal from various perspectives with sexuality are of great importance to the church. For example, psychologists, sociologists, anthropologists, and historians have studied family life. A Christian ethic for family life needs their wisdom. We need to know that the modern nuclear family (consisting of mother, father, and children only) is a relatively modern development arising largely out of economic patterns in an industrial society. We need to know something about the psychic strains on this form of family today. We need to know that there may be modifications or alternatives in family style that can faithfully nourish Christian values in our time. Information and alternatives from varied sources of human wisdom are important for Christian decision-making.

5. *Our norms and how we use them.* A norm is a criterion or standard of judgment that we can conceptualize, think and talk about, and use as a resource to make a decision. Our thoughtful moral decisions almost always make use of one or more norms. There are two basic types of norms: *principles* and *rules.*

A *principle* expresses qualities that ought to be present in any action without specifying exactly what action should or should not be done. A *rule* is action-specific; it points to particular classes or types of action that are morally approved or disapproved.

Here is a *sexual principle:* "Sexual acts ought always to express concern for the integrity and wholeness of the partner." This does not state which sex acts should or should not be done, but rather identifies the desired quality in any act. Here is a *sexual rule:* "Sexual intercourse ought to take place only between married partners." This is obviously more specific. It rules out all acts of intercourse between the unmarried.

At this point it is useful to recognize that there are several reasons why Christians might differ in their judgments about sexual morality—reasons connected to their use of these kinds of norms. First (and most obviously), they might simply disagree about the *content* appropriate to Christian standards. For instance, one might have a rule that masturbation is always wrong. Another, however, might have a rule that masturbation is morally permissible for the unmarried. Still another might use the rule that even in marriage, masturbation is a permissible act so long as it is not used as a preferred substitute for intercourse with one's spouse. The reasons behind the differences expressed in these three rules might stem from a variety of factors, including particular interpretations of the biblical notion of loving oneself, theological tradition, and differences in personal background and experience, in views about the purposes of human sexual expression, in views about the legitimacy of sexual autonomy and pleasure, in understandings of medical or psychological theories about masturbation, and in one's experience as a single or married person. For a variety of reasons, then, Christians can and do differ in the content of their moral norms.

Another area of sincere disagreement is this: whether general principles alone provide sufficient moral guidance, or whether more specific rules are necessary. One who opts for principles only might reason like this: "Sexual rules are clearly time-bound and culture-bound. As social conditions and scientific understandings change, sexual rules seem to change, too. By sticking with general principles, we recognize this relativity of human rules." For example, Old Testament people were taught that a menstruating woman was "unclean" and devised rules to prevent menstruating women from polluting the temple, the crops, and the warriors. Furthermore, this point of view contends that by refraining from specific rules we guard against moral legalism and can better express our freedom in Christ.

Another person, however, might reason this way: "Surely, some sexual rules in our religious heritage were wrong. But that does not mean they all were. Some sexual acts, by their very nature, are right, and certain others are intrinsically wrong, regardless of time or place. No changing social situation or scientific understanding will ever make rape a good or right thing to do."

Still another individual might believe this: "Yes, I recognize that sexual rules are culturally relative in large measure, and I am wary about claiming eternal validity for very many of them. But I know this: since I am notoriously prone to rationalize my behavior to suit my self-interest or my desires of the moment, I need something more specific than general principles to guide me. I need rules, too—perhaps more in the sexual area than in most other areas of my life."

For those who affirm sexual rules as well as sexual principles, at least three possibilities emerge as to their status and use. Thoughtful Christians disagree on this matter, too. Let us take as our example this rule: "Sexual intercourse ought to take place only between married partners." One possibility is to understand this rule as *universally prescriptive*. It is always obligatory. There are no legitimate exceptions to it. A second possibility is to understand the rule as a *useful guideline*. It expresses the wisdom of the Christian church as to what is generally right and good, but because rules cannot anticipate every unique circumstance, there may be exceptions when the rule should be ignored. The rule is only one useful factor to be considered in making one's judgment.

The third possibility lies somewhere between these two: *Presume in the rule's favor*. This position arises out of discomfort with the absolutism of the universally prescriptive approach and the flexibility of the useful guideline. To presume in the rule's favor means to affirm the truth in each of the other approaches without succumbing to their errors. Valid sexual rules express very serious matters, for example, marriage as the appropriate context for intercourse. Christians who are realistic about their finitude and sin, their limitations in knowledge and virtue will recognize the need to take rules seriously. However, given the complexity and rich uniqueness of human situations and given the freedom of God to will and do the new thing, no moral rule ought to be seen as barring exception. But having presumed in favor of the rule, the burden of proof is on the exception, *this* departure from the norm. How is it justified in reference to a higher good or higher loyalty than the rule itself expresses? With regard to the illustration, then, the bias of this position is in favor of restricting coitus to marriage. At the same time, this position admits that there could be premarital, extramarital, or postmarital exceptions. The Christian who would claim such exception, however, should willingly bear the burden of proof. In this unusual situation how could nonmarital intercourse be justified as faithful action? To live with important sexual rules that also are nonabsolute may well be to attempt to live creatively in that important but delicate balance between order and freedom.

6. *The church as a moral and sexual community.* One more element of our decision-making calls for emphasis—the Christian community. Christian morality, like Christian faith, must always be personal—willingly affirmed in free decision. But personal does not mean individualistic. As the New Testament affirms, we are surrounded by a great cloud of witnesses, both past and present. We need the give and take of shared ethical reflection. We need the challenge of opposing viewpoints as well as the nurture and support of our own identities and values.

Of course, as the church faces issues of sexuality it is fallible and sinful. At its best, the church knows a God of love, who delights in human sexuality and calls it good. The church is a community of persons of all ages called to be members one of another and to participate as the body of Christ, with all the richness of the bodily image. Yet, the church also participates in both doctrine and practice in dehumanizing forms of sexual rejection, oppression, and exploitation. As a result of sexual fears or stereotypes, the church has been excluding and judgmental.

However, the church is called to live in openness to that divine presence, which corrects and renews and sets our individual perspectives in the larger social context. As both moral and sexual community the church lives in penitence and hope, in contrition and gratitude. We know that as sexual beings we need the resources that the church can and does offer as normative agent and as a source of reconciliation and life.

WHAT ARE SOME PRINCIPLES FOR
SEXUAL MORALITY?

If sexuality is intrinsic to every human being, if sexuality expresses our desire for communion, and if the name of that communion is love, what, then, is love?

Three ancient Greek words for love can point us to its several dimensions: *Eros* (sensual attraction and desire for fulfillment), *Philia* (friendship and mutual affection), and *Agápe* (self-giving and other-regarding love). Authentic sexual love is multidimensional and involves all of these. It is attraction to another and the desire for sexual and personal fulfillment in and through the other. It is friendship and mutuality based upon an affectionate community of concern and shared interests. It is the desire to give to another out of the fullness of one's own personality and the willingness to receive from the depths of the other to whom one is committed in a close, trusting, faithful relationship. Love cannot be fully understood apart from its dimension of justice. Love without justice is only shallow sentimentality. Justice divorced from love cannot accurately be called justice. It is, rather, a balance of power relationships. Love, in expressing its dimension of justice, becomes concerned for power, but it is the empowerment of those who are in any way oppressed so that they have rightful access to the means for human fulfillment. Love with its justice dimension becomes our ongoing struggle for love's fullest possible expression in human relationships. This concern applies to ourselves and to our loved one, to the smallest communities and to the larger groups and institutions of our common life.

An attempt to express love's principles for guidance in specific questions of physical-emotional sexual expression would at least include these:

1. *Love's justice requires a single standard* rather than a double standard. This should mean that there is not one ethic for males and another for females, one for the unmarried and another for the married, one for the young and another for the old, nor one for those who are heterosexually oriented and another for those oriented toward their same sex. The same basic considerations of love ought to apply to all.

2. *The physical expression* of one's sexuality in relation to another ought to be *appropriate to the level of loving commitment* in the relationship. Human relationships exist on a continuum—from the fleeting and casual to the lasting and intense, from the relatively impersonal to the deeply personal. Physical expressions also exist on a continuum—from varied types of eye contact and casual touches to varied forms of embraces and kisses,

to bodily caresses and genital petting, to foreplay and genital intercourse. In some way or another we inevitably express our sexuality in every relationship. The morality of that expression, particularly its more physical expression, will depend upon its appropriateness to the shared level of commitment and the nature of the relationship.

3. *Genital sexual expression* ought to be evaluated in terms of the basic elements of a moral decision, informed by love:

Motive (why should I, or why shouldn't I, do this?): Each genital act should be motivated by love. This means love for one's partner. It also means a healthy love of oneself. Infusing both of those loves is love for God, whose good gift of sexuality is an invitation to communion.

Intention (*what* am I aiming at in this act?): Each genital act should aim at human fulfillment and wholeness, God's loving intentions for all persons. In marriage the procreation of children may at certain times be the intent of intercourse, but statistically those times will be in a small minority, and even then the desire for children is part of our quest for wholeness, for wholeness is known in relationships. Fulfillment also requires sexual pleasure. Good genital sex is highly erotic, warm, intimate, playful, and immensely pleasurable. At times it can also be almost mystical in its possibilities of communication and communion. In each of these ways it can contribute to wholeness—a deep sense of being at one with oneself, with the other, and with God.

The Act (are certain sexual acts intrinsically right and good and certain others inherently wrong and bad?): It is difficult to label whole classes of acts as inherently right or wrong, since the moral quality of any act hinges so heavily upon what is being communicated by it in the particular context. What are our intentions and what are their effects? We can surely say that sexual acts that are characterized by loving motives and intentions will exclude all acts that are coercive, debasing, harmful, or cruel to another.

Consequences (what will most likely result from this act, and in what ways will I be willingly accountable?): Responsibility for the results of a sexual act is a mark of love. This involves responsibility to the ongoing relationship, its commitments, and its promises. It means responsibility to the partner's emotional health insofar as that is linked with a given sexual act. If a child is conceived and born, it means responsibility for nurture. Responsibility also means that this particular act must be weighed in terms of its effect on the well-being of the wider human community. Will it endanger the love and justice by which communities must exist?

The above principles of sexual love or principles like them may well be sufficient moral guidance for some Christians. Others will find it important to elaborate more specific rules of sexual love. For example, many would insist that one crucial rule for genital intercourse is that it be confined to the permanently intended covenantal union. Others would agree with the rule but would permit exceptions. Whatever option is chosen, we need to remember that rules by themselves can never create love. They can protect persons at those boundaries of our experience where we express the still alienated dimensions of selfhood in exploitive and hurtful ways. However rules are used, they should nurture and strengthen our growth and that of others into Christian maturity and responsible freedom, not inhibit it.

Because we are not utterly whole persons, at times we will express our unhealed lives in sexual ways that hurt others and ourselves. And because our sexual socialization has been so surrounded by misinformation, fear, and guilt, these will mar our sexual expression. In our sexuality the final word of the gospel is always the word of gracious love: forgiveness, acceptance, empowerment for new life. The Word was made flesh and our flesh is confirmed. God is present and at work in all sexual loving. And God's promise is that we might yet become more joyously at one with our sexuality and thus more fully at one with life itself.

CHAPTER 4

Psychosexual Development

Throughout this book sexuality has been defined more broadly than male and female genitalia or the act of coitus. Sexuality is understood as the behaviors, attitudes, feelings, and life-style choices that are part of our personal and corporate life experiences as men and women. Psychosocial theories of sexual development result from the scientific study of people from several disciplines in order to increase our knowledge and understanding of what it means to be a sexual human being—male and female—in our time throughout various stages of life, in different cultures. The scientific study of sexual development involves observation of patterns of human thought, feelings, and behavior.

Naturally, we bring our own value structures to our understanding of psychosexual data. Our theological and biblical understandings influence our reading of these findings. At the same time, new scientific understanding challenges our values and assumptions. There is reciprocity here.

DEMYTHOLOGIZING PSYCHOSEXUAL DEVELOPMENT THEORIES

Sigmund Freud began the modern scientific study of human sexuality. Based on his work with disturbed individuals, he postulated far-reaching theories about the nature of sexuality. Although his theories are currently debated, Freud helped us understand sex as a complex motivating force in human personality. Building on this premise, therapists and researchers have added substantially to our knowledge about sexuality, especially during the last two decades. Our generation can experience being sexual without some of the crippling effects that ignorance produced in the past.

However, the pilgrimage has really just begun. Any cultural "savior" is also, by nature, idolatrous. In our search for immortality we use our talents and gifts to devise new life-creating skills, presuppositions, and mechanisms to replace the old. However, we can become enslaved to new dogmatisms. As we grow more comfortable and sophisticated in our notions about scientific study, we need to recognize that they are inevitably subject to the inadequacies of the human condition. No human venture is unprejudiced or untainted by the values of the therapist or researcher or broader culture. Psychosocial theories can enslave us to the new assumptions about sexual health and forms of behavior unless we recognize them as being imperfect and the object of critical judgment.

Many therapists and researchers are challenging established understandings. The following quotations from people immersed in sex research, education, and therapy indicate that there is much work to be done.

It should be stated at the outset that there is still no comprehensive, consistent theory of psychosexual development that is generally acceptable. We have many facts, but only a few can be explained; we have many explanations but only a few can be supported by facts.[1]

Until recently, . . . in contrast to the extensive information available regarding other bodily functions, such as excretion and respiration, sexuality was terra incognita. . . . Despite tremendous recent advances, sexuality still remains a mystery in many respects. Basic data, especially in the area of female sexuality, are incomplete; clear conceptual formulations on fundamental issues are still forthcoming.[2]

There is not really a great deal known about sex, particularly about sex as it falls into the normal or modal ranges. There is a great deal of talk, but the talk is based on very little information. There is little understanding of how a commitment to sexuality develops and the role it plays in general personality development. More is known in our society than any previous society about who does what to whom and how often, but little is known about the role it plays in organizing a life in which, even under the best of circumstances, sex tends to play a minor role. In many ways, the resistance to systematic research in the sexual area is greater than the resistance to sex education which is possibly defined as less threatening or less subversive. Indeed, what may produce the bankruptcy of the sex education movement is that, even among the advance guard, there is a tendency to believe that education without knowledge is possible.[3]

Beginning in the twenties and continuing into the forties, a systematic study of human sexual behavior was undertaken that focused on relatively normal people rather than on patients in a clinical psychological setting. This social bookkeeping approach to sexuality research moved away from individual case study and from populations defined as neurotic. Alfred C. Kinsey spent ten years collecting more than 16,000 case histories from people all over the United States and utilizing personal interviews. This body of data is still unmatched in scope and magnitude by subsequent studies. However, serious criticisms have been leveled at the sampling and interviewing methodology used.

Anthropology has also made a contribution to data about sexuality. Bronislaw Malinowski and Margaret Mead, through cross-cultural studies, helped people in this country to discover the fact that in some cultures norms other than ours exist.

Ethology has yielded significant information for the study of human sexuality. Whereas not all animal studies are transferable or analogous to studies of human sexuality, they have provided an important theoretical and practical basis for much work. Harlowe and his researchers found some significant correlations between adult sexual capability and early experiences of peer and mother nurturing as a result of their work with primate behaviors.

Child development and *family studies* have demonstrated the centrality of the family in sexual learning or the lack of it.

Sociological and *behavioral studies* have revealed data concerning understandings about our social roles as men and women.

Endocrinological research has also contributed to the understanding of both the importance and the limitations of the genetic determinants of human sexuality.

Sexual *anatomy* and *physiology* were meticulously studied by William H. Masters and Virginia E. Johnson under scientific laboratory conditions. For the first time accurate physiological findings are available to the lay person and to the scientific community.

Alan Gregg, in his introduction to the first Kinsey study, in 1948, indicated the importance of accurate information about sexuality.

Certainly no aspect of human biology in our current civilization stands in more need of scientific knowledge and courageous humility than that of sex. . . . As long as sex is dealt with in the current confusion of ignorance and sophistication, denial and indulgence, suppression and stimulation, punishment and exploitation, secrecy and display, it will be associated with a duplicity and indecency that lead neither to intellectual honesty nor human dignity.[4]

A REVIEW OF VARIANT THEORIES

The first theory of sex differences formally introduced was Freud's *instinct theory*, which proposed that the bases of all sexual attitudes are instinctual. "It seems certain that the newborn child brings with it the germs of sexual feelings which continue to develop to a progressive suppression, which in turn may be broken through by the regular advances of sexual development or may be checked by individual idiosyncrasies."[5]

The primary focus of this sexual drive is pleasure, and the goal of sexual development is "the so-called normal sexual life of the adult in whom the acquisition of pleasure has been put into the service of the function of propagation."[6]

This transformation from infantile sexuality to its "definite normal form" begins at puberty. For Freud, male and female sexuality are divergent in aim. A sexually mature male discharges sexual products in service of pleasure and propagation; a female is to serve as a sexual partner for man and as a mother (which is her compensation for lacking a penis). Any disturbance or deviance from these innate principles of sexuality were considered by Freud to be perversions.

We are indebted to Freud for the impact on popular thinking of his view that sexuality as central to identity formation beginning in infancy. He also made sex "legitimate" for scientific study. But his views of the inherently biological function of sex for procreation and his definitions of male and female differences are problematic in our day and age. Further study and personal experience also challenge his position concerning the necessity of sexual gratification and the tremendous power he ascribes to sex. It is an oversimplification of Freud to suggest that he rationalized and secularized the theological perceptions of sexuality that preceded him in power. However, in the end result there is a correlation between these two positions in that sex for other than procreation purposes was demonic (or—for Freud—perverse) and required the repression of sexual pleasure and the subordination of women.

Other theories of sex-role socialization have developed since then. In cognitive-developmental analysis it is first assumed that a child's view of the world and his or her way of thinking change qualitatively in the progression from childhood into adulthood. Sex roles in children begin with the establishment early in life of a gender identity, a child's self-categorization of the self as boy or girl, forming the basis of future evaluations. Lawrence Kohlberg (1966) notes that although parents are models for their children, this identification comes after gender identity is established. That is, a boy might say, "I am a boy; therefore, I want to do boy things; therefore, the opportunity to do boy things (and to gain approval for doing them) is rewarding." The child's self-determined gender identity is continually reinforced. In this cognitive-development analysis the initial process of determination of one's gender identity *and* of gender-typed activities remains unclear. Exactly how and why a girl comes to realize that she is a girl, different from boys, and in what manner female-stereotyped activities become labeled female to her is left unexplained.

Social learning theory provides an answer to these questions. It states that a child is initially dependent on others and consequently achieves self-understanding as a boy or a girl in response to offered rewards. In social learning terminology, a sex-typed behavior is one that typically results in different rewards from self or others for each sex. Terms that are used to analyze any aspect of behavior (for example, discrimination, generalization, reinforcement punishment) can also effectively describe the process by which children acquire and perform sex-typed behaviors.

The concept of observational learning is fundamental or the "tendency for a person to reproduce the actions, attitudes, and emotional responses exhibited by a real-life or symbolic model [Mischel, 1966]." Some of the characteristics of a situation which may influence the amount of modeling that takes place are:

the model's power and willingness to reinforce the child;

the frequency, rate and clarity of presentation of the particular behavior to be modeled;

the degree to which a model makes verbal declarations concerning the appropriateness of the behavior;

the child's motivation (deprivation level, the potency of the reinforcers being used).[7]

Since contrary concrete and reliable findings are limited in number (DeLucia, 1961; Epstein and Leverant, 1963), a social learning framework seems, at present, to better accommodate the facets of the acquisition and maintenance of sex-role socialization. Therefore, nurture, not nature (biology), must be regarded as the important factor in gender identity and sex-role definition.

Social learning theories are less complicated than analytical theories. The social learning approach has also provided us with the impetus to study sexual behavior. According to this more flexible approach, one can change the patterns of behavior by changing patterns of reinforcement and punishment. But these theories provide no answer to the meaning or purpose of sexuality. Individual difference, independence, and the unconscious or biological aspects of sexuality are ignored completely.

TOWARD A NEW UNDERSTANDING

Each of these theories falls short of our experience of the complexity and totality of sexuality. Thus, new approaches and various interactional theories have developed in recent years that incorporate a multidisciplinary approach. Only a few of these are reviewed here in order to glimpse the contemporary debate that presents the nature/nurture motif in different although controversial new constructs. Hopefully, they reflect the dynamic new possibilities for the near future in transforming traditional wisdom incorporated with new insights.

William Simon and John H. Gagnon (1973) offer a partial *interactional theory*, which emphasizes the interaction of nature and nurture in psychosocial aspects of sexual development. They emphasize that a sexual act has meaning in a particular sociocultural setting. Sexual activity is scripted behavior.

> Marital coitus, the most common form of sexual conduct in our society, involves a vast array of human learning and the coordination of physiological, psychological, and social elements, practically none of which can be attributed to nature writ large as evaluation or nature writ small as a morality play based on glandular secretions.[8]

Thus, all sexual activity is the outcome of a complex process of psychosocial development. No developmental sequence is fated either in nature or in the sexual organs, since all sexual processes are learned.

And physical sexual acts become possible only because they are embodied in and legitimized by social scripts.

> Our use of the term script with reference to the sexual has two major dimensions. One deals with the external, interpersonal—

the Script as the organization of mutually shared conventions that allows two or more actors to participate in a complex act involving mutual dependence. The second deals with the internal, the motivational elements that produce arousal or at least commitment to the activity.[9]

Simon and Gagnon offer a commonsense, nonideological approach to sexuality that takes into account more fully than others the unique character and importance of human relationships that integrate sexual activity with sexual meaning and purpose as well as internal/external factors. In this view, neither the biological nor the social can unilaterally write the script for given individual sexual behavior. In fact, the primary basis for a critique of this theory is that biological factors are underestimated and the nature/nurture polarity is oversimplified. Nevertheless, Simon and Gagnon have made an important beginning in suggesting an interactional theory. More recent research into both the biological and social dimensions of sexuality confirm this direction.

THE OLD AND THE NEW

It is important to underline the obvious: psychological research has played a historical role in shaping how society has thought about sex roles, even to determining the kind of questions considered appropriate to ask. The increasing sophistication and application of psychological theory has heightened respect for its importance and has enhanced its influence. People's behavior often follows psychologists' theories about it, and nowhere has this been more apparent than in the psychology of sex roles.

Before we turn our attention to new developments in research, we need to see traditional theories within the broader cultural context that is familiar to all of us.

Joseph Pleck, in an article entitled "The Psychology of Sex Roles: Traditional and New Views," outlines the traditional propositions about women's and men's personalities and psychological development:

[1] Women and men differ substantially on a wide variety of personality traits, attitudes, and interests.

[2] These differences, to a large degree, are biologically based.

[3] A major part of these psychological differences between the sexes results from a psychological process called "sex identity

development." In this hypothetical process, males and females psychologically *need* to develop the constellation of "masculine" or "feminine" traits that society defines as appropriate for their sex, in order to have a "secure" sex identity. This process is consistent with, but goes beyond the psychological sex differences which are directly biologically based.

[4] Developing sex identity is a risky affair. Many individuals, particularly males, fail to develop the psychological traits traditionally appropriate for their sex, or develop traits traditionally appropriate to the other sex. These individuals have profound difficulties in their personality and life adjustment, including homosexuality.

[5] Psychological differences between the sexes, as well as individuals' psychological need to develop and maintain a normal sex identity, simultaneously account for and justify the traditional division by sex of work and family responsibilities.[10]

Pleck emphasizes that propositions three and four are less familiar and more subtle in their implications than propositions one, two, and five. In explanation, he says,

It is well known that many traditional psychologists have maintained that there are psychological differences between men and women, and that these differences are biologically based. But while traditional psychology interpreted sex differences in personality as partly based in biology, it also saw these differences as partly learned. *To the traditional psychologist,* however, the partly learned nature of sex differences in personality does *not* mean that society is free to teach men and women to have different traits than it teaches at present. Rather, to them, the partly learned nature of sex differences in personality means that societies have to take extra care to insure that individuals learn only the right traits, that is, the ones that are appropriately masculine or feminine. *Instead of giving males and females greater psychological freedom in their development, the partly learned nature of sex differences puts men and women at a greater psychological risk,* because the development of sex-appropriate traits is not a foolproof process directly controlled by biology alone.[11]

Pleck argues that these two propositions (three and four) about the psychological *need* to learn sex-typed traits have ultimately

113

had a more conservative effect on attitudes toward sex roles than have the first two propositions about the extent of psychological sex differences and their biological basis. This means that we face difficulty in trying to change traditional sex roles for men and women, more because we have been taught to believe that men and women psychologically need to be different than because of the belief that men and women *are* different due to their biology.

As our previous critiques have suggested, these traditional theories were developed and elaborated by talented and persuasive psychologists.

Pleck admits that if these five propositions of American psychology are valid, "the efforts to bring about changes in sex roles taking place in society today will not only fail, but will lead to social disaster."[12]

Recent research and challenges to traditional theory suggest otherwise, however.

TRANSCENDING THE STATUS QUO
Five years ago, Marcia Millman criticized sociologists for reinforcing the status quo in the field of sex-role research. She points out that

> almost all the researchers we hear from have expressed a major interest in finding out whether or not change is occurring in American sex roles. It is ironic, then, that most of the research which has been reported focuses on those places in society which are most stable and where we are least likely to observe changes in sex roles. It is not surprising that researchers conclude that little change has taken place, but the accuracy of these conclusions seems questionable.[13]

Surveying the sociological research on sex roles Millman mentions the 1970 Garland and Poloma Study, which examined the effect on family structure of a wife working as a professional by looking at only two career families. The study concluded that American males are not emasculated or dominated by wives who hold prestigious jobs, because most of the marital partners Garland questioned said the man should be the breadwinner and the wife primarily the homemaker. Therefore, there was no reason for these men to feel threatened, since traditional sex roles had not changed. T. Neal Garland and Margaret M. Poloma looked only at couples that had reached a stable and traditional solution (they studied only married couples and left out of their study all the dual career couples who were divorced or separated).

Millman suggests that individuals not included in the study would be "more likely to express non-traditional ideas about sex roles and more importantly would be likely to identify their conflicting feelings about their respective roles as having contributed significantly to the disruption of their marriages or relationships."[14]

She argues that if we are interested in finding out whether or not sex roles are changing, we should concentrate on those places in society most likely to change or at least make comparative analyses.

Millman also refers to four other studies, which only examine women's sex roles either through interviews exclusively with women or by questioning men *only* about the changing roles of women. She suggests that even though these researchers stress the need to study men as well as women, their research focuses heavily on women (the implication being that sex-role change only has to do with women), and that this imbalance is characteristic of sex-role research in general. (The five study papers referred to here were presented at the American Sociological Association meetings in 1970.)

Millman argues that:

> It would be important to explore what sex roles have to do with the operation of institutions such as government agencies, political organizations, military groups, and corporation settings. For some reason, however, sociologists have not thought to study sex roles in relation to men and non-familial settings.[15]

Pauline Bart, another sociologist, reinforces Millman's critique by suggesting that sociological studies tend to support cultural biases, because a large portion of the research consists of measurements of how poorly or well individuals "adjust" to their appropriate role, generally assuming that adjustment is a good thing.

This harsh evaluation of sex-role research is not meant to minimize its importance. The behavioral sciences have helped dispel many traditional myths. And certainly, many studies such as those that Millman calls for have been done since 1970. However, it is important for us to remember—even when looking at more recent studies, which Millman would find supportable—that unless sociologists examine not only what sex roles are but ask what social, economic, and political purposes they serve, the likelihood is increased that research will sustain the stereotypical assumptions and biases that prevail in the general culture.

SCIENCE CORRECTING SCIENCE

Thomas Kuhn's 1962 analysis of the development of the sciences, in his book *The Structure of Scientific Revolutions*, would support Millman's challenge as necessary for a scientific revolution to take place. According to Kuhn, science has not grown by the orderly acquisition of knowledge. Instead, reigning theories or models (what he calls paradigms) are successful only as long as research generates results that are interpretable within the paradigm. But research may yield results that cannot be explained by the prevailing paradigm. Such departures from regular research findings build up until a new paradigm emerges that accounts for the new results. (Examples of such scientific resolutions include the overthrow of the Ptolemaic conception of the universe by the Copernican model and of Newtonian physics by Einsteinian physics.)[16] Thus, it is the dynamic nature of scientific debate that challenges old assumptions with new observations and results, leading to new formulations that create "new knowledge." We are in the midst of just such a revolutionary period as Kuhn describes.

In 1970, even before Millman, psychosocial researchers, therapists, and theorists were challenging traditional paradigms. By 1972, research existed that reached beyond the outlined propositions of the reigning psychosexual theories. A look at these recent studies reveals why Joseph Pleck and James Harrison (1975) argue that a new paradigm is being created—a new psychology of sex roles. "Two myths have predominated in the thinking about psychosexual development: one is that there is a necessary and important conflict between the 'innate' and the 'learned' aspects of psychosexual development. The other is that the male and female reproductive/sexual systems are extremely different from each other."[17]

CURRENT RESEARCH IN
PSYCHOSEXUAL DEVELOPMENT

John Money and Anke Ehrhardt's book, *Man and Woman, Boy and Girl* (1972), summarizes research conducted on gender identity by Money and his colleagues at Johns Hopkins University since the early 1950s.

With regard to the innate-learned controversy, Money says:

> In the theory of psychosexual differentiation, it is now outmoded to juxtapose nature versus nurture, the genetic versus the environmental, the innate versus the acquired, the biological versus the psychological, or the instinctive versus the

learned. . . . The basic proposition should not be a dichoto-mization of genetics and environment, but their interaction.[18]

Money's research reveals that genetic sex is established at the moment of fertilization (through the X or Y sex chromosomes), but that the genital structures of both sexes develop from the same structure or cell mass. There is a marked likeness in the form and function of the male and female sexual systems.

Thus, there are two sets of sexual structures in all developing embryos—the male (Wolffian ducts) and the female (Müllerian ducts). The external genitalia are identical in male and female embryos up to the third month of development, after which one ductal system disappears.

Through the first two months the undifferentiated genitalia in the embryo most resemble the mature female genitalia. In fact, androgens must be present for male structures to develop. If no androgens are present, the embryo will develop a female form.

Money's research, therefore, suggests that

the "natural differences" between males and females are not so evident as is often implied by those who have a vested interest in maintaining the differences in society. . . .

The "Adam's rib" explanation of the origin of women, when used in a literal sense, is contradicted in a literal sense by the priority in nature of female form and structure. Without androgen, nature's primary impulse is to make a female—morphologically speaking at least.[19]

In recent years research has been carried out at Johns Hopkins with persons whose sexual differentiation proceeded abnormally before birth. Inconsistencies among the gender indicators can occur at any point in the long chain of events leading to final adult self-definition as male or female. This series of events in-cludes (1) the development of sex glands in the fetus in response to the chromosomal pattern; (2) the production of sex hormones by the sex glands; (3) the effect of these hormones on the de-velopment of the internal and external genital organs and on the brain of the fetus; (4) adults' classification of the infant's sex based on the appearance of the infant's external genital organs; (5) adults' behavior toward the infant based on this classification of sex; (6) the child's classification of his or her own sex; (7) the production of sex hormones during adolescence; (8) the effect of these sex hormones on genital growth and erotic feelings; (9) and the effect of this genital growth and eroticism on the adolescent's classification of her or his biological sex.

These individual patterns of sex chromosomes (XX or XY) may not cause them to develop into an adult female or male. Possibly, this is due to chromosomal abnormalities (Turner's syndrome or the Klinefelter's syndrome) or because of disorders due to inappropriate levels of androgen, resulting in contradictory or incomplete differentiation of some part of the reproductive system. Some XY chromosomal males are androgen-insensitive and therefore develop female external genitalia, but no uterus, and incompletely operative testes. Some XX chromosomal females have received excessive amounts of androgens (formerly administered to mothers to prevent miscarriage), and they are born with male-appearing genitalia but have functional ovaries. Adults also may misclassify the child's sex at birth.

Money showed that if, as a result of any of these factors, a child is raised as a member of the "wrong" sex, the child will always experience himself or herself as a member of that sex in later life, no matter how different the self-classification is from the individual's sex chromosomes, hormones, or genitals and no matter what efforts are made to change that self-classification.

Money and Ehrhardt's research shows the powerful effect of socialization on an individual's sense of being male or female, since whatever happens before birth can be changed after birth. Most important, Money identifies a different critical event in the psychological development than tends to be the case with the traditional psychology of sex roles.

The traditional theory of sex identity holds that the critical event in development is the child's acquisition of "masculine" or "feminine" personality traits, attitudes, and interests. These traits are learned through a variety of psychological processes, but these processes often fail and many individuals, therefore, have insecure sex identities and are maladjusted. Money and Ehrhardt's analysis, by contrast, holds that the critical event in development is the child's early self-classification as male or female. After the child classifies the self as male or female, he or she can have many different traits, attitudes, and interests, be they "masculine" or "feminine," without threatening the basic self-definition. The critical event, then, is not developing masculine or feminine traits during childhood that affirm one's biological gender. Rather, the critical event is the development of the sense of being male or female, a feat that is accomplished quite early in life.[20]

James Harrison analyzes the import of the Johns Hopkins and related research. He believes that it points to seven distinguishable

118

criteria for differentiation between men and women. The five *biological* characteristics are these:

The first is *chromosomal* (XX, XY, or other variations). The second criterion is *gonadal sex*—the presence of ovaries or testicles. The third is *hormonal sex*, including secondary sex characteristics, such as facial hair distribution and breast development. Each sex produces both male and female hormones, though in different proportions, and since glands other than the gonads also produce hormones, hormonal sex is not always concordant with gonadal sex. The fourth criterion is the *internal sex organs*—the uterus and prostate. The fifth is the *external genitalia*.

The other two criteria are social and psychological factors that are based on the biological foundations. The sixth criterion is the *sex of assignment and rearing*, a process that begins with the announcement of the child's sex at birth and includes all sex-differentiated treatment throughout childhood. The seventh is *gender identity*, for example, a person's self-awareness of being male or female.

Harrison suggests that there are two other significant categories in which persons differ:

> One of these is the adoption of sex-roles, i.e., the differential expression of behaviors, attitudes, and interests by men and women or in Brown's (1958) term, "sex-role preference." The other is, to use the psychoanalytic language, the sex of object choice, i.e., the sex of persons with whom primary libidinal attachments are made, or to use the more popular term, "sexual orientation." The assumption, in psychology and psychiatry, that these two categories of behavior are always concordant has led to no end of confusion, even to damage of human beings. The assumption that either of them is always concordant with the first seven criteria is also unsupportable.[21]

In summary, Money's research reveals that gender identity (whether persons understand themselves to be male or female) happens approximately by age three. The most significant determinant of gender identity is sex of assignment. This is revealed through Money's work with intersexed (both sex) persons whose chromosomal and hormonal sex are different from their sex of assignment—which usually overrides these biological determinants. Hence, the most important factor in determining one's sex (gender) identity is *learned*.

Hormones may have an effect on the differential behaviors which are stereotypically associated with men and women.

These studies, however, do not demonstrate such an effect. Rather, they represent the attempt of researchers, like Money, to leave open the possibility that there may be such a hormonal effect which offsets the experiential determinants which consistently prevail over the biological ones in the establishment of gender identity and sex role behavior. . . .

The two non-biological criteria—the social sex of assignment and the resultant psychological sex of gender identity—have the capacity to override the biological determinants of personality differentiation between the sexes. It is not my intention, nor that of any of the researchers whom I have cited, to deny the significance of genetic or hormonal influence. Rather, my aim is to emphasize the interactive character of all these determinants.[22]

We are still left with many questions, but Money's research certainly has made a critical impact on the traditional nature/nurture controversy (the biological vs. social learning). James Harrison explains:

To use the old language, both nature and nurture have had their effect. Nature apparently cannot produce a man or a woman without the mediation of nurture. Nurture takes place in the context of the biological anlagen. The effect, however, does not seem to be simply additive. The contribution of experience is not simply added to the empty structure. . . . Both the biochemical and social environments seem to have an effect on the structure of the organism. The resulting human being is the product of multiple forces which play a role in his/her development and differentiation. It seems safe to conclude from this line of research that the effort to determine the absolute primacy of either biological or social factors is essentially a misguided quest. It is more likely that each individual person represents an unique combination of multiple factors that contribute to the formation of his/her personality.[23]

SEX-ROLE STEREOTYPING
Other research challenges traditional theories and provides new information for the development of an interactionalist theory. Eleanor Maccoby and Carol Jacklin's *The Psychology of Sex Differences* (1974) is a major review of the literature (2,000 books and articles) on psychological similarities and differences between men and women.

Maccoby and Jacklin conclude that within the limits of available research there are no average differences between the sexes in many areas in which differences have been widely believed to exist. For instance, the research results *do not* support common beliefs that women are less analytical than men, have a lower motivation to achieve, have lower self-esteem, and are more suggestible, socially oriented, and nurturant.

Also, evidence from current research leads them to infer that average differences between the sexes are confirmed in two areas —certain intellectual skills and aggression. Women have greater verbal ability than men on the average but have less ability at visual-spatial and mathematical tasks. In spite of the common differences between men and women in these intellectual skills, the distribution of women's and men's abilities overlap substantially.

On the average, men are more aggressive than women. However, Maccoby and Jacklin distinguish aggression from dominance, competitiveness, and overall activity level.

> Maccoby and Jacklin believe that the greater physical aggression observed in males has a biological basis in part, but this biological basis appears to be a greater readiness to learn aggressive behavior, rather than greater aggression per se. In light of recent claims that males' greater aggression makes male dominance over women inevitable (Goldberg, 1973), Maccoby and Jacklin note, with great common sense, that physical aggression is not the method most often or most effectively employed to influence other people. Aggression is a primitive way of exerting influence over others, and one which declines in importance as individuals mature and become more intimate with each other. The more mature forms of social influence that play a more significant role in adult life than simple physical aggression, by contrast, are relatively equally distributed between women and men.[24]

Careful consideration of the few differences between men and women that occur in a context of basic psychological similarities suggests that they are not significant enough to account for the different roles that women and men play in society, especially when one weighs the importance of verbal ability (higher in women) in professional status positions and the current inappropriateness of physically aggressive behavior as a means of control.

Maccoby and Jacklin have summarized their findings in an

article, "What We Know and Don't Know About Sex Differences," for *Psychology Today*. Some excerpts follow*:

MYTH: Girls are more "social" than boys.
There is no evidence that girls are more likely than boys to be concerned with people, as opposed to impersonal objects or abstract ideas.

In childhood, girls are no more dependent than boys on their caretakers, and boys are no more willing than girls to remain alone. The two sexes appear to be equally adept at understanding the emotional reactions and needs of others, although measures of this ability have been narrow.

Any differences that do exist in the sociability of the two sexes are more of kind than of degree, and may be somewhat more oriented toward adults, although evidence on this is weak.

MYTH: Girls are more suggestible than boys.
Boys are as likely as girls to imitate other people spontaneously. Girls are somewhat more likely to adapt their own judgments to those of the group, although some studies find the reverse. Boys, on the other hand, appear to be more likely to accept peer group values when these conflict with their own.

MYTH: Girls have lower self-esteem than boys.
Boys and girls are very similar in overall self-satisfaction and self-confidence throughout childhood and adolescence. The sexes do differ in the areas in which they report greatest self-confidence. Girls rate themselves higher in the area of social competence, while boys more often see themselves as strong, powerful, dominant, potent.

Through most of the school years, boys and girls are equally likely to believe they can influence their own fate, as opposed to falling victim to chance. During the college years (not earlier or later) men have a greater sense of control over their destiny, and are more optimistic in predicting their own performance on a variety of school-related tasks.

MYTH: Girls lack motivation to achieve.
In the pioneering studies of achievement motivation, girls were more likely to report imagery about achievement when asked

* Adapted and reprinted from *The Psychology of Sex Differences*, by Eleanor Emmons Maccoby and Carol Nagy Jacklin, with the permission of the publishers, Stanford University Press. © 1974 by the Board of Trustees of the Leland Stanford Junior University.

122

to make up stories to describe ambiguous pictures, as long as the instructions did not stress either competition or social comparison. Boys need to be challenged by appeals to their ego or competitive feelings for their achievement imagery to reach the level of girls'. Although boys' achievement motivation does not appear to be more responsive to competition arousal, that does not imply that they have a higher level of achievement motivation in general. In fact, when researchers observe behavior that denotes a male to achieve, they find no sex differences or find girls to be superior.

MYTH: Girls are better at rote learning and simple repetitive tasks. Boys are better at high-level tasks that require them to inhibit previously learned responses.

Neither sex is more susceptible to simple conditioning, in which stimuli become connected with responses in what is assumed to be a rather automatic process. Neither sex excels in rote-learning tasks, such as learning to associate one word with another. Boys and girls are equally proficient at tasks that call on them to inhibit various responses, e.g., discrimination of certain items from others, a task requiring the subject to avoid attending or responding to irrelevant cues.

Boys are somewhat more impulsive during the preschool years, but after that the sexes do not differ in ability to wait for a delayed reward or inhibit early, incorrect responses, or on other measures of impulsivity.

MYTH: Boys are more "analytic" than girls.

The sexes do not differ on tests of cognitive style that measure one's ability to analyze, i.e., the ability to respond to a particular aspect of a situation without being influenced by the context, or restructure the elements of a problem in order to achieve a solution. Boys and girls are equally likely to respond to contextual aspects of a situation that are irrelevant to the task at hand. Boys are superior only on problems that require visual discrimination or manipulation of objects set in a larger context; this superiority seems to be accounted for by spatial ability.

MYTH: Girls are "auditory," boys "visual."

From infancy to adulthood, the sexes exhibit a similar degree of interest in visual stimuli. They also seem to be alike in ability to discriminate among objects, identify shapes, estimate distances, and perform on a variety of other tests of visual perception.

Sex differences that are fairly well established:

DIFFERENCE: Males are more aggressive than females.
In all cultures in which aggressive behavior has been observed, boys are more aggressive physically and verbally. The sex difference manifests itself as soon as social play begins, at age two or two and a half. From an early age, the primary victims of male aggressions are other males, not females.

DIFFERENCE: Girls have greater verbal ability than boys.
During the period from preschool to early adolescence, the sexes are very similar in their verbal abilities. But at about age 11, they begin to diverge, female superiority increases through high school, and possibly beyond. Girls score higher on tasks that involve understanding and producing language, and on "high-level" verbal tasks (analogies, comprehension of difficult written material, creative writing) as well as "lower-level" measures (such as fluency and spelling).

DIFFERENCE: Boys excel in visual-spatial ability.
Visual-spatial ability involves the visual perception of figures or objects in space and how they are related to each other. One visual-spatial test has the subject inspect a three-dimensional pile of blocks, and estimate the number of surfaces visible from a perspective different than his own. Male superiority on visual-spatial tasks is not found in childhood, but appears fairly consistently in adolescence and adulthood, and increases through the high school years. The sex differences are approximately equal on analytic tasks (those that require separation of an element from its background) and nonanalytic ones.

DIFFERENCE: Boys excel in mathematical ability.
Beginning at about age 12 or 13, boys' mathematical skills increase faster than girls'. The greater rate of improvement does not seem to be entirely due to the fact that boys take more math courses, although the question has not been extensively studied. The magnitude of the sex difference varies depending on the study, and is probably not as great as the difference in spatial ability.

124

QUESTION: Is one sex more competitive than the other?
Some studies find boys to be more competitive than girls, but
many find the sexes to be similar in this regard.

In settings where competitiveness produces greater individual
rewards, males might be more competitive than females, but
this is a guess based on common sense considerations, such as
the male interest in competitive sports, and not on research in
controlled settings. The age of the subject and the identity of
the opponent no doubt make a difference too; there is evidence
that young women hesitate to compete against their boyfriends.

QUESTION: Is one sex more dominant than the other?
The dominance relations between the sexes are complex. In
childhood the segregation of play groups by sex means that
neither sex frequently tries to dominate the other; there is
little opportunity. When experimental situations bring the two
sexes together, it is not clear whether one sex is more successful
in influencing the behavior of the other. In mixed adult groups
or pairs, formal leadership tends to go to the males in the early
stages of an interaction, but the longer the relationship lasts,
the more equal influence becomes.

QUESTION: Is one sex more compliant than the other?
During childhood, girls tend to be more obedient to the commands and directions of adults. But this compliance does not
carry over into relationships with peers. Boys are especially
concerned with maintaining their status in their peer group,
and, therefore, are probably more vulnerable than girls to
pressures and challenges from that group, although this has
not been well established. It is not clear that in adult interactions, one sex is consistently more willing to comply with
the wishes of the other.

QUESTION: Are nurturance and "maternal" behavior more
typical of one sex?
There is very little information about the tendencies of boys
and girls to be nurturant or helpful toward younger children
or animals.

Very little information exists on how adult men respond to
infants and children, so we can't say whether adult females are
more disposed to behave maternally than adult males are to
behave paternally. But if there is a sex difference, it does not
generalize to a greater female tendency to behave altruistically.

Studies of people's willingness to help others in distress have sometimes found men to be more helpful, sometimes women, depending on the identity of the person needing help and the kind of help that is required. Overall the sexes seem similar in degree of altruism.

QUESTION: Are females more passive than males?
The answer is complex, but for the most part negative. The two sexes are highly alike in their willingness to explore a novel environment, when they both have freedom to do so. Both sexes are highly responsive to social situations of all kinds, and although some individuals tend to withdraw from social interaction and simply watch from the sidelines, they are as likely to be male as female.

Young boys seem more prone than girls to put out energy in bursts of strenuous physical activity, but the girls are not sitting idly by while the boys act; they are simply playing more quietly. Their play is fully as organized and planned, possibly more so. When girls play, they actively impose their own design upon their surroundings as much as boys do. It is true that boys and men are more aggressive, but this does not mean that females are the passive victims of aggression—they do not yield or withdraw in the face of aggression any more frequently than males do, at least during the phases of childhood that have been observed. We have already noted the curious fact that while males are more dominant, females are not especially submissive, at least not to boys and girls their own age. In sum, the term "passive" does not accurately describe the most common female personality attributes.[25]

We might ask, then, why do particular myths continue to exist when they have no basis in fact? Maccoby and Jacklin's conjecture is that a person's attention is selective. In other words, when a person behaves the way an observer expects him/her to, this is noted, and the observer's prior beliefs are confirmed and reinforced. But when a person behaves in a way that is not consistent with an observer's expectations, the behavior is likely to go unnoticed. Thus, beliefs remain the same. Myths live on that would otherwise die if we paid closer attention!

It is important at this point to highlight the findings of another study, conducted by Lisa Serbin and Daniel O'Leary, that put Maccoby and Jacklin's survey in a different light and that support their conjecture about the effects of reinforcing typical sex roles, while nonstereotypical behavior goes unnoticed. This research would also challenge any contention that Maccoby and Jacklin's average "differences" are absolute.

There has been widespread conjecture about when and how sex-role stereotypes develop. Serbin and O'Leary looked at fifteen preschool classrooms and concluded that

> as nursery school children busily mold clay, their teachers are molding behavior. Unwittingly, teachers create an environment where children learn that boys are aggressive and able to solve problems, while girls are submissive and passive. The clay impressions are transient, but the behavioral ones last into adulthood and present us with people of both sexes who have developed only parts of their psychological and intellectual capabilities.[26]

They suggest that "bullies are made not born," observing in these classroom settings that teachers responded over three times as often to males as to females who acted in aggressive disruptive behavior (hitting or breaking things). Boys usually received a loud public reprimand, while teacher's response to girls was most often a brief, soft rebuke that others could not hear. Consistent public rebukes of male aggressiveness did not inhibit this behavior. The researchers suggested that the teacher could resolve this problem by ignoring aggressive acts except to prevent harm to a victim and, in fact, to concentrate attention and concern on the child that has been harmed. Their advice proved accurate: in one case, the boys stopped bullying. Apparently, when children learn that they will be ignored for their misbehavior, they will stop it almost immediately.

Instead of aggression, girls rely on dependency or withdrawal to get adult attention. Serbin and O'Leary observed that teachers also reinforce this sex stereotypical behavior.

> We found that teachers were more likely to react to girls when they were within arms' reach, either literally or figuratively clinging to the teacher's skirts (all the teachers we observed were women). Sheila, for example, was so frequently underfoot, that Mrs. Cox constantly stumbled over her. Sheila was a bright, attractive child who asked many interesting questions, but she refused to play with other children. Except for her extreme dependency, Sheila's development was normal for her age.[27]

The teacher dealt with this problem by talking privately with Sheila constantly in order to build more self-confidence and by approaching Sheila when she was alone to encourage her to play with other children. None of these efforts produced any change. It was then suggested that for a few days the teacher only respond to Sheila when she was with other children. Sheila's extreme dependency vanished within two weeks.

A brief summary of some of the other results of this interesting study includes these findings:

—First, in assigning tasks, teachers would give boys directions and then encourage them to do it on their own, while they would assist the girls but not send them off to work by themselves.

—Second, teachers actually teach boys more than they teach girls. Academic abilities may be nurtured or nullified in the classroom. All teachers gave more verbal and physical rewards to male students who were academically oriented. Boys also receive more directions than girls do.

—Third, boys learn to do. In one exercise, the teacher consistently encouraged boys to practice a skill, while she also consistently fulfilled this task for the girls herself. The only exception to this general pattern of more instruction and encouragement for skill-building for boys happened when the class engaged in explicitly feminine sex-typed activity.

In summary, Serbin and O'Leary observed that teachers are less likely to give public attention or instruction to girls, whether their behavior is appropriate or not, than to boys. In fact, a girl's behavior seemed to secure limited adult reaction. It is important for us to ask at this point whether there is not a correlation between Maccoby and Jacklin's findings (that boys, on the average, tend to have better analytic problem-solving abilities, to be better at spatial reasoning, and to have higher mathematical abilities than girls) and the kind of "nurturing" boys and girls receive in the classroom.

Evidence from other studies shows clear relationships between problem-solving ability and the amount of instruction and direction a child receives.

So the superiority of boys over girls in spatial and analytical reasoning is at least partially a result of the way each sex learns to manipulate the environment—learning that begins in nursery schools with boys who staple and pour, and girls who must sit passively by and watch.

Boys are shown how lawn mowers and erector sets work, and

they wind up with better spatial and analytic skills. Girls are encouraged to stay by their mothers and teachers, where they talk and read. It's the girls who rate higher in verbal and reading ability.[28]

These researchers do not suggest that teachers "reverse their prejudices" in order to resolve this problem, but instead suggest that it would be best if none of the children learned to be too dependent or too aggressive. They feel that differential treatment of boys and girls can ultimately limit their creativity and adaptability to various situations, and that they should have access through encouragement and instruction to various modes of human behavior.

TOWARD A NEW DEFINITION OF MENTAL HEALTH

John Money's research dealt with intersexed persons—those whose chromosomal, hormonal, and postnatal sexual development were not consonant (some contradiction or ambiguity between "biology and personality"). A third body of research, done in 1974 and 1975 by Sandra Bem and her colleagues at Stanford University, considers another "contradiction." They looked at the consequences of having psychological traits that do or do not conform to the cultural expectations of one's sex.

Their results present a challenge to the traditional view of the psychology of sex roles, which holds that well-adjusted men have masculine traits and that well-adjusted women have feminine ones. In contrast to this notion, Bem's research demonstrates that if both sexes have only the "appropriate" trait for their sex, it can have psychologically negative effects.

Before looking at the results of Bem's study, let's consider a number of evaluations of our traditional notions of psychological health as well as methods of scientific observation.

Gloria Hirsch, in an article entitled "Non-Sexist Childrearing: De-Mythifying Normative Data," published in *The Family Co-ordinator* (April 1974), points out that researchers look at "what is" in the culture to obtain "normative data." She argues that the subjects being observed have already adapted to traditional sex-role behavior as men and women. She further suggests (as did Millman) that research approaches and instruments are devised that only support these sex stereotypes. Normative data reveals that people's attitudes about what is innately male and female simply reflect their own stereotypical roles and the broader societal separation of men and women and does not necessarily

129

reveal any new information about the "real" nature of men and women. Not only does normative data support traditional attitudes about male and female differences but also the notion that men are superior and healthy and women inferior and deviant. Thus, societally, a higher value is placed on "male" characteristics, values, and tasks.

Money's research supports Hirsch's challenge that biological differences do not inherently lead to personality differences, but how do psychologists and the broader public evaluate male and female traits with regard to mental health? Two studies support Hirsch's contention that a double standard of mental health exists.

In 1968 Inga Broverman and her associates at Worcester State Hospital in Massachusetts tested seventy-nine clinically trained psychologists, psychiatrists, and social workers (forty-six men and thirty-three women), using a Sex-Stereotype Questionnaire consisting of 122 items—characteristically known as male or female traits. The professionals were divided into three matched groups and each was given different instructions. One was told to choose traits that characterize the healthy adult male, another to choose those of the healthy adult female, the third to choose those of the healthy adult. The results showed the "clinically healthy male" and the "clinically healthy adult" as identical and totally different from the "clinically healthy female." Thus, the general standard of mental health applies to men.

The researchers conclude:

The double standard of health for men and women stems from clinicians' acceptance of an "adjustment" notion of health, for example, health consists of a good adjustment to one's environment. In our society, men and women are systematically trained, practically from birth on, to fulfill different social roles. An adjustment notion of health, plus the existence of differential norms of male and female behavior in our society, automatically lead to a double standard of health. Thus, for a woman to be healthy, from an adjustment viewpoint, she must adjust to and accept the behavioral norms for her sex, even though these behaviors are generally less socially desirable and considered to be less healthy for the generalized competent, mature adult.

By way of analogy, one could argue that a black person who conformed to the "pre-civil rights" southern Negro stereotype, that is, a docile, unambitious, childlike . . . person, was well adjusted to his environment and, therefore, a healthy and mature adult. Our recent history testifies to the bankruptcy of this concept. Alternative definitions of mental health and maturity are implied by concepts of innate drives toward self-actualization, toward mastery of the environment, and toward fulfillment of one's potential (Allport, 1955; Buhler, 1959; Erikson, 1950; Maslow, 1954; Roger, 1951). Such innate drives, in both Blacks and women, are certainly in conflict with becoming adjusted to a social environment with associated restrictive stereotypes. Acceptance of an adjustment notion of health, then, places women in the conflictual position of having to decide whether to exhibit those positive characteristics considered desirable for men and adults, and thus have their "femininity" questioned; that is, be deviant in terms of being a woman; or to behave in the prescribed feminine manner, accept second class adult status, and possibly live a lie to boot.[29]

This double standard also exists in the broader culture. According to psychologist Philip Goldberg, by the time young women reach college they have come to believe that women are inferior, even when the facts do not support this belief.

In 1968 Goldberg asked a group of female college students to rate a number of professional articles from what are considered traditionally male, female, and neutral fields. Students were given identical booklets containing these articles. The only difference was that the same article bore a male name as author in one set of booklets, a female name in the other set. Each booklet included three articles by "men" and three articles by "women." The students were asked to rate each article for value, competence, persuasiveness, and writing style. The "male" authors fared better in *every* field in these evaluations, even in such "feminine" areas as elementary school teaching and dietetics. Goldberg concluded that

since the articles supposedly written by men were exactly the same as those supposedly written by women, the perception that the men's articles were superior was obviously a distortion. Women—at least these young college women—are prejudiced against female professionals and, regardless of the actual accomplishments of these professionals, will firmly refuse to recognize them as the equal of their colleagues.[30]

MASCULINE, FEMININE, OR BOTH
Sandra Bem chose to test the traditional notion of mental health or "adjustment" along sex-stereotyped lines. First of all, she

challenged the assumption that masculine and feminine traits are opposites in human personality as reflected in available personality scales. On a psychological test, one scores as either masculine or feminine, but the test does not allow a person to say that he or she is both.

According to traditional theoretical understandings, if persons are high on masculinity, then they must be low on femininity. Bem wished to test the idea that so-called masculine and feminine traits were actually independent of each other—that one can have a high level of feminine traits.

> I have come to believe that we need a new standard of psychological health for the sexes, one that removes the burden of stereotype and allows people to feel free to express the best traits of men and women. As many feminists have argued, freeing people from rigid sex roles and allowing them to be androgynous (from "andro" male and "gyne," female), should make them more flexible in meeting new situations, and less restricted in what they can do and how they can express themselves.[31]

Bem pointed out that there was already considerable evidence that traditional sex typing is unhealthy. For instance, high masculinity, although a traditional sign of psychological adjustment in adolescence, may correlate high anxiety in adult life and low self-acceptance. The results can be similar for women who are very feminine. And greater intellectual development has quite constantly correlated with cross-sex typing (masculinity in girls, femininity in boys), since boys who are strongly masculine and girls who are strongly feminine tend to have lower overall intelligence, lower spatial ability, and show lower creativity.

She argues further that traditional sexual typing necessarily restricts behavior, since persons are taught to repress any behavior which is inappropriate for their sex—sex attributes typical of the opposite sex. "Men are afraid to do 'women's work,' and women are afraid to enter 'man's world.' " Men are reluctant to be gentle, and women to be assertive. In contrast, androgynous people are not limited by labels. They are able to do whatever they want, both in their behavior and in their feelings.[32]

In order to measure how masculine, feminine, or androgynous people are, Bem devised the Bem Sex Role Inventory, which consists of a list of sixty personality characteristics: twenty traditionally masculine (ambitious, self-reliant, independent, assertive); twenty traditionally feminine (affectionate, gentle, sensitive); and twenty neutral (truthful, friendly, likeable). All sixty traits are listed in random order. A person indicates on a scale of one (never or almost never true) to seven (always or almost always true) how accurate each word is as a self-description. The difference between the total points assigned to masculine and feminine adjectives indicates the degree of a person's sex typing. If masculinity and femininity scores are approximately equal, the individual has an androgynous sex role. This test was given to more than 1,500 undergraduate students at Stanford University. Fifty percent of the students adhere to appropriate sex roles (sex-typed, having only those traits traditionally considered appropriate for their sex), 15% are cross sex-typed (having only the traits traditionally considered appropriate for the other sex), and 35% are androgynous (having both masculine and feminine traits.)

Bem then tested her prediction that androgynous individuals of both sexes would perform well tasks requiring skills usually thought masculine and tasks calling on traits usually considered feminine. She suggested that sex-typed or cross sex-typed individuals, on the other hand, would do well on only one of these kinds of tasks.

> In one of the experiments Bem conducted to prove these points, subjects faced group pressure to change their judgment on a perceptual task—to go along with the group even though the group's judgment was clearly wrong. Here, being able to resist group pressure was considered to be a "masculine" skill. In several other experiments designed to assess "feminine" nurturant skills, subjects played with a kitten, played with a baby, or were instructed to listen supportively to another student describing problems encountered in adjusting to college. In each case, subjects were rated on how comfortably and skillfully they carried out these activities.[33]

Bem's assumptions were basically confirmed. Feminine women conformed to group pressure more frequently than masculine men and androgynous students of either sex. Highly masculine males resisted conformist pressure but were less adept at tasks requiring nurturance and emotional sensitivity, while androgynous males did well at both tasks.

The women's results for the exercises testing feminine traits were somewhat surprising. Androgynous women did well, as mentioned before, at resisting group pressure and at nurturing activities and showed high sensitivity to others. But the highly feminine women not only had difficulty resisting group pressure but were also inhibited to varying degrees in the tasks requiring nurturance or emotional sensitivity—playing with a kitten or baby or listening to another student's problems. Bem speculated that feminine women were inhibited because they were required to take initiative in an ambiguous situation and were fearful of negative evaluation; they lacked assertiveness even in attempting traditionally feminine tasks.

However, in testing adeptness at what are thought of as typically feminine and masculine tasks, both the androgynous men and women did equally well.

This research supports Bem's theory that traditional concepts of masculinity and femininity do restrict a person's behavior in important ways.

> In a modern complex society like ours, an adult has to be assertive, independent and self-reliant, but traditional femininity makes many women unable to behave in these ways. On the other hand, an adult must also be able to relate to other people, to be sensitive to their needs and concerned about their welfare, as well as to be able to depend on them for emotional support. But traditional masculinity keeps men from responding in such supposedly feminine ways.
>
> Androgyny, in contrast, allows an individual to be both independent and tender, assertive and yielding, masculine and feminine. Thus androgyny greatly expands the range of behavior open to everyone, permitting people to cope more effectively with diverse situations. As such, I hope that androgyny will some day come to define a new and more human standard of psychological health.[34]

A COMPARISON OF OLD AND
NEW PERSPECTIVES

How does the new psychology of sex roles, based particularly on findings of the Money, Bem, and Maccoby and Jacklin research, compare to traditional theories? Pleck offers the following comparison:

First, the new psychology of sex roles agrees with the old, in holding that men and women do differ on the average on certain psychological traits. But the new understanding finds these differences smaller, less biologically based, and less socially significant than the traditional paradigm.

Second, the new psychology of sex roles agrees with the older view that to a large extent men and women learn "appropriate" sex traits. However, the new approach rejects the old view that men and women need these particular sex-appropriate traits to be secure as men or women. Instead, this social learning is viewed as a result of social expectations. We are taught that we *ought* to act according to certain ways in order to validate our biological sex identity.

Third, according to the new psychology of sex roles, the critical event in psychological development is learning one's biological gender, which usually occurs by age three. If one argues according to traditional theory, the critical task of development is to achieve the behavior, attitudes, and feelings that are defined as appropriate to one's sex. In fact, current research indicates that learning *only* behavior deemed appropriate for one's sex can be a handicap.

Fourth, although the new psychology of sex-role research outlines particular differences between men and women, they are not strong enough to account for or justify the differences or inequities in the social roles of men and women.

The table on page 136 shows Pleck's typology.

The findings of this new research will help to shape different perspectives of psychosexual adjustment. For many people this "new knowledge" is not startling but an important scientific confirmation of what we already know—that men and women are, first of all, persons, and that the most rewarding relationships between men and women as friends, lovers, or workers are ones that embody a mutual commitment of respect, sensitivity, challenge, and mystery.

The apparent dialogues happening in scientific approach and in thinking about what it means to be male and female reflect the impact and power of human experience transformed from man-superior and women-inferior to the new creation: man/woman in God's image. This is the demand of love: to appreciate the full humanity of the "other."

The old psychosexual paradigms of male and female do not encompass the strength of our mothers, the tears of our fathers, the intimacy of lovers, or the trust between men and women who are friends. Our need for each other's gifts and, thus, our mutual vision is greater than the old separation of sexes. And science may—if its function is to serve humanity—heal itself, in order that it might serve.

ADDITIONAL QUESTIONS FOR CONSIDERATION
Our attention has focused on psychosexual consideration with regard to social behavior, attitudes, and roles of men and women.

COMPARISON OF TRADITIONAL AND NEW PERSPECTIVES ON THE PSYCHOLOGY OF SEX ROLES

	Traditional Perspective	New Perspective
Extent of psychological sex differences	Large differences between men and women on most traits.	Some sex differences on some traits (certain intellectual skills and aggression), but considerable overlap between the sexes.
Biological basis for psychological sex differences	Psychological sex differences rooted in biological differences.	Psychological sex differences are biologically based in part, but are nonetheless highly trainable and influenced by environment.
Psychological needs in personality development	Innate psychological need to learn sex-appropriate personality traits and interests, thus establishing secure "sex identity."	Psychological need to have accurate self-classification of one's gender (i.e., male or female), but no psychological need to have sex-appropriate masculine or feminine traits; such traits are learned because of societal pressure, not innate psychological need.
Potential problem in personality development	Failure to develop sex-appropriate masculine or feminine traits, resulting in psychological maladjustment; relatively frequent.	(1) Failure to develop accurate self-classification of one's gender, occurring only in a small minority (1 to 2 percent). (2) Developing *only* sex-appropriate masculine or feminine traits, leading to psychological handicaps.
Implications of psychology for women's and men's social roles	Psychological sex differences and needs for sex identity account for and justify women's and men's social roles.	Psychological sex differences and presumed need for sex identity do not account for women's and men's different social roles; sources of these differences in social roles lie elsewhere.[35]

However, there are a number of particular questions about psychosexual theory that are of particular concern to people in the church as well as in the broader culture; these questions relate to genital sexuality or the broader issues of sexual preference or sexual attraction.

One of these matters is homosexuality, which literally means the same sex. Culturally, homosexuality is easy to define. Popularly, it explicitly focuses upon sexual relationships. However, we need to distinguish homosexual acts from homosexual orientation, which may involve sexual acts but also feelings, needs, and commitments. One who engages in homosexual experiences at some time in life is not thereby primarily homosexual.

Kinsey found that more than one in three white men and about one in eight white women in the United States engaged in some same-sex sexual activity, although most of these persons were heterosexual. Therefore, homosexuality and heterosexuality are not always fixed patterns but are matters of degree. Some people are bisexual—attracted to both sexes. Most of us, to some extent, have both homo- and heterosexual traits.

All of us are, first of all, persons. For the homosexual, sexual desire and experience are no more or less a controlling factor in life than sexual desire and experience are for the heterosexual. This means that homosexual persons are as different from one another in beliefs, values, and talents as are heterosexuals.

Like heterosexuals, some homosexuals are promiscuous and some faithful; some seek self-gratification and others lasting commitment and mutual fulfillment. Researchers are beginning to realize that the majority of stable homosexual relationships stay hidden in order to avoid the pressure of society's lack of acceptance. Therefore, data about the stability of homosexual liaisons is, for all practical purposes, impossible to obtain. Homosexuals and heterosexuals alike are of diverse political opinion, religious belief, racial or ethnic background, and economic status. In other words, the only general difference between heterosexuals and homosexuals is sexual preference.

The majority of authors dealing with the short-term nature of homosexual relationships recognize that the primary reason for this problem is the guilt and self-hatred felt by homosexuals.

Homosexuality has existed since ancient times and has been present in many different cultures. In fact, the majority of societies that have been studied have condoned homosexual behavior. This is generally not true of modern Western culture, however.

After years of research the questions of where and how a homosexual pattern of life originates are unanswered. At least, there is little agreement. Some researchers suggest that there are chromosomal and/or hormonal differences between homosexuals and heterosexuals, but attempts to treat homosexuality with sex hormones have merely increased sexual desire without altering its object. Even recent studies offer no basic proof of genetic or hormonal differences.

Some authorities believe that homo- or heterosexual orientations are learned, although diverse opinions exist as to how and why. There are a number of theories which suggest that people become homosexual because of their negative relationships with parents early in childhood and/or because of the relationships between their parents. In addition to familial factors there may also be certain social factors, since we learn a great deal about how to behave both in a masculine and feminine way from our peers. A number of sociologists suggest that one who experiences social rejection because he or she is not typically masculine or feminine may seek and find acceptance in a homosexual relationship.

None of these theories is universally accepted. Probably many different factors can account for either homosexuality or heterosexuality; they may be different for different people. Most likely little will be known about what makes one a homosexual until we understand more fully how one becomes heterosexual.

Behavioral scientists' evaluations of homosexuality are as diverse as their theories about what causes it. A number of psychiatrists are convinced that homosexuality is an illness. Edmund Bergler, in his book *Homosexuality: Disease or Way of Life?*, defines homosexuality as "a neurotic distortion of the whole personality. . . . There are no healthy homosexuals. The entire personality structure of the homosexual is pervaded by the unconscious wish to suffer. This wish is gratified by self-created troublemaking (psychic masochism) . . . he is an emotionally sick person."[36]

This neurotic disorder is believed to stem from disturbed family relationships, particularly for males, representing a combination of a domineering, seductive mother and an unloving father. Lesbianism (female homosexuality) is seen as sometimes resulting from lack of mother love or father love. Other theories suggest that it results from the disillusionment and pain women experience because of their second-class status in our culture.

Theories concerning family pattern as cause are not widely accepted, because many similarly disturbed families produce no homosexuals at all; there are many heterosexual children with similar family problems. The neurosis theory has been based on appraisals of small samples of homosexuals who seek therapy: a highly unrepresentative sample. One could argue that theories based solely on work with disturbed heterosexual patients would result in a similarly skewed impression of heterosexuality. Unfortunately, little research has been done in comparing homosexuals who enter therapy with homosexuals in the broader culture or with heterosexuals.

Some psychiatrists take a more neutral position, believing that homosexuality is simply a variation in sexual orientation. They recognize that some homosexuals may indeed be sick but do not consider their homosexuality the cause. They do not believe homosexuals to be any more lonely, anxious, or irresponsible than heterosexuals, although some may have unique problems stemming from cultural prejudice against them. Many homosexuals who seek psychotherapeutic help do so in order to ease their inner conflicts and to learn to cope with the social pressure they bear—not to change their sexual orientation.

Psychiatrist Judd Marmur suggests that "many homosexuals are well adjusted with their homosexuality. They have their own community, they are as happy as most of us are. After all, nobody is happy all the time and being heterosexual certainly does not guarantee happiness."[37]

Sigmund Freud did not regard homosexuality as an illness. He wrote, "Homosexuality is assuredly no advantage but it is nothing to be ashamed of, no vice, no degradation, it cannot be classified as an illness; we consider it to be a variation of the sexual development."[38]

It was not until 1957 that any research was done with homosexuals not in therapy. Psychologist Evelyn Hooker, of the University of California in Los Angeles, compared male homosexuals and heterosexuals by giving them a battery of personality tests. (Neither group of men were in therapy.) Clinical psychologists rated each person's test results without knowing the person's sexual orientation. Results showed that the analysts could not differentiate homosexuals from heterosexuals. Hooker concluded that

> the "disease" called homosexuality does not exist. The forms of homosexual experience are as varied as the forms of heterosexual experience.
>
> Homosexuality may be a deviation that is within the normal range of human behavior.
>
> Particular forms of sexual desire and expression may play a

less important role in personality structure than many psychiatrists assume.[39]

In 1974 the Trustees of the American Psychiatric Association took a similar position. They unanimously ruled that "homosexuality shall no longer be listed as a 'mental disorder.' " There is now a category called "sexual orientation disturbance," described as follows:

> This category is for individuals whose sexual interests are directed primarily toward people of the same sex and who are either disturbed by, in conflict with, or wish to change their sexual orientation. This diagnostic category is distinguished from homosexuality, which by itself does not necessarily constitute a psychiatric disorder. Homosexuality per se is one form of sexual behavior and, like other forms of sexual behavior which are not of themselves psychiatric disorders, is not listed in this nomenclature of mental disorder.

Still other psychiatrists take an openly affirmative position that homosexual persons should claim, honor, and responsibly live out their homosexuality. They believe it would be unhealthy for them to do otherwise, just as it would be for one to repress his or her heterosexuality. Wainwright Churchill testifies, "This author wishes to go on record as one clinician among a multitude of others who has had the opportunity to interview, and in several cases, to become acquainted with homosexual males who meet every reasonable standard of mental health in their relationships with themselves and with others."[40]

Psychologist Mark Freedman suggests that the homosexual personal quest for identity, purpose, and meaning can be quite intense, once he or she begins to appreciate the tremendous social pressures against gay persons. In 1967 he did research with lesbians and heterosexual women. The results were similar to Hooker's findings and demonstrated that lesbians are no more neurotic or disturbed than heterosexual women. However, some results were more provocative. He says, "My research on lesbians found them scoring higher than a control group on autonomy, spontaneity, orientation toward the present . . . and sensitivity to one's own needs and feelings."[41]

The results of comparable experiments done in 1969 (by June Hopkins) and in 1972 (by Marvin Siegelman) closely resemble Freedman's, with lesbians scoring higher on independence and self-acceptance.

Obviously, there are great discrepancies between the negative, neutral, and positive attitudes regarding cause and evaluation of homosexuality. Most researchers have modestly qualified their evaluation due to the limitations of their research and the data it has produced. Therefore, it is difficult to make broad generalizations about homosexuality, and at present the questions of causes and evaluation of homosexuality—or heterosexuality—are left unresolved until more substantive research can be done with nonclinical homo- and heterosexual populations.

CHAPTER 5

Sexuality and Public Policy—An Overview

The term public policy refers to the combination of decisions a society makes about the tension between the desire for individual rights and freedoms and the need for social consensus, on the one hand, and the distribution of goods, services, and experiences in the society, on the other.

Christians have a profound stake in the quality of life for all persons. Wise decision-making in the area of public policy as it affects sexuality is particularly difficult. Sometimes the difficulty arises because the views of an individual or those of a group differ substantially from those of the wider public. Sometimes the area is difficult because of the interplay of civil liberty and public good. Governmental expression and enforcement of public policies relating to sexuality inevitably run afoul of these elements. Sexual behavior between consenting adults is so personal that no element of governmental enforcement can avoid a threat to civil liberties. Christians concerned for sexuality need to keep the issues of public good and civil rights in balance.

Human sexuality is part of our experience, with significant implications for many arenas of life. Sexual awareness plays a role in decisions we make about politics, economics, law, medicine, and a large number of other institutions. We are often unaware of the impact of sexuality on these areas unless particular incidents arise that focus our attention on their interrelationships. When a neighborhood group becomes concerned about prostitution in its community, it may vigorously protest the connection of sexual experience and economic gain. At the same time, it may remain unaware of the more subtle but very similar connections between sexual allure and the sale of goods on television or in magazines. Similarly, a legislator whose support for civil rights for gay people is causing reelection problems is facing an obvious emergence of sexuality into the political arena. Yet, far more wide-ranging assumptions about sexuality and sex roles may be less overtly present in his or her stand on who should be covered by social security or what funding should go for medical research on birth control. We should be as aware as possible of the role sexuality plays in so much of our lives.

Social movements that aim at human liberation, such as feminism and gay activism, help us focus on our own sexuality and provide critiques of our assumptions about sexual expression. For example, when someone questions whether homosexual relationships are normal, they should be asked to examine how they decide what normalcy is and to question how much of their definition depends on their own interpretation of what is aesthetically appealing. When one raises objections to women performing certain jobs in the society, he or she should grapple with the question of whether it is physical or psychological limitations that cause the objections or merely social role stereotypes that have been built up over decades without independent or scientific validity.

This chapter attempts to take seriously the insights of many groups concerned about sexual expression. It will explore how the sexuality of particular kinds of people is affected by public policy decisions in a number of spheres.

The question of whether a society, acting through its legal system, should prohibit sexual expression that offends the common moral standards in that society has been debated for centuries. John Stuart Mill, a nineteenth-century philosopher, emphatically rejected the idea.

> The only purpose for which power can rightfully be exercised over any member of a civilized community against his will is to prevent harm to others. His own good either physical or moral is not a sufficient warrant. He cannot rightfully be compelled to do or forbear because it will be better for him to do so, because it will make him happier, or because in the opinions of others, to do so would be wise or even right.[1]

Other theorists, however, see the enforcement of majority moral principles by the legal system as a prerequisite for a stable society:

> What makes a society of any sort is community of ideas, not only political ideas but also ideas about the way its members should behave and govern their lives; these latter ideas are its morals. . . . If society has the right to make a judgment and has it on the basis that a recognized morality is as necessary to society as, say, a recognized government, then society may use

the law to preserve morality in the same way as it uses it to safeguard anything else that is essential to its existence.[2]

This tension emerges in a number of the areas discussed below. One example of this conflict arises in discussion of pornography. As a general principle, most of us want to uphold the freedom of speech and expression articulated by the First Amendment to the Constitution, yet we are personally offended by some specific products of that freedom, particularly in the realm of explicit sexual materials. At some stage the right to print or express an idea may come into open and serious conflict with other values in the society or may clearly interfere with the perceived rights of other persons. There is a point where the radical freedom to do or say one thing may harm the society. At that point individual freedom will have to be curtailed to meet a broader societal need. Determining that point is a major public policy decision in many areas related to human sexuality.

The other critical dimension of public policy is societal decisions about the distribution of resources. Such decisions may include whether mere equality of opportunity is to be a goal or whether past disparities should be corrected, as with "affirmative action"; to what groups should we (by race, sex, age, marital condition) provide the benefits of certain life experiences or the support of societal institutions; how should we allocate the "risks" in a society, be they the possibility of pregnancy or the possible side effects of developing new medical treatments.

The church can and must have a role in defining and implementing public policy. This may mean commenting upon decisions made legislatively or administratively at the federal, state, and local levels. It also involves deciding what other nongovernmental institutions we should focus our attention toward in raising the general consciousness of society on the nature and quality of human sexuality. Often the church, which is concerned for equal justice under law, must advocate personal functioning beyond the minimal standards expressed by the legal system in the direction of increased mutuality, creativity, and sensitivity in sexual relationships but should be very cautious in asking that legal system to control expressions of sexual conduct that cannot be determined to cause injury to the society.

SEXUALITY AND WOMEN

SEXUAL SELF-DETERMINATION
Historically, women have had less opportunity than men to control their own reproductive lives yet, paradoxically, were often

144

perceived as ultimately more responsible than men if unwanted conception occurred. The legal system prohibited access to birth control information and abortions, while the medical establishment screened out most of the women who wanted to become physicians, thus assuring that myths about women and their bodies would be perpetuated. Only recently a series of trends has emerged that begin to provide women with the right to medical services and the possibility of achieving genuine self-determination in relation to their bodies and their sexuality.

The early 1970s brought two extremely important Supreme Court decisions that affected sexual self-determination. *Eisenstadt v. Baird* involved the conviction of William Baird for distributing a package of vaginal foam after a lecture on contraception, an act in violation of a Massachusetts law that prohibited giving such products to single persons. The Supreme Court overturned the conviction and noted: "If the right of privacy means anything, it is the right of the *individual*, married or single, to be free from unwarranted governmental intrusion into matters so fundamentally affecting a person as the decision whether to bear or beget a child."[3]

The following year the court went one step further by establishing that the zone of privacy extended to many decisions involving the aborting of a fetus for any reason. *Roe v. Wade* established that during the first three months of pregnancy the abortion decision was to rest solely with the woman and her physician.[4] With regard to the second trimester, states could enact legislation to regulate the abortion procedure but only to promote the "health of the mother." Only during the final months of pregnancy could a state "in promoting its interest in the potentiality of human life" prohibit abortion except where the life or health of the mother was at stake. Subsequent decisions established that the biological father could not interfere to prevent an abortion if the woman desired one and limited the parents' control over an unwed daughter's decision to have an abortion. Regrettably, one third of the world's women live in countries where abortion is still totally illegal or is permitted only when a woman's life is clearly threatened.[5]

This is merely the state of the law. It does not answer the personal moral questions around a decision to have or not to have an abortion, or does not even describe optimal public policy in this area. Even within the broad permission granted by the law the church should attempt to continue to evaluate data about abortions and should suggest measures for institutions to undertake to alter trends or experiences that are destructive or problematic. For example, medical data indicates that some women suffer adverse psychological effects from their abortion experience. This may be related to the meaning they give to the act or to the atmosphere in which the procedure is performed. Either cause calls for better counseling and support related to this experience. Discussion prior to the procedure by empathetic counselors sometimes reveals women who are, in fact, being subtly or overtly coerced into abortions they do not desire. Likewise, postprocedure sessions, like those at Massachusetts General Hospital, which last thirteen weeks, permit women to deal with frequently unresolved religious and philosophical questions and resolve the sense of societal stigma many women feel. Such sessions frequently help women to develop more security about their own decision and about their future.[6] A serious effort to support such counseling would be one way for the church to move beyond minimal legal demands in this area. Other examples of steps the church might take would be to encourage continued research on possible risks in subsequent pregnancies after some types of abortion and to provide, or be advocates for, means through which women who want to have a child will not be forced merely because of economic circumstances to have an abortion. It is also estimated that 22 percent of the women seeking abortion in New York City had had at least one earlier abortion, which may indicate the need for increased availability of and access to methods of birth control.

Moving beyond legalisms, however, also calls for vigilance to see that the rights articulated by the courts are actually implemented by the responsible agencies. Laws have been passed in the United States during the past few years, which, although ultimately ruled unconstitutional, have seriously interfered with obtaining abortions, particularly by poorer women. One amendment to an appropriations bill in 1976 temporarily halted the use of federal funds to pay for abortions, thus curtailing service at free clinics in some cities, with the subsequent effect of sending poor women back to the same dangerous, nonmedical abortionists they turned to prior to the Supreme Court decision. In other states obviously unconstitutional statutes were passed as harassment (Louisiana passed a law making it a capital offense to participate in an abortion), or complex regulations were written that make obtaining an abortion unnecessarily traumatic. (In Missouri, women must be informed that if a live birth results from the abortion, the woman will lose custody of the child, the requirement being little more than a way to frighten women into not having the procedure done.) When the decision about the distribution of services is an element of public policy, the church must be sensitive to how disparate the availability of certain services may be.

Several important forces are also at work in the health care field. First, the greater influx of women into medical schools and into medical practice has the potential for beginning to change some misconceptions about women that have been perpetuated for centuries. In 1973 only 7 percent of all physicians in the United States were female; 26 percent of the medical students in 1976 were women. The medical profession, for a long time explicitly and today somewhat less overtly, considers menstruation an illness, looks upon pregnancy as a "disease" that requires a doctor's care (not merely a midwife's intervention), and sees menopause as the final, incurable illness (one book calls it the "death of the woman in the woman"). Since Freud, in much psychiatric theory women are viewed as fundamentally weak and as attempting a lifelong adjustment to the fact that they are not men. One widely used psychiatric textbook acknowledges the social acquisition of sexual roles to some extent but still notes certain feelings as normative:

> In school and college a girl may have sought unconsciously to show that her intellect was as good as a boy's, sometimes to use her intellect aggressively—phallically. Her ambition often changes when . . . she can displace her masculine identification onto a man whom she loves, and feels that she can gain satisfaction through his achievements.[7]

Demythologizing about women's roles and the reconceptualization of biological processes as health and not "disease" may likely be the outcome of a genuinely open medical establishment.

A second development that is assisting in the improvement of the relationship between women and the health care system is the so-called "self-help movement." This is the attempt by concerned women to teach their sisters ways to examine themselves for various signs of illness. Breast examinations for possible cancerous tumors and the use of the speculum to examine the cervix are the most widely adopted methods. Barbara Ehrenreich and Deirdre English, authors of several booklets on women and health care, note:

> Self-help, which emphasizes self-examination and self-knowledge, is an attempt to seize the technology without buying the ideology. Self-help has no limits beyond those imposed by our imagination and our resources. It could expand far beyond self-

examination to include lay (though not untrained) treatment for many common problems—lay prenatal and delivery assistance, and so on.[8]

In some churches, women's groups are already engaged in study sessions to learn about their bodies and to speak together about the role the health care system can and does play in their lives.

Increased protection of the law and the movement toward inclusiveness in medicine may also help to eliminate coercive medical interference with women's bodies. Coerced sterilization generally involves either poor women on welfare or persons alleged to be mentally retarded. In 1974 the US Department of Health, Education and Welfare produced guidelines on sterilization after a highly publicized court case was instituted involving sterilization without consent of two Black girls, age twelve and fourteen years old, in a family planning clinic. The girls won their case and the court noted there was "uncontroverted evidence in the record . . . that an indefinite number of poor people have been improperly coerced into accepting a sterilization operation under the threat that various federally supported welfare benefits would be withdrawn unless they submitted to irreversible sterilization."[9]

The Department of Health, Education and Welfare estimates that 100,000 to 150,000 low-income persons are sterilized each year. Many simply do not want more children. However, procedures are performed on others for reasons that are highly suspect. In some hospitals, residents in obstetrics and gynecology need to do a certain number of various sterilization procedures in order to become certified. Although the required quota of laparoscopies (in which a small incision is made below the navel in order to reach the Fallopian tubes to tie them shut) can be done on purely voluntary patients, hysterectomies (the actual removal of the uterus) are less desirable; doctors convince women to have these operations (often during labor or immediately after an abortion) for their certification rather than for any medical necessity. Thirty-five percent of the women in Puerto Rico have been sterilized; many of these were erroneously told that it is a reversible procedure. There is a high level of noncompliance around the country, even with the minimal Health, Education and Welfare guidelines. These guidelines require a three-day waiting period between the time "consent" is given and the operation, the free-will signing of consent forms, no sterilization for those under twenty-one, and notice and counseling about the permanence of the operation and the availability of other methods of birth control.

Sterilization is often perceived by medical practitioners as a kind of punishment for having too many children. Aside from giving the feeling this is close to cruel and unusual punishment, prohibited by the Eighth Amendment, it is not up to the medical profession to make such policy judgments. This is particularly true when one considers the significant maternal death rate associated with all sterilization methods (25/100,000 in laparoscopy; 300 to 500/100,000 in hysterectomies), the 2- to 4-percent frequency of infection and bleeding complications, and the exceedingly high "regret" rate reported (25 to 32 percent) in medical literature.[10]

Closely related with abuse of sterilization for the poor is the specter of coerced sterilization for those thought likely to produce physically or psychologically defective offspring. The Supreme Court, in *Buck v. Bell* (1927), upheld the right of a Virginia hospital to sterilize a "feebleminded white woman," whose mother and daughter were also adjudged mentally deficient.[11] The statute provided that a hospital superintendent could order sterilization whenever he was "of the opinion that it is for the best interest of society that an inmate under his care be sterilized." Justice Holmes noted the high value in preserving the quality of the human species and suggested that mentally ill people should be willing to sacrifice reproductivity. He concluded that "three generations of imbeciles are enough." This decision has never been reversed. Many states have similar laws on the books, and although they are only infrequently used, they provide an opportunity for serious abuse. In 1974 the deputy commissioner of the Virginia Department of Mental Health and Rehabilitation reported that two or three operations were still being done each year under the Virginia statute.[12]

A related matter is medical experimentation, performed in particular upon those most vulnerable in the society—the poor and the incarcerated. One highly criticized research program done on Mexican-American women in South Texas provided women with what they thought was a new kind of oral contraceptive. It turned out that half were receiving a placebo pill that had no medical effects, and many became pregnant precisely at a time when they had expressed a strong desire not to have another child. Although such blind studies may need to be done, they are impossible to justify where the participants were misled about the nature of the research. It should be noted that experimentation on reproduction is done almost completely on women. Although male researchers frequently alleged that this was merely because it was easier physiologically to control female ovulation (since even a 90 percent reduction in sperm does not always cause infertility), serious questions are being raised about whether a kind of chauvinism wasn't the decisive factor.

Some research on male fertility is now being conducted. Methods to lower sperm production by inhibition of hormone secretions of LH (luteinizing hormone) and FSH (follicle stimulating hormone) by drugs that act directly on the testes and by drugs that will inhibit the sperm's tail motility (and thus render them infertile) are presently being investigated by researchers. Although most of these techniques still provide some serious medical drawbacks or reduce sexual interest and create abnormal passivity, one review study concludes, "Limited clinical trials of several new methods have yielded encouraging results."[13] This research should be supported.

THE ECONOMICS OF FEMALE SEXUALITY

Prostitution is reputed to be the oldest and, with the alleged exception of China, the most ubiquitous profession. Author Ned Polsky defines prostitution as "the granting of nonmarital sex as a vocation." Although that definition seems to describe what most people consider prostitution, it does not make clear precisely why most societies have chosen to criminalize the practice or what element of the practice is seen as particularly reprehensible.

It seems unlikely that prostitution could ever be viewed as a loving act, yet the law in no other circumstance prohibits per se acts of intercourse without love. For example, the law does not inquire whether a marriage is loving or whether it is one for convenience or profit. Marrying for money may bring social opprobrium, but it does not invoke the censure of the legal system. It seems of use, therefore, to question why economically motivated sexual experience is prohibited in one form when it may be present in others.

Most prostitutes in the United States are not initially arrested for the act of prostitution but, rather, for soliciting for prostitution. Thus, the fact that it is an affront to the privacy of the public leads to most arrests. In England, on the other hand, soliciting is also illegal, but prostitution is not. Discreet advertising is permitted, so that persons interested in the services offered by prostitutes can locate them easily.

Prior to the 1976 Democratic National Convention, New York City passed an ordinance that prohibited loitering for the purpose of prostitution. It was worded so vaguely that within a few days of enactment, one woman who merely asked for a match and another simply waiting to use a pay telephone were either arrested or told to move on. Caution must be used even in drafting laws prohibiting solicitation by prostitutes or by their patrons, lest abuse occur in enforcement.

The way prostitution is practiced in the United States creates serious problems within the criminal justice system. It is, however, a multibillion dollar industry. As a result of several years of research, Gail Sheehy estimated that there are 200,000 to 250,000 prostitutes (mostly female) in this country. At the rate of six $20-or-more contacts each day, yearly profits from prostitution are between $7 and $9 billion.[14] The profiteers in this business are frequently not the prostitutes but the other parties who form the network that supports the business. These individuals include pimps (men who organize prostitutes and protect them from abuse by other men), operators of the cheap hotels that are frequented by prostitutes and landlords of such real estate, lawyers who specialize in the defense of prostitutes, and organized criminal elements that are connected with the process. Rarely do these other parties get involved in the criminal justice system. Even where state or local laws permit prosecutions for, say, landlords who knowingly allow their properties to be used for illegal activities, few offenders are ever formally charged.

The women, however, are frequently harassed and prosecuted. In San Francisco it is estimated that each arrest for prostitution costs the city $1,730. The first arrest there and in most jurisdictions never leads to imprisonment but to a ninety-day suspended sentence and a two-year probation. This lengthy probationary term makes a second arrest a serious matter. To avoid it, prostitutes may be blackmailed into sexual relations with police officers (the ultimate in hypocrisy) or may be forced to produce evidence or testify (accurately or fraudulently) against persons the police would like to convict for other reasons. An arrest record for prostitution makes it virtually impossible to find employment and is itself a difficult stigma to overcome. Many times women who were prostitutes discover that they cannot leave the "vocation." Margo St. James, a former prostitute, comments that it is much easier to hire an ex-convict for the shipping department than it is to hire an ex-prostitute for the secretarial pool.

The present system can hardly be viewed as victimless. The woman is stigmatized and humiliated. Likewise, the very sordidness of the payoff scheme and the involvement of organized crime bring an increased incidence of violence to areas of high prostitu-

151

tion. The number of assaults by and on prostitutes has gone up dramatically in large metropolitan areas over the past few years.

In taking a public stance, the church might advocate a continuation of the present system of law enforcement or might suggest that the customers of prostitutes should also be prosecuted as a deterrent to this sexual expression outside marriage. As another alternative, it could adopt the stance of legalization of prostitution so that states or localities could promulgate guidelines for the business. A third option is decriminalization, in which laws prohibiting consensual prostitution are repealed and the state takes no further regulatory action. Those who support decriminalization do not want to legitimate prostitution. At the same time, the equal enforcement of laws against prostitutes and their customers will not happen. It is possible, of course, to regulate public nuisance behavior without making prostitution itself a criminal act.

Pornography (from the Greek, meaning "writing of harlots") in America represents a multimillion dollar enterprise that capitalizes on sexual fantasy. In this area, too, there is a spectacular clash between the claims of the Constitution, which protect the promotion of all "ideas," and our sense that some visual and verbal images are so shocking and offensive that they should not be allowed to be disseminated.

After a series of confusing and often contradictory federal court decisions in the 1960s, the present test for when sexually explicit material is also obscene was set down in 1973 in *Miller v. California*:

> (a) whether "the average person, applying contemporary community standards" would find that the work, taken as a whole, appeals to the prurient interest, (b) whether the work depicts or describes, in a patently offensive way, sexual conduct specifically defined by the applicable state law, and (c) whether the work, as a whole, lacks serious literary, artistic, political, or scientific value. . . . It is possible to give a few plain examples of what a state statute could define for regulations under the second part (b) of the standard announced in this opinion: (a) Patently offensive representation or description of ultimate sexual acts, normal or perverted, real or simulated. (b) Patently offensive representations or descriptions of masturbation, excretory functions, and lewd exhibitions of the genitals.[15]

One year later the court clarified that "community" standards meant local standards, a decision that has prompted prosecutions for obscenity on a highly sporadic basis. The publisher of one particularly explicit magazine was sentenced in Cincinnati, Ohio to seven to twenty-five years in prison on an organized crime charge for an alleged conspiracy to distribute obscene literature, although the magazine is still sold in most other cities. In Fairfax County, Virginia an especially aggressive district attorney has recently obtained several convictions against merchants who operate adult book stores. The sale of five sexually explicit magazines to undercover police brought a four-year-two-month jail term, and the sale of two 8mm films led to a two-year sentence.

Underlying the Supreme Court decisions is the assumption that the First Amendment does not protect speech or expression that does not contain "ideas." For example, libelous statements (known false statements) or "fighting words" have long been considered unprotected speech. The claim that pornography does not contain "ideas," however, is challenged by many legal scholars:

> Pornography can be seen as the unique medium of a vision of sexuality, a "pornotopia"—a view of sexual delight in the erotic celebration of the body, a concept of easy freedom without consequences, a fantasy of endlessly repetitive indulgence.[16]

> The claim that pornography presents the debasement and dehumanization of man (sic) and that it contains no ideas is a contradiction. Surely the debasement of man is a serious moral idea, and not all men agree that a given sort of activity is dehumanizing.[17]

Other "ideas" claimed to be present in some types of explicit sexual materials are that nudity or specific sexual practices are acceptable modes of expression or that sexual experimentation is a healthy thing.

There is some debate about whether pornography gives people thoughts about rape and assault, which they then go out to practice. A few particularly hideous sexual crimes have been traced to specific explicit elements. Although some anecdotal material links sex crimes with erotic materials, empirical studies do not demonstrate the connection. One massive study conducted by Michael Goldstein and Harold Kant indicated that sex criminals actually saw less erotica during adolescence than a control group, and that unusually violent criminals often came from "very repressive family backgrounds regarding sexuality."[18]

Other observers, however, are concerned that it is not the specific one-to-one correspondence between explicit material and acts of violence against women that is the real problem, but the way pornographic images reinforce cultural stereotypes about women already present in the media. Psychologist Ernest van Den Haag discusses the psychological impact of pornography, specifically that which includes an element of violence:

> By de-individualizing and dehumanizing sexual acts, where this becomes impersonal, pornography reduces or removes the empathy and the mutual identity which restrains us from treating each other merely as objects or means. This empathy is an individual barrier to non-consensual acts, such as rape, torture, and assaultive crime in general. Without such empathy, we are not humane to each other; and finally, as we become wholly solipsistic, our own humanity is impaired. Pornography, thus, is antihuman and antisocial. . . . If we do not feel empathy, then others are easily relegated beyond the pale, to become merely means. By inviting us to reduce others to sources of sensation, pornography destroys the psychological bonds that bind society. . . . Pornography, in exalting the instrumental use we can make of each, depreciates and destroys the emotion that goes with devotion to or consideration for others as ends. Yet love and affection are precious—and precarious—heritages of our civilization and their socialized modes, compassion and empathy, are indispensable to it.[19]

The poles of thought about pornography, then, are that it all contains "ideas" that need to be protected, even though they may be personally offensive, or that in virtually all its forms it is so dehumanizing that its presence is an affront to love and mutual respect. In between are persons who draw distinctions between the types of explicit materials. James Phillips, Florida's assistant state attorney, noted: "There's so much out there, we go after only what is really revolting."[20]

Civil libertarians see genuine problems with any attempt to prohibit distribution of pornography. One reason is the fear that when some literature is stopped by censorship because the state wishes to maintain some minimal community consensus, the door is open to more dramatic moves. Justice Brennan, in a famous Supreme Court dissent, raised the question: "For if the state may, in an effort to maintain or create a moral tone, prescribe what its citizens cannot read or cannot see, then it would seem to follow that in pursuit of that same objective a State could decree that its citizens must read certain books or must view certain films."[21] In fact, in some communities where antipornography groups are strong, pressure is being brought on libraries to take certain sex education books from the shelves.

Another argument against control recognizes that human sexual experience is, in a real sense, a commodity distributed unequally in our society. The vital sexual encounter of the newly married or the myriad of sexual opportunities open to the attractive celebrity are denied to other elements of our society. Studies by the US Commission on Obscenity and Pornography found that in Denver, for example, 22 percent of the shoppers in adult bookstores were handicapped or of "poor physical appearance."[22] For them, pornography may represent their only form of sexual experience, lonely as it may be.

Even if one endorses the broad view against any censorship, there are ways to control the intrusiveness of such material into the lives of those who find it offensive. Unsolicited mail and bold public advertising should probably be controlled as nuisances, like offensive odors or loud noises that intrude into our lives unless legally curtailed. Some federal postal laws now provide means to stop explicit mail from being sent more than once to persons on mailing lists. In some communities various zoning ordinances have been passed to either curtail growth of adult entertainment businesses (Detroit prohibits opening a new business within 1,000 feet of another one or within 500 feet of a home unless 51 percent of the local people approve) or to put them all in one area (as Boston's so-called Combat Zone). The Supreme Court has upheld the validity of the former approach but has not yet ruled on the latter.

WOMEN'S SEXUALITY AND VIOLENCE

Our awareness of the number of public policy issues surrounding sexuality and violence is increasing as two forms of sexual violence—rape and wife-beating—become more and more prevalent in our society. Federal Bureau of Investigation statistics indicate that the incidence of rape increased 93 percent in the 1960s, while the rate of marital violence was three times higher by 1973. The FBI estimates that rape and wife-battering are the most underreported crimes in the country, and that these crimes actually occur ten times more frequently than statistics indicate. Even a conservative estimate puts the number of battered wives nationwide at well over a million each year.[23]

One of the difficulties in addressing issues of sexual violence is in first knowing how to define the subject. In recent years public discussion has tended to focus less on the sexual dimension of certain crimes and more on their violent nature. Often sexual violence has very little to do with sex but is simply assault and battery because of a person's gender, sexual identity, or orientation (female, wife, gay) or assault that uses a person's sexual organs as a tool or as a recipient of violence (as in rape). In a magazine entitled *The Police Chief: The Professional Voice of Law Enforcement* a special edition (May 1974) was devoted to "Crisis Intervention and Investigation of Forcible Rape." The following section makes this point:

> It is common to regard rape as sex crime. However, there is reason to question this view. Indeed, looking at it in the traditional way may well create a set in the police investigator's thinking that is dysfunctional. That is, to regard the act primarily as sexual in nature may distort the view of investigating officers, giving them a sense that they are dealing with something that really belongs in the area of morality. If one looks at rape as a crime against the person, one may be more disposed to see it as one would view other aggressive crimes, such as robbery, assault, etc. . . . Recent research on rape suggests that the intent of the offender is more often aggressive than sexual to prove his own masculinity and invulnerability by scapegoating and degrading the victim. Contrary to popular belief, the average rapist probably is not someone for whom normal sexual outlets are unavailable. Often, too, the crime may follow a fight with a mother, a girl friend or wife, and be a displacement of hostility against that woman.[24]

Thus, the emerging public consensus about a definition for sexual violence is that it has to do with physical or emotional abuse of persons' sexuality or abuse because of their gender or sexual identity. This definition would then allow a variety of crimes to be defined as crimes of sexual violence: rape, wife-beating, child molestation, forced sterilization, and the murder of gay persons in retaliation for their choice of sexual orientation.

This sort of definition has grown largely out of public research and reflection on the realities of rape and wife-beating. One of the common assumptions about rape is that it is a crime induced by women who are sexually seductive. This assumption is reflected in the popular phrase "she was asking for it"—a phrase that blames the victim of the rape and not the perpetrator.

Recent research, particularly that done by Susan Brownmiller for her book *Against Our Will: Men, Women and Rape* (1975), challenges this assumption and puts forth a new definition of rape. In studying the patterns of rape throughout history and in many different cultures, Brownmiller discovered that rape rarely has had anything to do with sex or the sexual seductiveness of women but has had everything to do with the power relations between women and men. Her thesis is that men have used their superior physical strength and their consequent ability to rape as a constant threat that keeps women dependent and in need of protection. Men do not rape for sexual enjoyment. They rape to demonstrate their power over women through violence. The practice of rape, then, is consciously or unconsciously intended to humiliate and control women—or to keep women in their place.

This definition is not meant to place the entire burden for rape on sensitive males in our society who do not intentionally want to control women, especially not through the use of sexual violence. But it does raise the significant question about the degree to which *all* men and women in American society participate, even unknowingly, in what is called a "rape culture" or a culture in which rape is the logical extension of the relationship of domination and subordination between women and men. The Rev. Donna Schaper provided a paper for this study in which she shared reflections on her ministry in Philadelphia, which has often focused on working with community groups that are organizing to prevent rape. In her words,

> whether or not a woman has been a victim of an actual rape, she is nonetheless affected by it. Whether or not a man has ever raped a woman, he is nonetheless affected by it. For most of us, our defense mechanisms work well enough that we are not constantly worried by fears of physical consequence. Layer upon layer of protective reality intervenes to keep us from acknowledging the fact of physical rape. But little rape, as opposed to big rape, is a part of all of our experience: courtship is predicated on a rape psychology, with me saying no so you can force me to say yes. Men who cannot play this game successfully lose out in courtship; women who say yes too soon are considered "aggressive" and "domineering." The power relationships in courtship are clear; for either partner to violate them by expressing too much power (female) or too little (male) is to court rejection rather than acceptance.[25]

She also goes on to say,

Individual men, while responsible for their own behavior and particularly at the moment of rape, are not responsible for the causes of their behavior. While responsible for the consequences, they are not responsible for the *causes*. For example, the eighteen-year-old school dropout who is unemployed, who steals for a living and who chooses the action of rape must be held accountable for this behavior. However, that same man is not responsible for the socialization which caused the option of rape to surface in his behavior. The society shares that responsibility with him and it is to that society that action against rape must turn.[26]

Rape, in this sense, results from economic frustration taken out on women, therefore calling for action to alleviate the unjust economic suffering of men in our society—particularly when men are expected to be the breadwinners.

Similarly, images that portray women as powerless, in need of protection and dependent on men for economic and emotional survival feed into the socialization in which we *all* participate and thus must be addressed at the level of public policy in relation to the role and status of women in society. Some women, through centuries of conditioning, participate in the promotion of these images and, therefore, challenge all of us to take responsibility for educating the society about their destructive impact. While sexual and seductive images of women in all forms of the media may not arouse a young man to rape an old woman, still those images contribute to a general public image of women as passive, weak, and easy targets for gratuitous violent abuse.

For instance, films and television programs often portray women as wanting to be raped or as actually enjoying the act. The rape and violence fantasies of women are even the subject of several books. And *Time* magazine (February 7, 1977) ran a feature article entitled "Really Socking It to Women," which portrayed many women "modeling" for scenes that displayed sexual violence against them. *Time* found that "images of women being physically abused are becoming increasingly common. In record album photos, fashion and men's magazine layouts, and even a few department store windows and billboards, women are shown bound, gagged, beaten, whipped, chained, or as victims of murder or gang rape."[27]

Writer Molly Haskell raises an important critique of the assumption that all women want to be raped or that all women willingly participate in their own humiliation. In her article entitled "Rape Fantasy: The 2,000-year-old Misunderstanding" in the November 1976 edition of *Ms.*, she makes the following point: no one has ever assumed that because men have castration anxieties and fantasies they want to be castrated![28]

Ironically, many theorists agree that until women can be viewed as persons who no longer need protection from men, who have the strength to protect themselves and possibly others, male violence will continue. Until that time, groups of women and men are actively working to change the ways legal, medical, and counseling groups deal with the victim and the rapist, as well as with the wife and the husband who beats her.

Progress has been made in all areas of public response to the crime of rape. In November 1975 the US Department of Justice published a large manual entitled *Rape and Its Victims: A Report for Citizens, Health Facilities, and Criminal Justice Agencies.*[29] Gerald M. Caplan, director of the National Institute of Law Enforcement and Criminal Justice, writes in the foreword of the book:

> The woman who is raped is doubly victimized—first by the attacker and again by the attitudes of society. Until very recently, sexual attacks and their aftermath were not even topics for open discussion. But that has changed, partly through the initiative of concerned citizens. With that change has come the opportunity to analyze and improve the treatment of the rape victim. . . . The National Institute believes this manual can contribute to more enlightened and sensitive procedures in an area heretofore characterized by a preoccupation with the credibility of the victim rather than her needs.[30]

The first task of the manual is to state the problem, which it does in the prologue:

> Rape is one of the ugliest crimes. Its very nature is humiliating to the victim, and it is frequently accompanied by violence, forced sodomy, and similar acts that additionally traumatize and humiliate. The victimization of the woman does not necessarily cease with the termination of the attack itself. Pregnancy, venereal disease, hospitalization, loss of employment, imputations of wantonness, and even ostracism by family or neighbors may follow.
>
> Should the victim report the offense to the police, her

suffering may be continued or even exacerbated by the justice system. She may be exposed to police skepticism, tactlessness, or outright prurience; inadequate, delayed, or nonexistent medical care; and the need to repeatedly describe details of the attack to a seemingly endless assortment of police, doctors, prosecutors, judges, most if not all of whom are men. If she should continue her cooperation to the point of trial, court rules can open her chastity, character, and choice of companions to scrutiny and, often, disparagement. And, after all the victim's anguish, defendants in rape cases are seldom convicted as charged.[31]

After stating the case dramatically, a series of guidelines is offered to help police, hospital administrators, prosecutors, and citizens involved in community action reexamine their agencies' response to rape. As an example, these guidelines call for the organization of rape investigation units; the use of women officers on sex crime squads; the provision for immediate medical examination upon arrival at the emergency room to minimize trauma; a confidential medical history to protect the victim's privacy; limiting the need for the victim to testify to any prior sexual history; changing mandatory death sentences for any kind of rape to more flexible sentencing options; the development and support of rape crisis centers run by women; and advocacy on the part of citizen action groups for adequate victim services (hotline, crisis counseling, assistance with housing, transportation, child care, anonymous reporting), public education, catalyzing change within the criminal justice system, and law reform.

While a great deal of progress has been made by citizen action groups in working toward implementation of change in the way rape victims are treated, much of that progress is now endangered by recent budget cuts and personnel layoffs in law enforcement agencies and hospitals. There is also some evidence that women's health centers and rape crisis centers are not receiving the support they need to function well. Arrest rates for rapes committed remain low and conviction rates far lower. Though massive efforts have been made to support and encourage women to come forward to make charges and testify against their assailants, the prospects for successful prosecution are so remote and the ordeal women must go through in testifying sufficiently great that rape remains largely an unpunished crime.

Part of the problem in getting a rape conviction is that the traditional penalty has been so high—in some states the death penalty—that courts refuse to impose it. In 1975 the Center for

Constitutional Rights, the American Civil Liberties Union, the Women's Law Project, and other groups interested in both civil liberties and women's issues filed an amici curiae brief in the United States Supreme Court on behalf of a man who was sentenced to death for rape in Georgia. The brief says in its Summary of Argument:

> The historical origin of the death penalty for rape lies in the long-standing view of rape as a crime of property where the aggrieved was not the woman but her husband or father. In the Southern states this view coalesced with a tradition which valued white women according to their purity and chastity and assigned them exclusively to white men.
>
> As a result, a double standard of justice developed for weighing and punishing rape by white and black men. This double standard of justice was reflected in Georgia's penalty structure for rape which, until the abolition of slavery, reserved the death penalty exclusively for black men. Ever since 1861, the death sentence has rarely been imposed on white men. . . . *Amici*, interested in effective enforcement of laws against rape, urge that the death penalty for rape be invalidated because it stems from archaic notions which demean women and gross racial injustice.[32]

The writers of the brief finally conclude:

> The death penalty for rape should be rejected as a vestige of an ancient, patriarchal system in which women were viewed both as the property of men and as entitled to a crippling "chivalric protection." *It is part of the fabric of laws and enforcement practices surrounding rape which in fact hamper prosecution and convictions for that crime thus leaving women with little protection from rape.*[33]

Even when adequate reform of the judicial system has been made to enable legal structures to respond more quickly and fully to the crime of rape, the perception of rape as a positive act of male machismo may still operate until thorough public reeducation has been accomplished. In the meantime, one highly unusual legal remedy has been reported by San Francisco columnist Charles McCabe: The suggestion is that the rape victims not report the crime against them as a rape, but that they charge the assailant with indecent exposure, thus mobilizing the machismo outrage of law enforcement officers and the disdain of all those men who might otherwise find reason not to condemn his behavior! While indecent exposure is only a misdemeanor, there are a number of states where a second conviction becomes a felony. So long as rape, wife-beating, and child molestation are seen as sexual issues, it will be difficult to take adequate preventive measures. Thus, many people contend that these offenses should be treated as general crimes of violence, such as assault and battery.

Rape is not confined to anonymous or nonmarital sexual violence. In fact, the magnitude of sexual violence within conventional marital relations has been a growing topic of public discussion over the last several years, as wife-beating has increased among *all* socioeconomic groups. This study has looked at such questions as: Is rape possible within marriage, and if so, why are there no legal remedies available if it occurs? What is the relationship between male and female socialization and violence? Does violence grow out of frustration and an unwillingness or an inability to play one's prescribed role? What is the relationship between hardship and violence directed against members of one's own family? Are patterns of wife-beating similar within different socioeconomic and racial groups? While our search for the answers to these questions is just beginning, we concur with Del Martin's analysis of what needs to be done, as stated in her book *Battered Wives:* the launch of a massive education program to make the public more aware of the prevalence of marital violence; the formation of coalitions between women's organizations and civic groups (and we would add, church groups) to establish emergency shelters for victims; and lobbying for remedial legislation.[34]

In Chicago, a police survey conducted between September 1965 and March 1966 demonstrated that 46.1 percent of all the major crimes except murder perpetrated against women took place at home.[35] The study also revealed that police response to domestic disturbance calls exceeded total response for murder, rape, aggravated assault, and other serious crimes.[36]

A study in Oakland, California, in 1970 showed that police there responded to more than 16,000 family disturbance calls during a six month period.[37]

The 46,137 domestic disturbance calls received by Kansas City, Missouri, police represented 82 percent of all disturbance calls received by them in 1972.[38]

In Detroit, 4,900 wife assault complaints were filed in 1972.[39]

In New York 14,167 wife abuse complaints were handled in Family Court throughout the state during the judicial year 1972-73.[40]

In 1974, Boston police responded to 11,081 family disturbance calls, most of which involved physical violence.[41] At the end of the first quarter of 1975, 5,589 such calls were received—half the previous year's figure in one-quarter the time. (As an aside to these figures, Boston City Hospital reports that approximately 70 percent of the assault victims received in its emergency room are known to be women who have been attacked in their homes, usually by a husband or lover.[42])

In Atlanta, Georgia, 60 percent of all police calls on the night shift are domestic disputes.[43]

The Citizen's Complaint Center in the District of Columbia receives between 7,500 and 10,000 complaints of marital violence each year. Approximately 75 percent of the complainants are women.[44]

Trends in domestic violence are similar in city after city. But the problem is not just an urban one; it is to be found in rural areas as well. For example, the police chief in a small Washtenaw County (Michigan) town of 6,000 reports that family assault calls come in every day.[45] Another police official with extensive rural experience estimates that police calls for "family fights" are exceeded only by calls relating to automobile accidents.[46]

Del Martin explains that "the terms 'domestic violence' or 'domestic disturbance' are not synonymous with 'wife-battering.'" But she adds:

You don't need a degree in criminology to realize that the police are not called into a domestic situation unless the weaker person(s) involved need help or are perceived to need help by witnesses. . . . In most relationships the woman is physically weaker than the man. We can assume that a good many of the domestic disturbance calls that do not involve juveniles concern women being intimidated, frightened, or assaulted by men

163

to the point where someone decides that help is needed from the police. This assumption is borne out by statistics. Of the figures available on complaints, 82 percent in New York,[47] 75 percent in Washington, D.C.,[48] 85.4 percent in Detroit,[49] and 95 percent in Montgomery, Maryland,[50] were filed by female victims.[51]

Perhaps the most disturbing discovery made by researchers in the field is that an astonishing number of men and women are not disturbed by marital violence.

Sociologist Howard Erlanger . . . found that 25 percent of his sample of American adults actually approved of husband-wife battles. . . . [In fact,] the greater the educational level, the greater was the acceptance of marital violence. Approval ranged from 17 percent of grade-school graduates to 32 percent of college postgraduate students, with a slightly lower 30 percent for those who had completed just four years of college. The study also showed that, contrary to popular belief, low-income respondents were no more prone to nor more readily accepting of violence in the home than were middle- or upper-income respondents.[52]

The popular assumption by the middle class that marital violence occurs more frequently in the ghetto and among lower-class families reflects the inability of middle-class investigators to face the universality of the problem. Evidence of wife-beating exists wherever one cares to look for it. Fairfax County, Virginia, for instance, is a suburb of the District of Columbia and considered to be one of the wealthiest counties in the United States. Police there received 4,073 family disturbance calls in 1974. They estimated that thirty assault warrants are sought by Fairfax County wives each week.[53]

As it is now, women have very little protection from marital abuse, because the police and family courts simply refuse to interfere by arresting or prosecuting the husband. Laws that govern this sensitive and complex area of human behavior need to be modified to protect growing numbers of women who experience flagrant physical and emotional battering.

WOMEN AND ECONOMIC JUSTICE
Beverly Wildung Harrison, in a memo on human sexuality and public policy written for the study, reflects on the relationship between women's sexuality and economics. It is her view that the way women perceive themselves and their sexuality, particularly

in terms of their relationships to men and to the social order, depends greatly upon their economic status. She says:

> I want to stress again that the single most important social policy issue affecting women's sexual liberation is the need for economic equality—and that not merely as equal pay for equal work. The prohibition against sex discrimination in employment contained in the Civil Rights Act of 1964, and the Equal Pay Act, provide a legal framework for that minimalist demand. Economic justice for women, however, will *not* be a reality until everything from earliest socialization to actual practice changes in two directions: 1) The overcoming of the caste-like character of the work women are permitted to do in the economy for wages. This requires reversal of employment patterns which permit women to serve in the work force only in "domestic" roles—waitresses, laundresses, nurses, stewardesses, cooks, sales clerks, seamstresses, teachers, maids, producers of non-durable goods, not to mention our exclusive recruitment as secretaries, typists, file clerks. . . .
>
> 2) Ending the practice of not remunerating domestic work in the home. At present house work and child-care are not officially recognized *in any way* as value-producing work in this society. At a minimum we must have Social Security coverage for full-time homemakers (male or female) and some sort of wage-structure (or tax credit) for those who do housework and raise children. . . . I am quite serious when I say that there will never be real economic justice for women until *both* conditions are met. The fact is that women's psychic, sexual, and social vulnerability is so deeply conditioned economically (and women's reputed "conservatism" follows from this) that only this two-pronged strategy will touch the problem.[54]

Dr. Harrison goes on to say that substantial economic change will not happen suddenly. Recent Department of Labor statistics signal a renewed downward trend in average per capita wages of women in relation to men—indicators that make clear that the small gains of recent years were superficial adjustments resulting from token inclusion of a few women at the upper end of the scale. And the proportion of women to men in the labor force will continue to increase, with the largest proportional increase happening among women within the Hispanic community. For many of these women one of the key issues, in addition to equal pay, is the availability of quality day care. Working women need to be able to trust that their children are well provided for during their working hours. A Child and Family Services Act that will federally sponsor parent-controlled child care, offering medical, nutritional, and educational care as well as shelter for any child, has been previously defeated but now is again before Congress.

Women who have worked within the home doing housework and child-rearing are also in a difficult position, because their services have not been fiscally valued. Several pieces of proposed legislation speak to the particular needs of women who have never been able to claim remuneration for their work. One is the Displaced Homemakers Act, which will seek to provide transition services (job training and counseling) to homemakers who find themselves without support through death or divorce. Other proposals focus on laws that will ensure some independence for the homemaker. Such proposals range from a move to make the property truly joint for couples eligible to file a joint income tax return (so that the wife "owns" 50 percent of property, income, assets, and debts) to a much more modest proposal to make tax-deductible contributions to pensions for homemakers.

Still other reform proposals focus directly on pension and social security laws for women. Under present law a woman divorced before twenty years of marriage collects no social security through her husband's work record. If she's never worked for pay, she gets no social security benefits. Since private pensions are often even less generous with divorcees, many women are left with nothing for their old age. The Women's Lobby reports that 14 percent of older women have *no* income, and 42 percent have incomes of less than $120 per month. Clearly, legislative reform in this area will be a first step toward the promotion of justice for women.

SEXUALITY AND MEN
In the extensive discussions about women's roles and their socialization, it is sometimes overlooked that many men suffer also from the stereotypes that have been developed over the past centuries. The socialization process for men often restricts choices of vocations, hobbies, and interests because of societal pressures to conform to fairly rigid expectations of what is masculine behavior. Virtually all the major institutions of American life still perpetuate an image of men as aggressive, nonemotional, and competitive. Men of any age who do not wish to conform to these traditional views face adjustment difficulties with their peers, their coworkers, and even some of the women with whom they come in contact. Although there are many consciousness-raising groups that assist women in overcoming rigid role behavior, similarly designed support groups for men are much rarer. The

church can take leadership in assisting men to find ways to respond positively to the questions the women's movement is raising for women and for men and to free themselves from the necessity of fitting into familiar patterns.

One manifestation of the tension that develops for men confronted by challenges to their jobs or roles is sexual dysfunction. William Masters and Virginia Johnson comment on the most frequent problem, impotency:

> With each opportunity for sexual connection, the immediate and overpowering concern is whether or not he will be able to achieve an erection. Will he be capable of "performing" as a "normal" man? . . . Actually, the impotent man is gravely concerned about functional failure of a physical response which is not only naturally occurring, but in many phases involuntary in development. To oversimplify, it is his concern which discourages the natural occurrence of erection. Achievement of an erection is something over which he has absolutely no voluntary control.[55]

Although women, too, suffer fears about sexual adequacy, the performance anxieties of men are probably more pronounced. Regrettably, there are still relatively few competent and experienced therapists who are able to deal with these anxieties and to relate them to the broader changes in the society that may make men feel so threatened that dysfunction results.

Men who want to share more fully in the parenting of children also find themselves with difficulties. Although maternity leaves are becoming increasingly common, paternity leaves for the birth of a child are very rare. Similarly, most jobs held predominantly by men are based on the assumption of full-time service. There is little recognition that a father might want to work only part-time and raise his children the rest of the time. Rigid time schedules in business and industry may even make it difficult to coordinate time with one's spouse who is also working, but on a different schedule. More humane arrangements in work time should be explored by all institutions, including the church, at all levels to make it easier for men, in particular, to spend more time with their families and to play a significant role in the nurture of children.

YOUNG PEOPLE AND SEXUALITY
Beverly Harrison, of Union Theological Seminary, contends that "all children in this society are socialized in a situation of intense

sexual stimulation and peer pressure to conformity in sexual experimentation. Yet the pressure against providing children with accurate information even regarding venereal disease is also great."[56] That is the heart of the dilemma for young people today. They are unable to avoid contact with a barrage of sexual images and generally unable to find out what healthy sexuality is.

Drs. Goldstein and Kant found, incredibly, that for most children the only real education about sexual functioning is derived from explicit pornography.[57] Although they concluded that a reasonable exposure to such material "correlates with adult patterns of acceptable heterosexual practice," we certainly find disturbing the fact that this was the only—or at least "best"—source available for learning the mechanics of sexual relations, and that it offers little explanation of values in human relationships. Certainly, sex education programs have grown in number in schools and churches over the past few decades. However, a 1969 study found that parents and students were in remarkable disagreement as to whether a sex education program even existed in the child's school. The conclusion was that "some courses are apparently so antiseptic that the children are not aware of the presence of sex education."[58]

Frequently, children are denied access to information allegedly because of the need to "protect" them from data they could not yet assimilate. It has been noted by some observers that one reason adults deny access to information about sexuality is because they, consciously or unconsciously, want to "punish" sexual feelings and experiences by generating feelings of guilt, or in the extreme, by denying access to means to prevent pregnancy. Ethicist Daniel Callahan, director of the Institute of Society, Ethics and the Life Sciences, suggests a more affirmative response:

As adults we have to pay a high price for the kind of power we have. For we are morally obliged to seek not our welfare but theirs. They are dependents, and they depend upon *us*. To be sure, they have some freedom. They can and do make choices and, despite what parents or society might like, they can make sexual choices—no way has ever been found to prevent them from so doing. Unfortunately, they do not always make very responsible choices, especially when it comes to as powerful a force as sex. Why should we expect them to? It is hard enough for us as adults to do so, only after a much longer course of experience than they have had. The most we can do —because we are responsible for the world they live in—is to help avoid those things we know will hurt them, help to reduce the impact of those acts (even of folly) which they have already done, help them in a word to make it through the teenage years with as little lasting harm as possible.[59]

In the sex education area, local communities are given broad discretion in deciding how their schools should deal with this subject matter. In 1976, prior to several Supreme Court rulings, only twenty-six states permitted doctors to provide birth control services without parental consent. In June 1977 the Supreme Court struck down a New York State law that prohibited distribution of contraceptives to persons under sixteen.[60] The court noted that the state had not produced any evidence that teenage sexual activity increased in proportion to the availability of contraceptives. It commented further that unwanted pregnancy should not be the "punishment for fornication." Essentially, purely age-based denial of contraceptive information and devices is now unconstitutional. In actual practice, many physicians will be reluctant to provide such devices (particularly if not asked). It is estimated that 46 percent of the 3.7 million fifteen- to nineteen-year-old women, at risk of unintended pregnancy, receive no assistance from clinics or family physicians.[61] Callahan again comments:

> If we make sex education and contraceptives and abortion available to teenagers, and if we help those teenagers who decide to give birth to a child, will we not simply create a casual tolerance and permissiveness toward teenage sexual activities which in the long run will only make things worse? While I personally believe our society is too sexually casual, it became that way before we even thought of providing services and sex education and I have seen no evidence that providing education and help *does* make the problem worse.[62]

Young people become victimized in today's world not only by ignorance, but by direct and overt acts of adults as well. The exact dimension of the problem of physical child abuse is not known. However, good reporting methods in New York City and in Denver, Colorado indicate an incidence of 250 to 300 cases per million population reported each year.[63] A large percentage, if not the majority of cases, are seen by no one and thus go unnoticed in such statistics. This wanton torture of thousands of children every year is found throughout every socioeconomic level in the nation. Too often the legal machinery tends to be overly protective of the reputations of the parents or other adults involved in the abuse. As a result, children are often returned to the same homes in which they were beaten, burned, or incestuously sexually abused without any positive indication that it will not occur again.

Another more recently unearthed phenomenon is the coercive use of extremely young children, who could not possibly have given "consent," in pornographic films and as prostitutes. This, along with child molestation (pedophilia), represents the most blatant intrusions of adult power into the sphere of youthful sexuality. Molestation generally is done by persons who know the child, not strangers, and who tend to be passive heterosexual individuals who rarely appear in court again if caught once. Some studies have concluded that "the children often come from homes in which they lack care and attention; they seem to need the attentions offered by the adult who eventually molests them."[64] Psychological disturbances and even sexual dysfunction may result from such incidents; frequently, the way parents and doctors react to learning of the incident is even more traumatic than the molestation itself (unless there is real physical damage done, a rare occurrence).

Young people are terribly vulnerable in today's world. In most countries they have few legal rights, little economic power, and only minimal defenses against the powerful adult forces that can distort their perceptions of their own sexuality.

SEXUALITY AND OLDER PERSONS

There are 22.4 million persons over sixty-five years of age, representing over 10 percent of the US population. The evidence clearly suggests that many older persons suffer from negative attitudes toward sexuality. A common stereotype holds that active sexuality is only the prerogative of youth and that women and men who are aging have no interest in sexual relations. In terms of specific social policies this problem is most acute where older people are institutionalized and are left in hospitals and nursing homes without space and/or moral support for the expression of physical intimacy. Important physical support is withdrawn just at the time in life when human need for intimacy that nourishes the capacity for life-affirmation, self-worth, and the avoidance of isolation is the greatest.

Alex Comfort states this dilemma clearly:

Aging induces some changes in human sexual performance. These are chiefly in the male where orgasm becomes less frequent and where more direct stimulation is required to produce erection, but compared with age changes in other body systems, such as muscular strength or vital capacity, these changes are functionally minimal. In fact, in the absence of disease, sexual capacity is lifelong, and even if and when actual intercourse fails through infirmity, the need for other aspects of the sexual relationship such as closeness, sensuality and being valued persists. This is totally contrary to the pre-conceptions of hospital and nursing administrators. It is even contrary to the beliefs of many older people themselves, who have been hoodwinked out of continuing sexual activity by a society which disallows it for the old, as they have been hoodwinked out of so many other valuable activities of which they are fully capable—useful work, social involvement, and even continued life—through being wished away by well meaning relatives.[65]

Changes in the policies of hospitals and nursing homes that will allow greater privacy for older persons can be effected at the administrative level through such church organizations as the United Church of Christ Council for Health and Welfare Services and through such community organizations as the Grey Panthers and the American Association of Retired People. Local churches can play a particularly helpful role in developing a new public awareness of the movements to support the intimacy needs of older persons in our society.

Among those over sixty-five, there are 1,000 women for every 724 men. Many of these women are widows, who are forced into a single living situation that creates severe isolation, as well as economic stress. Women who have not previously learned to define themselves as full persons apart from marriage and family relationships may find aging destructive to their sense of identity and worth. Or older women whose primary orientation is toward heterosexual intimacy will experience frustration as fewer men are available for relationships. Even if remarriage is a possibility, social security policies make it difficult for a woman to do so without taking economic loss if she receives benefits as a dependent of her previous husband. The Gray Panthers and groups such as the Women's Lobby in Washington, D.C. are working to develop and support legislation that will make important changes in social security and in income tax policies that discriminate against older people.

In the meantime, the church could actively support the development of alternative institutions that would allow older people who are not in need of medical care to live together in community homes or with an extended family of all ages. An experiment of this sort was reported in *The New York Times Magazine*.[66] A group of twelve older people (eleven women and one man) decided to pool their resources and live together in a town house complex in Evanston, Illinois rather than alone or in nursing homes. This model appears to be extremely successful and is one answer to the problems of isolation and economic deprivation.

SEXUALITY AND SINGLE PERSONS

A dramatic shift in public policy in relation to single persons in our society may be in the making, as a result of some of President Carter's recent remarks. He has said publicly that he wants to encourage marriage for those who are now single and living together. To do so he will recommend a tax break for married households. While this strategy may accomplish his stated task, it may also cause hardships for persons who choose to remain single or for persons of the same sex who live together and should be eligible for similar tax benefits.

A subtle discriminatory perception of single people is common in our society. Most of our major institutions, including the church, are organized socially around the traditional nuclear family unit. The numbers of single persons in our church and society, however, are growing. As the numbers of nonmarried persons, widows, widowers, divorced persons, and gay people increase, this organization of church and public life around the normal family unit and the couple will create even greater alienation than in the past. In addition, single parents will be subtly conditioned to think of themselves as misfits within the church and society. Ministry in this area of public policy urges us to find ways to support persons in their real-life situations as well as to explore new options for relationship and sexual expression for persons who are single.

One of the most difficult problems encountered by single parents is the lack of available quality day care. Poor and non-white women are often forced to take welfare rather than work because day care is simply not available or because they do not trust that their children will receive quality care and nurturance. For other single persons the problem of parenting is even more basic: some single people find it tremendously difficult to adopt children or to participate in the process of artificial insemination in order to bear children. While marriage may or may not be an option for some single women and men, parenting is a responsibility that they welcome and may want an opportunity to exercise.

SEXUALITY AND THE GAY COMMUNITY

Although nowhere is the status of being a homosexual per se a crime, in all but eighteen states most sexual conduct between same-sex persons is in violation of sodomy statutes, which prohibit any oral or anal sex. Other state laws are even more vague. Maryland prohibits any "unnatural or perverted sexual practices" and considers all homosexual acts to be included. Many states do not punish gay people for sodomy, which requires proof of some overt act, but for "solicitation for engaging in prohibited behavior," loitering (being in an area frequented by other gay persons for no apparent licit purpose), or "disorderly conduct" (which may include dancing with someone of the same sex). Obviously, some of these statutes are so broad that they could be used to punish the conduct of heterosexual persons as well. However, it is extremely rare that any of these laws are used against anyone who is not gay or bisexual. Since sodomy is generally a felony, gay persons who are charged with it (and who fear that a conviction could cause them to lose civil or political rights or licenses in their chosen profession) will often plead guilty to a lesser misdemeanor charge simply to avoid the possible consequences of trial on the felony charge. Elimination of sodomy laws and the curtailed use of other laws to punish gay persons mentioned above are two legislative priorities of gay activists for the immediate future.

A serious setback to the rapid elimination of all such restrictive laws occurred in 1976, when the Supreme Court affirmed without comment (although three members wanted to consider the case on the merits) a decision of a Virginia Federal District Court that held the Virginia sodomy statute to be constitutional and not an invasion of legally protected privacy interests. The court noted that previous cases dealt principally with marital privacy or the sanctity of home and family. Further, it said the state could pass such legislation after merely establishing "that the conduct is likely to end in a contribution to moral delinquency."[67]

In the lower court decision there was a strong dissent by Judge Merhige, who stated that the *Eisenstadt* decision specifically protected the privacy of individuals, married or unmarried, and was not based on protecting the family. He stated that there is no authority for intrusion by the state into the private dwelling of a citizen, and there was no evidence presented that homosexuality causes society any significant harm: "A mature individual's choice of an adult sexual partner, in the privacy of his or her own home, would appear to me to be a decision of the utmost private and intimate concern."[68]

The second major legislative change would be the passage of federal, state, and local legislation that would prohibit employment or licensing discrimination on the basis of "affectional or sexual preference." Presently, private employers (including churches) can openly discriminate on the basis of sexual orientation, except in the very few localities where it is prohibited by local ordinances.[69]

On the federal level the Civil Service Commission, in theory, may not arbitrarily dismiss employees for being gay. Several recent court decisions seem to indicate that the commission must be able to demonstrate an actual connection between the alleged conduct and a loss of efficiency in the agency employing the individual before dismissal is permitted. It is not sufficient for the agency to argue that retention of the employee will bring public contempt upon the agency.

In state and local government circles hostility toward gay employees is frequently much greater. For example, on very little evidence public school teachers are often dismissed for "unfitness" to teach merely because they are advocates of a gay lifestyle outside the classroom. The fear seems to be that the teachers' affectional preference will be contagious, although actual cases of the seduction of pupils by teachers of any persuasion are very few. In one instance a state court held that it was acceptable for the Board of Regents to refuse employment as a university librarian to a known gay activist, because the board should not be required to place its "tacit approval" on the "socially repugnant concept" the individual represented.[70] In many other situations where good moral character is required in order to obtain various kinds of occupational licenses, many jurisdictions still consider gay orientation to be proof of moral turpitude.

This association of moral turpitude and homosexual orientation has deep historical and psychological roots. Cultural intolerance, especially of gay men, reflects our culture's sexism. That is, the same attitudes that perceive women as weak and subordinate perceive gay men as weak and subordinate because they do not choose to fulfill the traditional masculine role as the dominant partner in relationship to a woman. The frequent derision of gay men, who are called sissies and girls, points out the depth of our culture's anxiety about men who do not conform to a machismo image. Historically, gay men have been persecuted alongside lesbians and heterosexual women who were considered dangerous to the society—often because they were stepping out of the bounds of their own roles and were challenging the dominant male culture.

The difficulty of employment for gay people makes the fear of disclosure for covert gays a serious problem. This opens up the possibility of blackmail (financial or even sexual) from others who discover their affectional preference. The threat of disclosure to one's family, for example, is so traumatic because of the lack of support services for any of the involved parties that large payments for silence can be elicited. Civil rights legislation that prohibits firing on the basis of sexual or affectional preference would go a long way toward reducing the coercive pressure in the possibility of blackmail.

Although employment is still the key civil liberties issue for most gay organizations, there are other civil rights issues that are receiving attention. Many times gay people still find it difficult to gain access to some housing, particularly where local ordinances do not permit occupancy by persons unrelated by blood or marriage. Similarly, under many federal public housing statutes gay couples are not eligible for such low-income housing, and persons with convictions for sodomy have additional difficulties. Present immigration laws also discriminate against gay people. The Supreme Court has upheld the denial of entry for aliens who have a psychopathic personality, which includes being a homosexual.[71] Similarly, a large number of courts will not permit an openly gay person to become a naturalized citizen, arguing that her or his beliefs and/or actions demonstrate bad moral character.

For a minority of gay persons matters of family law are of great personal significance. First, no states presently recognize the legality of marriages (often called holy unions) between persons of the same sex. The Minnesota Supreme Court noted that their statute specifically defined marriage as a union between persons of different sexes. They denied a marriage license to two men because, they said, one of the objectives of marriage was the procreation and raising of children, something this couple could not do.[72] A Kentucky court noted that although the statute didn't say marriage must be between members of the opposite sex, "common usage" would be implied, and therefore two women could not obtain a marriage license.[73]

The unwillingness of states to recognize gay unions leads to other difficulties. If one member of a gay couple dies without a will, his or her property will be distributed according to the laws of the state, which generally means it will go to parents, brothers and sisters, or more distant relatives. If gays living together do make a will naming each other as beneficiaries, it is open to (often successful) challenge by the deceased person's relatives on the ground that there was undue influence in the making of the agreement. Thus, the will can be broken and the intentions of the writer nullified. Gay persons living together also suffer disadvantages under federal income tax laws (because they cannot file a joint return, usually desirable), the federal estate tax (because they cannot avail themselves of the marital deduction), and the federal gift tax. The problem with this sort of marriage prevention is that it does not support the efforts of gay men and lesbians to establish long-term, committed relationships based upon values of permanence and fidelity—values that the church works hard to promote for heterosexuals. There is much discussion within the gay community about establishing new forms of relational contracts based upon equal partnerships.

For gays to obtain custody of their children by former heterosexual marriages is also a serious, often insurmountable, problem. Courts have taken a wide variety of approaches to this question. Some believe that since gay life is a bad role model, homosexuality per se is cause for a declaration of unfitness as a parent. Others note that sexual orientation is only one factor to be considered in the overall "best interests of the child." A third series of decisions permits custody by a gay parent if the parent will not live with his or her lover or even visit with him or her except under very circumscribed conditions. On rare occasions courts seem to consider sexual orientation completely irrelevant to custody decisions. The most liberal decisions reached so far granted two politically active lesbians unconditional custody of their respective children over strong objections by both former husbands that their "flaunting" of their sexual preferences would embarrass the children.[74] The Oregon Supreme Court permitted a gay father to retain custody of his two sons, because there was no proof that there was substantial harm to the welfare of the boys, but it conditioned custody on continuing supervision by the family court.[75]

Courts are generally most concerned with whether the child will be unduly influenced by the life-style of the parent so as to be unable to make a choice about his or her sexual orientation, and whether knowledge of the parent's preference will cause the children to be ridiculed by their peers. Frankly, research on granting child custody to gay parents has only begun. We feel

176

that the actual "best interests of the child" is the most viable criterion for custody; this requires that no single belief or practice of either parent can be the sole grounds for disapproval of custody. After our discussions with many gay persons inside and outside the church, the conclusion drawn by John Money seems highly appropriate.

Society's apprehensions notwithstanding, it is not inevitably psychically dangerous for children, boys or girls, to live with a divorced parent who sets up a new household with a partner of the same sex. Children are rather readily able to equate such a situation with that of living with a widowed mother and her sister, or a father and grandfather, for example. It is not the sameness or difference of the sex of the adults that counts, but the quality of the relationship between them, and the quality of the relationship they establish with the child.[76]

HANDICAPPED PERSONS AND SEXUALITY

Increasing attention in the medical, church, and sexual counseling communities is being given to handicapped persons. Frederick E. Bidgood states the problem:

Although it may be true in the abstract that handicapped individuals share in all aspects of . . . humanity—that they are just as "normal" as non-handicapped individuals, and that their specific disabilities or incapacities and their adjustments to them are the only differences between them and other people—the vast majority of the handicapped are nevertheless denied their full humanity, are hindered from becoming fulfilled human beings by the fears, guilts, and misconceptions of society. While the details may vary with the specific individual, society has placed an added handicap on the already handicapped person by helping to deny two basic needs—a realistic and positive identity as a sexual being, and the opportunity for sexual expression and fulfilling sexual relationships.[77]

We have found in our conversations with handicapped persons that they, like many women and men, suffer from the beautiful body syndrome of our culture, which defines physical beauty in a very particular and dehumanizing manner. In fact, one of the key problems identified by handicapped persons is that society assumes that because they are handicapped they are not sexual

177

beings at all and therefore does not prepare them to lead lives that include affectional or sexual dimensions. This would again be especially true for handicapped persons who live in total institutions.

A group of United Church of Christ persons who are handicapped participated in the study process. They identified a number of issues that point to the need for change in public policy, primarily at the administrative level:

—The right to information about themselves, their sexuality, their sexual expression, their bodies, and their bodily functions. Often information is withheld, beginning with early childhood education, out of the assumption that handicapped persons do not need to know. Special programs in sex education may need to be developed to address their unique needs.

—The opportunity for sexual expression, autosexual and relational. This opportunity is closely related to the issue of privacy but is also related to the provision of opportunities for handicapped persons to develop meaningful intimate relationships. In some cases institutions may need to create physical space to accommodate the possibility of handicapped persons marrying and living together within the institution. And under some circumstances adjustment may need to be made to a variety of possible relationships. Mobility or short-term residency within a series of institutions raises a question for some handicapped persons about the possibility of short-term relationships and appropriate sexual expression. In other instances homosexual relationships may be the only physically possible option, and institutions may, therefore, need to consider the possibility of enabling committed partners to live together in an atmosphere of support and encouragement.

—The right to knowledge of surgical processes that would make intercourse possible if surgically alterable impediments exist.

—Access to medical and counseling personnel who are trained to deal with the specific needs of the handicapped.

—Third-party assistance or use of relational surrogates. Often married couples with certain physical disabilities are not physically capable of relating to their partner or to themselves sexually. This opens up a question about the possibility of the use of third-party assistance in sexual expression. This concern creates some obvious difficulties for public and private institutions to address as well as for members of families or friends of handicapped persons. The basic issue for church, person, and culture seems to be: Does a person have a right to caring, mutual sexual expression regardless of physical handicap?

—The need for social contact and varieties of human relationship. Many times the contexts in which handicapped persons can meet one another as well as other members of society are limited. While many institutions are beginning to bring handicapped children into nonspecialized programs (called mainstreaming) within both public and private schools, these opportunities tend to be rare. Special effort will need to be made by those who care to create more adequate opportunities for social interaction.

SEXUALITY AND INSTITUTIONALIZED PERSONS
Certain kinds of institutions in today's world present unique problems for the expression of human sexuality. We refer here not only to what Irving Goffman calls "total institutions," such as asylums and prisons, where all components of one's life are regimented, but also to institutions such as the military, where one has more freedom of movement but in which patterns of conduct and thinking are still deeply ingrained.

PRISONS
The sexual experiences of prisoners in America and most other nations are, at best, solitary masturbation and, at worst, vicious coercive assaults. Studies from all over the United States indicate a widespread pattern of sexual assault on inmates by other inmates, often within minutes of arrival at the jail or even in the sheriff's van that takes them to the institution. There are few remedies for such attacks in the present system. Prison guards frequently discourage even reporting such incidents or "solve" the problem by placing the assault *victim* in virtual solitary confinement and permanent lockup to "protect" him. Courts generally will not provide injunctions to prevent future brutality, will not award civil damages or take criminal action against jail officials who permit such assaults to occur (unless there is gross negligence), and do not consider the fear of sexual assault to be a valid defense for escape from the institution (although this defense has been raised successfully at least once).

Little is known about the extent of same-sex "rape" in women's institutions (although Winston Moore, director of the Cook County Department of Corrections, refers to them as "veritable bastions of openly conducted lesbianism"[78] but does not distinguish between consensual and coerced acts) or about the level of coercive abuse by jailers on inmates. In male prisons, at least, the inmate-on-inmate assaults may serve several purposes and mirror attitudes about sex in the outside world.

Only two states, Mississippi and California, permit conjugal visits from spouses or lovers. For fifty years the Mississippi State Prison at Parchman was the only institution to permit this. In 1970 Columbus Hopper did a study of the Parchman system by interviewing former inmates and prison officials. Officials indicated that the system made inmates friendlier to guards but did not significantly lower the level of assaults or the level of homosexuality. The most important thing for the inmates (listed by 50 percent) was how the visits were able to keep their marriages together. One lawyer who reviewed the study noted that "these findings suggest that the stress in these programs is not to be placed on the conjugal aspect of the visit, but on the privacy and intimacy of the visit itself—the ability of the inmate and his family to converse, at length, about major issues in their lives."[79]

In a few other countries the need for privacy and intimacy is recognized as part of the rehabilitative scheme for prisoners. Sweden allows frequent conjugal visits and permits seventy-two-hour home furloughs after a specific amount of time has been served (even though 8 percent of the inmates do not return). For a long time Mexico has had the Tres Marias Colony, on an island ninety miles offshore, where dangerous criminals are committed to exile but are permitted to take their families with them.

Although we might not choose to adopt any of the specific techniques of other nations, it seems that the United States needs to assess its responsibility toward the sexuality of those we incarcerate, for the sake of inmates and their families.

INSTITUTIONS FOR THE MENTALLY ILL AND/OR MENTALLY RETARDED

Although there is a medical difference between those determined to be mentally ill and those considered to be retarded, many states treat both the same in terms of sexual behavior and family obligations, particularly if they are institutionalized.

Most states do not permit those who are allegedly mentally ill or retarded to marry, arguing that they cannot understand the contractual nature of their commitment. Patricia Wald, a prominent advocate for legal rights for the retarded, raises a serious question, however, about the underlying assumption of such laws:

The critical policy question is who among those who function at a lower intellectual and social level present such an intolerable risk to themselves or their mates that they should be forbidden to marry? Some mental retardation experts say, categorically, none. We certainly need far more refined data than we now have to pick out which ones. We can't even make accurate predictions about how normal people will function in a domestic liaison. One out of four marriages ends in divorce and an unknown number of the rest generate misery, murder, mayhem, mental breakdowns, and child abuse. On what basis then can we tell retarded persons they can't marry? Many already do so and successfully. Either we must come up with data to show that some (and we must know who they are) retarded persons will almost certainly disastrously injure themselves or others by entering a marital relationship or we must keep our hands off.[80]

Some of the marital adjustment problems retarded persons do have result precisely from the nature of their early institutionalization. They are generally denied the normal freedom of association with members of the opposite sex and are virtually never given any information about the moral or physical components of human sexuality.

Well over half the states permit the development of a mental illness to be grounds for divorce. In general, such statutes provide that the illness must be incurable by present therapies and that the spouse has been institutionalized for a period of time, usually three to five years. We find it unacceptable, however, that many states do not supply legal counsel to the allegedly ill spouse and that, in a few cases, there is no notification that a divorce action is under way, assuming he or she will not be able to understand what is happening anyway. Attorney Robert Farmer, author of *The Rights of the Mentally Ill*, believes that "resting all on the good faith of the petitioner, who wants the divorce, and on the judge's ability to ferret out pertinent facts independently seems to be a lamentable situation."[81]

When a finding of mental illness is made about parents, the majority of states also permit the children in the family to be put up for adoption without the parents' consent. In these states it is generally not required that any evidence of neglect be shown; the mental illness is sufficient cause to remove the child. Given the serious questions now being raised about the nature of mental illness, extreme caution should be used in dividing a family in this manner.

THE MILITARY
Although women are now a part of all branches of the service, there is still an overriding element of traditional masculine

imagery in the institution. This leads to several serious sexuality-related problems.

First, the military services do not permit the enlistment of or continued service of admittedly gay persons. In one major decision in 1976 Air Force Sergeant Leonard Matlovich, who desired to stay in the service although he was openly gay, was denied the right to serve. Similarly, persons are still discharged under other-than-fully-honorable conditions for engaging in homosexual activity or for being suspected of homosexual tendencies. (It is estimated that over 20,000 persons were given such discharges over the past decade.) In a few cases (particularly those involving officers and enlisted personnel, where coercion is clearly possible) courts-martial are still conducted for homosexual acts. Most practicing gays are discharged with general or undesirable discharges, although some honorable discharges are given. Only in instances where there is evidence that the homosexual act was a first-time occurrence or was done as experimentation will an individual be retained.[82]

A second problem that relates to the masculine stereotypes present in the military is the high level of rapes during wartime. Official estimates from the Vietnam War show several hundred courts-martial convictions for rape and related charges, but Susan Brownmiller's exhaustive study of rape raises serious doubts about whether the magnitude was not much greater. "If in the United States a mere one in five rapes is reported, what percentage might have been reported in Vietnam, where a victim who survived the assault knew no English, had little or no recourse to the law, and was considered an enemy?"[83] For Brownmiller, rape in wartime is a grotesque example of the male assertion of dominance over all women. "In the name of victory and the power of the gun, war provides men with a tacit license to rape. In the act and in the excuse, rape in war reveals the male psyche in its baldest form, without the veneer of 'chivalry' or civilization."[84] According to the Uniform Code of Military Justice, rape is a crime, and a person found guilty of rape "shall be punished by death or such other punishment as a court-martial may direct [Article 120]." Rape is also a violation of the international laws of war, which are codified for American soldiers in the Army Field Manual.

For a fuller treatment of these issues see the report of the United Church of Christ Task Force on Ministries to Military Personnel, which was approved in principle by the Tenth General Synod (1975) under the title *In Order to Establish Justice*.[85]

182

ISSUES AFFECTING SEXUAL PRACTICE AND UNDERSTANDING

SEXUALITY AND THE MASS MEDIA

Sexist and racist stereotypes continue to dominate the advertising and the entertainment sections of public media. What, if anything, is more disturbing than the existence of such stereotypes is the relative absence of other images that portray the sexes and alternate life-styles in nontraditional and positive ways. The women portrayed on commercial television programs tend to have either very traditional roles and occupations or are superwomen endowed with strength matched only by their seductiveness ("Charlie's Angels," "The Bionic Woman," and others).

Men retain violent or ruthless characterizations as detectives, frontiersmen, or corporate executives or are viewed as bumblers not far removed from the days of Dagwood. Although the networks and the Public Broadcasting System have presented occasional portrayals of independent women, well-adjusted gay persons, and sensitive nonmanipulative men, it is lamentable that such images are still infrequent.

Advertising also plays upon sexual stereotypes to sell products. It is undoubtedly by design, for example, that luxury cars, which are sold predominantly to men, are hawked by beautiful women. The clear implication is that men who crave and then purchase such cars will be able to get such women as well.

Children's toys offer another good example. Several toy companies, in response to concerns of parents and preschool educators, have recently begun to manufacture anatomically correct boy dolls and girl dolls, which provide helpful self-understanding for young boys and girls. At the same time, advertising for children's toys furthers many stereotypes. Rose K. Goldsen comments:

These breasts are strictly to drape clothes around, to suggest fantasies having to do with self-decoration. They have nothing to do with fantasies about providing milk for infants, nothing to do with succorance and nurturance of babies. The fashion-doll scenario the toy companies target to girls casts the vote for number-one female sex role, and it's not the role of wife and mother, not by a long shot. Sex object in charge of consumption is more to the point.[86]

Toys designed for boys heavily emphasize warfare (G.I. Joe), competition (racing sets), and conspicuous consumption (add-ons to many toys so that a full set of equipment may include dozens of elaborate pieces).

Although many images in the entertainment and advertising sections of the media are derogatory or restrictive, it is unusual that some products directly related to human sexuality are not advertised at all. Nonprescription contraceptives cannot now be advertised on television or on the radio. The National Council of Churches recently recommended that these devices not be advertised, but given the epidemic proportions of venereal disease and unwanted pregnancies in the United States, we believe that there is sufficient chance for usefulness in these advertisements and that they should be permitted.

SEXUALITY AND NEW BIRTH TECHNOLOGIES

Each year thousands of children are born as a result of the process of artificial insemination. Many theologians, physicians, lawyers, and other policy-makers see great promise in this technique for childless couples and for those whose genetic background makes conceiving a genetically defective child a serious possibility. The technique itself is relatively simple. Sperm is collected through masturbation or catheterization and is deposited in the vagina, cervical canal, or uterus of the woman to be impregnated. Most operations of this sort involve impregnation by the husband's own sperm (AIH) and are done to overcome low sperm counts, malfunctions of the sexual organs, or painful intercourse (dyspareunia).

Artificial insemination by an anonymous donor (AID) raises more serious ethical and policy considerations, but it is often used if there is a likelihood of genetic illness because of incompatibility between husband and wife. Children born by AID are still not legally considered legitimate in many states. Not all problems of infertility or genetic incompatibility can be solved by artificial insemination. For example, some women are not capable of producing viable eggs, while others have congenital problems that make it impossible to safely carry a fetus to term. Several methods are described briefly below that could, in the future, provide assistance—egg transfer, ectogenesis, and cloning. Major policy decisions must be made now, however, as to whether research on all or any of these methods should be conducted.

Egg transfers might be of several types. An ovum fertilized by a husband's sperm might be transferred to another woman's uterus for development if the biological mother could not safely conceive. In another method, an egg could be donated (inseminated or not) for implantation into an unfertile mother's Fallopian tubes (prenatal adoption). Finally, a woman with blocked oviducts might have an egg fertilized outside her body (in vitro) and then have it returned to her uterus for development.

There is considerable skepticism in the medical community about how far along these methods have been developed. In 1972 Dr. Douglas Bevis announced publicly that three children had successfully been born through an embryo transfer. Precise details have not been forthcoming. Nevertheless, it is highly probable that these delicate egg transfers will be performed soon, if they have not been already.

Few would question the anguish suffered by parents who are unable to conceive a much wanted child. However, a major policy question is whether the parents' desire for a child entitles them to have it by methods that deliberately impose upon that child an unknown and untested risk of deformity or malformation.

Dr. Leon Kass notes that even if gross malformations would not occur with egg transfers, there is the real possibility of some form of mental retardation—something that might never be anticipated from animal experiment results.[87]

A more radical step is ectogenesis, development of the embryo in vitro—entirely outside the woman's body. Dr. Daniele Petrucci, of Italy, claims to have destroyed a fifty-nine-day-old embryo, which was becoming deformed, that had been developed in vitro. Similarly, Dr. Pyotr Anakhin, of the Moscow Academy of Medical Sciences, claims to have destroyed some 250 embryo/fetuses developed in vitro, one of which had developed for six months! In the summer of 1974 Dr. Landrun Shettles, of the University of California, agreed to perform artificial inovulation for a childless couple. (He had previously succeeded at getting a fertilized egg to implant, but it was deliberately destroyed a few days later, when the woman subject had an operation for cervical cancer.) Several eggs were aspirated and fertilized in a test tube. Before implantation was made, the chairperson of the Obstetrics Department determined to his satisfaction that the planned test was in violation of federal regulations and destroyed the contents of the test tube. Shettles left after twenty-seven years at the university, and the couple sued the chairperson for $1.5 million for "malicious destruction" of the contents of the test tube.[88]

A final type of artificial birth technology is cloning, the process of obtaining a near genetic duplicate of a parent organism through totally asexual means. One early experiment involved removing the nuclei of frog egg cells, thereby eliminating the female set of chromosomes in the nuclei, and replacing them with nuclei from body cells of other frog embryos or tadpoles that had a double set of chromosomes. In general, these cells developed into frogs that genetically were copies of the frogs which donated the new nuclei. Occasionally, the tests went awry and frog monstrosities were created. Exactly how feasible this is for humans has become more and more unclear. The process starts out much more difficult just because human egg cells are so much smaller than those of frogs and becomes increasingly complex as science attempts to find a way to delete the nucleus of the "parent" cell for implantation in the egg cell. Dr. Robert Edwards, an egg transfer specialist, doubts the feasibility of any human cloning. "It might be feasible, but all the results so far show that when the nucleus is taken from an adult cell and is placed in an egg, many of the offspring will die. It now seems doubtful that the transferred nucleus is incorporated into the embryo."[89]

Many other geneticists, however, are much more optimistic, at least about the technological feasibility. Dr. Jones F. Bonner, of Caltech, has indicated a belief that in the next few decades we will be able to "order up carbon copies of people" in a kind of "human mass production."[90]

Although most of the methods discussed above are being considered as means of preventing disease or "correcting" childlessness, it is also possible to conceive of their use to affirmatively alter the whole human species.

Catholic theologian Bernard Häring describes his view of the need to do affirmative work toward guiding the future.

> Creation is an unfinished work that calls for man's cooperation to bring it to greater perfection. And man himself is an unfinished work, called to become an even better image of God. Therefore he can be faithful to himself and to his Creator only by striving for progress in a creative way. His is a cultural being. He never simply adjusts to nature. Rather, as co-creator and co-revealer with God, he has to take into his hands to transform it in accordance with his goal to grow in his capacity to reciprocate love and to discern what enhances human dignity and what blocks it.[91]

For the late geneticist Herman J. Muller this creative effort was to be taken as far as possible. He advocated use of artificial in-

semination, for example, as a way to improve the general pro-
clivities, at least, of the race.

> Well-endowed children would be far more desired if the
> couples were allowed to exercise the deciding voice in the
> choice of the genetic father after seeing the records concerning
> a wide range of possibilities, considering counsel concerning
> them, and judging which of them have shown more of the
> traits preferred by the couples themselves.[92]

The mechanics of these approaches are not as significant as
deciding the basic policy question: Is it valid or not to work to
control our genetic future?

TRANSSEXUALS

In 1976 the sports pages (as well as the front pages) of most news-
papers contained stories about Renee Richards, a fine tennis
player, who was discovered to be a former male ophthalmologist
and tennis player, Richard Raskind. Dr. Richards was denied
participation in one prestigious women's tournament because a
sports association decided that a woman was defined by genetic
makeup, something Richards could not alter.

There are now approximately forty clinics in the United States
alone where sex alteration operations are performed, usually
male to female because they are relatively easier to accomplish.
Dr. Richards explained her feelings to author Andrew Kopkind:

> I've known that I was a transsexual ever since I was an infant.
> I've had an absolutely overwhelming desire to become the
> woman I felt I am. It's a kind of emotional malignancy—not
> a disease, of course—but the desire grows and grows, and
> there's no stopping it. I tried for years and years to deny it. I
> tried to grow a beard. I joined the Navy. I tried psychoanalysis,
> marriage, having a child—all kinds of male endeavors.[93]

The major public policy decision about transsexuals has to do
with how we should deal with the legal recognition of their new
sex. Social security regulations will permit the change of sex
for purposes of obtaining benefits, and states will authorize a
change of name. Many states, however, do not allow individuals
to change the designation of sex on their birth certificates, and
it is this designation that creates the legal establishment of
gender for marriage and other purposes.

In one 1974 court decision in New York a woman got her marriage annulled on the grounds that her "husband" was actually a female who had undergone a sex change operation. The court held that there was no valid marriage, because he could not "function" as a male.[94] Although the misrepresentation practiced by the "husband" is hardly to be condoned, the failure of states to make birth certificate changes serves to create unnecessary psychological adjustment problems. According to Dr. Harry Benjamin, "After [sex-reassignment surgery] has been done and we are dealing with a fait accompli, it should be made as easy as possible for the patient to succeed in his or her new life. And the legal recognition of this new life is a very essential part indeed."[95]

THE FAMILY AND HUMAN SEXUALITY
Toward the end of our study, it became clear that major reforms in marriage, divorce, and child custody laws would be needed if we were to move toward a more just and humane society. We also became aware that many of society's institutions work against the stability of the nuclear family and against any acceptance of the validity of long-term living arrangements not formalized as legal marriage. We did not feel prepared to suggest very specific alterations in family law, but we do propose that the following two areas need to be closely examined.

THE DE FACTO FAMILY
For most practical purposes the only legally protected form of family is that consisting of parents (preferably two) and the children they have borne or adopted since their marriage. Obviously, there are many persons today who live together under relatively stable, but informal, conditions. Some of these individuals live communally; others in situations that closely resemble a marital arrangement. Historically, persons who lived together for lengthy periods were considered to be involved in common law marriages, which, in theory, created the same kind of contractual obligations as a more formal marriage. This concept and a number of other judicial fictions are practiced somewhat today, but generally only when they are required to prevent gross injustice to women and/or children who have been part of a stable relationship but who find themselves needing some "proof" of that relationship. This can occur when a woman wishes to bring suit for the wrongful death of the man she has

been living with, when she seeks workman's compensation, or when she seeks social security benefits. There is, therefore, in many states a way to "create" a marriage when it is expeditious to do so.

Insofar as the state has legitimate interests in the regulation of marriage (health, protection of young children and dependent spouses, and inheritance, for example), it should pursue these in the regulation of nontraditional living arrangements. However, we feel the need for the church to explore more critically the policies that limit or preclude the existence of nontraditional, yet relatively stable, living arrangements. For example, local communities can restrict, through zoning, the number of persons unrelated by blood or marriage who can live in the same house. Similarly, the multiple parenting of children (as in Israel's kibbutzim) and the idea of having children "exchanged" between sets of parents so that they can gain a variety of life experiences are hampered by present social and legal restrictions.

PRESSURES ON THE FAMILY
The fact that over a third of the marriages end in divorce is itself a comment on the growing instability in traditional ideas about marital commitments. The statistics, however, do not begin to measure the trauma that divorces present to the parties directly involved and to their children. Family counselors, frequently visited by the more affluent who are considering divorce, no longer try to keep marriages together at any cost but recognize that sometimes the best counseling for all the people involved is to work to make the separation hurt as little as possible. Regrettably, such counseling is not presently accessible to all who could benefit by it.

In most states specific grounds for divorce are still required; one party must become vilified as mentally cruel, adulterous, or a host of other labels, while the other is exonerated. As early as 1967 the National Conference of Commissioners on Uniform State Laws urged a movement toward a "breakdown of marriage" perspective, where the proof of a "breakdown" is no more than the fact of a separation for a specific length of time. No one has to prove something terrible about the other party, not even incompatibility, and one partner can initiate the separation simply by moving out. To the argument that this makes marital dissolution too easy, sociologist Jessie Bernard says, "But if one party is adamant in his or her insistence on divorce, the marriage has actually broken down; living together under legal duress does not reconstitute the marriage. The no-fault divorce recognizes this bitter reality." When these no-fault cases are heard in court, they are a motion "in the interest of the Jones family" and not as "Mary Jones versus John Jones."[96]

This approach leaves major questions open concerning the protection of the children and the nonworking spouse. There are several possibilities. A task force of the Citizens' Advisory Council on the Status of Women looked at property distribution systems in other countries. In West Germany, for example, after certain kinds of property were removed from the total (that owned before the marriage, gifts, and inheritances), the remaining estate was divided equally. Another system, which also replaces the combination of alimony and child support payments now in existence, would be a monthly cash payment to the parent who is keeping the children by the other party (assuming that he/she is working steadily) in recognition that raising children means they must be supported and that the newly single parent-guardian must be maintained properly as well.

Under these newer schemes, child custody is viewed in a new way. In close to 90 percent of the cases the child is now given to the woman, under the presumption that she will be a better parent. The reality that follows is that the father ends up seeing less and less of the child. Reform systems recognize that neither parent should be presumed, merely by sex, to be the best for the child, but that a nonadversary method should be designed that will, among other things, take into serious account the wishes of the child. As with no-fault divorce, this system would not require that a father prove that his wife is unfit before he could realistically have a chance to gain custody, which is now the case in many states.

TOWARD HUMANE PUBLIC POLICY

The analyses of selected public policy issues presented in this chapter rest upon the conviction that sexuality has to do with the quality of life of the whole human community and that this is the serious business of Christians. Many present public policies came into being in an earlier time under church influence or religious values (including some of the most repressive and dehumanizing ones).

On the one hand, the efforts of individuals and of church bodies in the public arena are directed toward healing the brokenness in human relationships and being the advocate for the defenseless, the uninformed, and the victimized.

On the other hand, our approach is toward affirmative action—

190

creating a humane social order, strengthening relationships of fidelity and caring, establishing structures of sexual justice.

The Christian's mandate in the search for justice is given in Jesus' reading of Isaiah as he entered the synagogue in Nazareth:

The Spirit of the Lord is upon me,
because [God] has anointed me to preach good news to the poor.
[God] has sent me to proclaim release to the captives
and recovering of sight to the blind.

—Luke 4:18

CHAPTER 6

Some Perspectives on Sex Education

This chapter describes approaches to sex education, particularly as they affect public education. Some of the principles and approaches can be modified for use in church-sponsored programs which reflect the church's unique role in sex education.

Generally, we tend to think of sex education, whether for good or ill, as a controversial product of the so-called sexual revolution or new morality of the seventies. For some persons the introduction of sex education in public schools in the United States heralded a cataclysmic breakdown in the country's moral character, accompanying the increasing secularization of the schools and the encroachment of public institutions into private lives.

In 1969 these private fears culminated in a public attack launched against sex education efforts in public schools. At the time, the failure of this movement was attributed to the closed minds, unyielding authoritarianism, and paranoia of its supporters, who ultimately could not dissuade a more rational and temperate majority. However, in our more enlightened age, we might admit that we're not so sure.

We might consider that the intentions, however valid, of those parents and teachers advocating sex education in the schools were also reactionary and ill-advised. A closer look at some of the earlier curriculum models shows a general uncomfortableness with sexuality, a strong emphasis on the biological or "plumbing" aspects of sexuality, and an overriding emphasis on our cultural understanding of sexual dos and don'ts through more pragmatic than moralistic fear tactics, such as using information about the rising VD rates as a deterrent to sexual behavior. We still hear about teachers who "make sex so clean it's dirty" or the boys' hygiene teacher who says, "See this thing between your legs? Well, it's not a muscle; don't exercise it." The movement, in part, was a panic reaction to the supposedly increasing sexual freedom of our younger generation. We were not ready to recognize and address the complexity of human sexuality nor to respect the authentic feelings, differences in values, and questioning about sexuality of our young people or ourselves.

We are only beginning, more cautiously and respectfully, to create safe situations for talking and learning about sexuality, which produce more informed and yet very diverse approaches to sexual experience. We have become only a bit more aware of the value of our physical differences, personal experiences, religious diversity, the fluidity of human relationship, and the complexity of moral decision-making.

Side by side within our communities live those who still anticipate moral destruction, those who seek simple solutions to complex problems, those who have made sex a contemporary golden calf, and those who look to new possibilities in human expression and fulfillment. None of us is immune to this subject, for we embody it. We have been more or less familiar with sex since birth. It is not a new "issue," even publicly.

A BRIEF HISTORY OF SEX EDUCATION

The present controversy reflects the attitudes of an earlier time. The Calvinist tradition, which equated sexuality with sin, was carried to America by the Puritans. Loyalty to God was consistent with a negative attitude toward human sexuality. The pleasures of sex were pleasures of the world and, therefore, were to be shunned. The puritanical moral code set the legislative pattern for many colonial laws and, later, statutes throughout the United States, such as the Comstock laws of 1873, which embodied anticontraception and antiobscenity laws. (This act took its name from Anthony Comstock, secretary of the New York Society for the Suppression of Vice, for whom obscenity was "a poison to soul and body, and anything remotely touching upon sex was to his mind obscene."[1])

Successive waves of immigration during the nineteenth century brought a variety of new cultural and religious attitudes toward human sexuality. During the late 1800s many voluntary organizations, such as the YMCA and YWCA, sponsored lectures and panel discussions dealing with sex-related topics. In 1892 the National Education Association discussed the place of sex education in the curriculum. About the same time, the National Congress of Parents and Teachers examined methods of implementing sex education in the schools. The purpose of the American Society for Sanitary and Moral Prophylaxes, organized in 1905, focused on the eradication of diseases of the social order (specifically, venereal disease) through public education. This emphasis created the initial thrust for sex education programs in the schools.

The beginning of World War I is usually identified as the time when new attitudes and patterns of behavior began to emerge to a significant degree. The war brought with it a more concerted attempt by the US Army to curtail the incidence of venereal disease.

Women's clothes, popular music and dance, and bobbed hair all represented the freedom of the flapper and the emergence into respectability of the, working woman. The 1920s saw a dramatic change in attitudes about public expression of sexuality. At this time, the Federal Council of Churches expressed the view that sex is a positive and stimulating force for good. And the US Public Health Service began conducting sex education conferences in high schools.

Studies by Robert and Helen Lynd show evidence that from 1920 to 1930 the new sexuality was reflected in films, in the naming of the automobile as the "passion wagon," and in the increase of premarital sex, divorce, and children born out of wedlock.

Freudian findings concerning biology and psychosexual behavior certainly heightened public desire for more understanding and openness about sexuality. Freud's new understandings about sex soon became accessible to the broad public through magazines and paperbacks. By the 1940s all these changes were having their impact. Gallup polls conducted in 1943 and 1948 showed substantial support for the inclusion of sex education in public schools.

Through interviews with people from a variety of socioeconomic backgrounds, Alfred Kinsey and others made new data available about attitudes toward masturbation, homosexuality, sex play, and female orgasm that reflected the similarities and differences in need and attitude present in the culture. Studies done during the 1960s by Masters and Johnson brought sexuality to the attention of the health-related professions by highlighting the impact of feelings on the adequacy of sexual relations. Thus, public attitudes began to reflect not only the position that sex is "naughty but nice" but also that sexuality is an integral part of all human relations.

During the last decade sex education as an educational concern came a long way toward realization. A 1972 Gallup poll indicated that 71 percent of the respondents would approve of a nationwide program of birth control education in the public schools.

THE NEED FOR SEX EDUCATION

The polls show that a majority of the American public want sex education in the schools. However, we don't have it. Some people still believe that what children don't know they won't do or that the less they know the better off they'll be, although doing what comes naturally and keeping quiet about it hasn't worked too well. The fact that our young people aren't being taught doesn't mean they aren't learning; on the contrary, the statistics indicate that they are. In 1974 there were 2.5 million new cases of VD, one fourth of them among teenagers. More than one million pregnancies occur to teenagers each year. These figures are shocking and troublesome in a culture that disapproves of premarital sex for a variety of reasons. But some recent changes that are shedding light on these statistics are also creating additional pressure on teenagers. Our society, with its ever increasing emphasis on education and self-fulfillment, has extended the nurturing process and has put off recognition of adulthood until the early twenties, thereby discouraging teenage marriage.

Only a few generations ago, girls married at age sixteen—if not before—and were considered old maids if they remained unmarried after twenty. But today marriage is most common for girls in the early or midtwenties, and the age is rising. For earlier generations the average age for the onset of menses was thirteen, whereas now the age is eleven. This means that we as a society expect teenagers to wait a minimum of seven years longer than past generations to become sexually active after sexual maturity is reached. Hence, our educational and social systems postpone maturity, while causing frustration and resentment among adolescents who are physically and sexually mature.

The problem is aggravated even further by the increasing change in the role of women over the last century. Educational and social systems have been increasingly more open to women. Therefore, girls are in close association with boys, without the traditional modes of protection.

To ignore these factors as if they will have no effect on the conduct of young people is to be unrealistic. Studies done by Herbert S. Sorenson, Melvin Zelnick and John F. Kantner, and Morton M. Hunt present somewhat contradictory findings about adolescent sexual behavior. All of them, however, suggest that teenagers are having sexual relations at a younger age and are having them more frequently than before. A 1971 study by Kantner and Zelnick, of the Johns Hopkins School of Public Health, surveyed 4,240 never-married teenage women, age fifteen to nineteen. More than half of the sexually experienced teenagers surveyed reported having used no contraceptive method the last time they had intercourse. Some adults worry that adolescents with access to such reliable contraception as the Pill, IUD, and diaphragm will become promiscuous. Yet less than one in ten of those sexually active youths interviewed in the Kantner-Zelnick study used any of these methods.[2] It seems that by not putting correct facts into the minds of children, they manage to get other, incorrect facts elsewhere. The preponderance of evidence suggests that there is a correlation between adequate sex information and responsible behavior. Those neighborhoods with parents, school, and church involved in providing comprehensive settings for sex education have the lowest rates of VD and unwanted pregnancy and birth.

Sex education is a reality, whether it be through experience or through peer group information. The issue, then, is what kind of education—adequate or inadequate. Most miseducation happens on the street, through peer group communication. A study by Sol Gordon in 1973 reports that the more sexual experience a young person has had, the less knowledge that person tends to have about the facts of life. Furthermore, self-concept informs one's decisions about what he or she will or will not do sexually.

A girl who thinks of herself as master of her behavior, who takes pride in being a person who cannot be manipulated by others, and who feels that being used for someone else's pleasure is beneath her dignity and standards, is unlikely to indulge in behavior that would injure that self-concept. Similarly, the boy who thinks of himself as a responsible person of honor and integrity, who feels contempt for preying on weaker or less knowledgeable people, and who takes pride in the honesty of his dealings with everyone, is unlikely to attempt to persuade a girl to engage in activities which might expose her to injury or criticism.[3]

This dilemma about more experience and less information is not unique to teenagers. It is a dilemma of contradiction and confusion in values and pressures for adults as well. Psychologists have helped us to realize that some of our sexual attitudes have inhibited us from living fuller lives as marriage partners, friends, and parents.

Bruno Bettelheim points out that "the traditional sexual morality which used to bind anxieties, inasmuch as it protected real dangers (undesired pregnancy and venereal disease), now creates anxiety." He adds, "Today to be afraid of sex now signifies neurosis, for when traditional mores clash, the results can be psychologically devastating. Clearly, if a morality designed to protect against anxiety now endangers it, then such a morality has become unworkable and is in need of radical reform."[4]

At the same time, our society glorifies sexuality. While teen-agers are denied easy access to objective, accurate information about sexuality, society sells products through the mass media by using sex. We present youth with distorted views of the impor-tance of sex.

William Simon points out that

for many, including many of the young, sex continues to be a fearful test that must confirm what it can only provisionally. For males, the fear of socio-sexual inadequacy and incom-petence and for females the double fear of being too little sexual and too much sexual will keep the sexual game precisely that. A game in which the costs of losing often outweigh the rewards of victory.[5]

Thus, as individuals we must deal with contradictory social forces—pressures that distort the importance of sex and at the same time demean it—as well as with personal values that may lead to a distorted and guilt-ridden experience.

THE ROLE OF THE FAMILY

Our first sex education does not come from peers but from our parents through subconscious or conscious nurturing. The family is our first exposure to reality about sex. Through questioning and through observing relationships at home children receive their first understandings of sexuality in the broader sense as the sensual, erotic, physical, communal, and marital. It is in the home that we learn about love and intimacy and develop a sense of the celebration of life through joyful embracing and numerous forms of affection and of the essence of our humanity as we grow to understand what it means to be men and women. This broader definition of sexuality as affecting all of life informs our under-standing of sex education as something more than just a safe-guard against such disasters as unwanted pregnancy or venereal disease. Parents help to shape our psychosexual attitudes and values. Within the home parents can support the positive aspects of our sexuality that serve to strengthen self-esteem, respect for others, and quality of relationships, which may help us to face potential life crises. Data from the Gordon study mentioned earlier supports the premise that there is a positive correlation between informed adolescents and sexual responsibility.

Children's curiosity and questioning about sexuality (although not always explicit) begins much earlier than puberty. Infants are born not only human but sexual. The warmth and manner of their reception into the world are part of their sex education. As early as age six months, children have been known to learn the sensual pleasure of fondling their genitals. Since much of a person's future sexual attitudes and preferences is determined by the age of six years, the importance of parents in this shaping process is obvious. Through their marital relationship and their relationships with their children and with others parents obviously affect their children's later psychosexual behavior.

However, desirable values with regard to sexuality are rarely taught through the traditional "heavy" talks initiated by parents. Such experiences are usually so embarrassing for children that the information is not remembered. What is remembered is that talking about sex is embarrassing, uncomfortable, unexpected, and probably a no-no.

True feelings expressed at natural times at home are important. If sex *never* gets discussed at home, naturally children will not feel as if they can talk openly about this important part of their feelings.

But how does an adult communicate comfortableness about sexuality? First of all, by being comfortable in discussing sexuality as husband or wife. Ideally, couples do this within a context of their shared value systems.

It isn't enough for children to know the biological facts, nor is it necessary for young children to comprehend every intricacy of sexual reproduction, functioning, and behavior. The answers are not found in one or even a set of books. Instead, we learn continually throughout our lives by observing, communicating, and experiencing.

It is also important for parents to accept that sexuality is personal and individual; it is helpful in their marital relations and with children as well. Like adults, not all children are the same. They have different levels of interest, curiosity, and intellectual and emotional development. No child needs to be burdened by the expectation of stereotypes about sexual needs and desires, whether male or female. Thus, it is the parents' judgment that determines what information and values a child is ready for next.

This chapter has suggested that if parents truly wish to prepare their children more fully for a responsible and happy sexual life, they will look at their own marital relationship and what it may be communicating and share their understanding of love for each other with their children, as well as the values by which they live as sexual beings, in an explorative and comfortable way.

Are there other ways parents can help their children? They can answer questions honestly and provide basic, accurate information about their own bodies. Too much pain, with regard to sexuality, is still due to misinformation, whether it results in sexual dysfunction or in false expectation or fear of unwanted pregnancy. Such information can be provided at appropriate and comfortable times throughout childhood—when children ask questions, when they have confusing experiences, when they explore their own bodies.

Street language about sex is often degrading, insensitive, and incorrect. Parents who are troubled by crude or offensive ways of talking about sexuality should not avoid the problem but instead provide children with more acceptable, yet accurate, language for talking about sex. So much of our dilemma in talking about sex is in not knowing how and in not feeling good about it.

Sex education does not happen by five years of age, nor with the story of the egg and the sperm or the penis and the vagina. It is about masculinity and femininity, feelings about ourselves, relationships, love, consideration, affection, and contraception. No five-year-old child could possibly even have touched upon these subjects in their complexity, much less comprehend them. Comfortableness and openness about sex does not mean that we thrust our children into observing or experiencing all adult forms of sexuality. This may only lead to harmful experimentation without understanding. Observing marital expressions of affection is basic for the young child, to learn what love is all about.

Parenting responsibility is a continuing and difficult one, a lifelong learning, decision-making process. A large number of parents find it hard to work out such considerations alone and need additional information and broader support. Many segments of society are becoming increasingly aware of the importance of parenting education and training. Churches, parent-teacher associations, and other voluntary organizations have encouraged this effort and have developed resources for use within their own organizations. High school and college curricula reflect the significance of preparing for the parenting role. It is important that we encourage and initiate these types of supportive programs in our communities, particularly in those groups and institutions that have access to parents.

THE ROLE OF THE SCHOOL

If the family is so important, why, then, is any other form of sex education needed? Parents often worry about what roles the schools and religion play. We've already recognized the importance of the home and also that sex education is a lifelong process, a sequence of experiences through adolescence, adulthood, marriage, and menopause and a variety of sexual functions and dysfunctions that nearly everyone encounters. No child can comprehend all this in childhood, not even after one or several talks. Churches, schools, and parents have insisted for a long time that sex education is a combination of their individual responsibilities. And they're right. Other sources—the locker room or the street, for example—usually dispense inaccurate or inappropriate information and behavior, which need to be countered or set in context.

Sex is about moral decision-making and, therefore, is an "agenda" for the church. A number of churches and synagogues have only very recently moved away from their historical positions on sexuality and have issued reevaluations. There are fundamental differences in position between Jewish, Protestant, and Catholic groups—and *within* each of these traditions as well. Given this diversity, a monolithic religious norm with regard to sexuality cannot be presented. This affects public approaches to all sexual issues—abortion, contraception, homosexuality. Pluralism requires that, without our public education institutions, arenas be provided for presenting these different positions in an unbiased, respectful manner.

What is the role of the school? The teaching of the values of responsibility, justice, and equality happens within many subject areas. Moral decision-making in areas of human sexuality must be broadly understood.

Our rich and diverse religious and cultural history makes it difficult to achieve consensus about sexual values. However, these traditions deserve truthful and critical presentation. Isadore Rubin urges that the same attitudes that are unquestionably the foundation of sound scholarship and pedagogy—critical intelligence, a respect for truth, the right of individuals to self-determination—be applied to the area of education about sexuality. Rubin states that "in teaching politics and government, we do not feel the need to indoctrinate all students into being members of one or another political party. Rather we try to teach them skills and attitudes which they require to make intelligent choices as adults when faced with a changing world and an array of alternatives."[6] Given unique cultural and personal differences, such an educational approach is fundamental.

The public school is a socializing as well as a nurturing agent. It can provide an arena for discussion about what makes for a good community. Sexuality, in its negative and positive manifestations, is certainly integral to our understanding of human adjustment and of community responsibility. The school can bring together varying opinions, beliefs, and experiences about sexuality in a setting where persons can consider each position and develop some common understandings about personal and public needs. In this setting, students may learn objective and accurate information, as well as varying feelings about approaches to sexual behavior—physically, emotionally, and morally—that they would otherwise be unprepared to confront in the broader community.

WHAT IS SEX EDUCATION?

Recognizing this as the primary reason for public education in sexuality, what specifically are the goals of sex education? The words sex education conjure up different images and concepts for different individuals. Within the context of understanding sexuality as part of human and humane community development, sex education is

not merely "reproductive" education
not solely "prophylactic" education
not something imposed
not simply a "telling" process
not "insurance against disaster"
not moral indoctrination.[7]

If a major objective of sex education is to improve the quality of life, and if sexuality is a basic part of our human personality, then the following sex education program guidelines seem applicable:

To provide for the individual an adequate knowledge of his/her own physical, mental, and emotional maturation process as related to sex.

To eliminate fears and anxieties relative to individual sexual development and adjustments.

To develop objective and understanding attitudes toward sex in all of its various manifestations—in the individual and others.

To give the individual insight concerning relationships to members of both sexes and to help in understanding obligations and responsibilities to others.

To provide an appreciation of the positive satisfaction that wholesome human relations can bring in both individual and family living.

To build an understanding of the need for the moral values that are essential to provide rational bases for making decisions.

To provide enough knowledge about the misuses and aberrations of sex to enable the individual to protect him/herself against exploitation and against injury to his/her physical and mental health.

To provide the understanding and conditioning that will enable each individual to utilize his/her sexuality effectively and creatively in his/her several roles, e.g., as spouse, parent, community member, and citizen.[8]

Another list of objectives, suggested by a group of young people, might also be considered:

To provide whatever factual information the individual desires on all aspects of sex.

To increase self-understanding so that individuals may become self-confident members of their own sex.

To increase understanding of the opposite sex in order to promote positive relationships between the sexes.

To understand better other patterns of sex behavior among peers, among the adult generation, and in other cultures, so as to prepare individuals to live with others who believe differently.

To open up communication and promote understanding between adults and youth.

To develop an appreciation of sex as an integral part of life, and see it in the perspective of one's whole life.

To allow and enable each individual to develop a personal standard based on an understanding of and concern for others.

To see sex education as a continuous process to prepare individuals mentally and emotionally for their biological development through maturity.[9]

Those concerned with educating preadolescents may find helpful the following objectives established in 1968 by the Family Living Advisory Committee of the Community School Board, Staten Island School District 31, New York:

To help each youngster appreciate his or her own role, as well as that of other members in the family structure.

To help each youngster see the need for thoughtfulness, kindness and respect in his or her relationship with family as well as others.

To provide each youngster with knowledge about his or her physical and emotional development and to prepare him or her for further changes that will occur.

To establish the use of correct terminology in reference to body parts and their functions.

To provide honest and sensitive answers to youngsters' questions on such topics as reproduction and sex differences.

To help youngsters understand the need for careful consideration of decisions involved in their behavior towards others and the acceptance of responsibilities for these decisions.

To encourage youngsters to view their decisions in light of their own family values and ethics, which may involve their religious affiliation.

To encourage community involvement by means of parent workshops and community meetings so that parents may increase their understanding of their role in the child's total development.[10]

APPROACHES TO SEX EDUCATION

Once principles and objectives for a sex education program have been established, an approach must be developed. Several different approaches have been utilized by schools attempting to do something positive. No single method is best for every situation, nor should one method be used exclusively. Variations and adaptations should be determined by the needs, the personnel, and the unique characteristics of each school and community.

Since sexuality is a function of the total personality, an effective sex education program concerns itself with the biological, sociological, and psychological and, therefore, might include:

A cognitive component—dealing with factual information that will provide one with a sound and comprehensive information base about sexuality.

An affective component—participating in activities leading to the development of insights and understandings about one's own sexuality and the implications of this knowledge for personal relationships.

A skills component—learning to make decisions and to determine values and behaviors when dealing with issues of sexuality.

If information is accurate and is offered objectively, followed by discussion and appraisal, then it is likely that these three components will evolve quite naturally.

A number of teachers have developed courses that approach understanding of the totality of sexuality and the real needs of the students. One high school teacher says:

During the first year, we taught a sex information course—giving out a lot of information about anatomy, conception, birth, contraception, venereal disease, abortion, and masturbation. During our second year, we taught a sex education course, emphasizing the uniqueness of each individual's sexual values and focusing more on sexual decisions, interpersonal relationships and sex roles. Since then, we've been teaching a human sexuality course—dealing primarily with feelings and values. Information is still important, but we focus almost exclusively on that information which students consider "need to know."[11]

In earlier decades public schools that approached the subject of sex education used outside lectures, filmstrips, printed resources, or personal counseling, all of which required little involvement on the part of school administrators, teachers, parents, or students. The special and infrequent use of these techniques reinforced the understanding that sex is something one can't discuss like other topics. Much of the time these techniques, with the exception of counseling, offered little opportunity for questions, discussion, interchange of opinions, or personal, individual work with students.

Individual counseling reaches only a few and possibly not those most in need of help. Furthermore, for the development of their own objectivity and insight, students need the experience of participating in a group setting.

A constructive curriculum approach has already been alluded to—a continuing comprehensive course on human sexuality. Ideally, such a course could help to meet the objectives outlined earlier. The scope of our understanding of sexuality, needs of the students, and aforementioned objectives and principles suggests many viable options.

The alternative or complementary approach is to include sexuality considerations in other courses in the curriculum where appropriate. Some subjects in which sexuality plays a role are literature (T.S. Eliot, James Joyce, D.H. Lawrence), history (the Victorian era, the roaring twenties, the impact of women's suffrage and liberation movements), the social sciences, biology, home economics, health and physical education. This approach is not meant to overemphasize the importance of sexuality but to recognize it as a social, psychological, and political force throughout human history.

As a complementary approach particularly applicable to high school or college programs, Lester Kirkendall suggests in his classic *Sex Education as Human Relations* the inclusion of sex education in functional courses that help students to make decisions about their own social and family situations and their personal futures. Kirkendall says, "The content must be firmly grounded in the needs of young people and help them specifically with questions of a personal and social nature, not stressing pathological materials but a positive, constructive approach which explores the possibilities of happier, better living."[12] He outlines a series of particular topics to be included in this type of course, which moves from simple analysis of human behavior to preparation for parenthood. Kirkendall believes that the topics of these courses should be determined by the interests of students. Such courses could be introduced as early as preadolescence and could be continued through college and into adult education programs. This concept of sex education as being integral to our learning about biology and literature as well as preparation for life-style decision-making is compatible with the understanding of sexuality as a complex lifelong process.

Eleanor Morrison and Mila Underhill Price agree. In their book *Values in Sexuality* they write:

> The fundamental issues relating to human sexuality encompass the personal value system, life style, self-image, communication mode, and philosophy about how persons in relationships act toward each other. Any course of study in sex education must deal with all these individual realities, in addition to information or external facts, if the learner is to live as a responsible citizen and sexual being in our pluralistic society.[13]

IMPLEMENTING A SEX EDUCATION PROGRAM

Those beginning a sex education program can do their work more constructively if they consider from the outset these elements:

—the uniqueness of their situation and some flexibility with regard to planning;

—the importance of community support and involvement;

—consideration for the needs of students not only as perceived by adults but also as self-determined by youth;

—ongoing planning, evaluation, and informed commitment to the program concerning the probable problems involved at every stage.

Careful thought about the how-to's of implementing any program is important. Three considerations are particularly critical: decisions regarding who will participate, careful assessment of needs, and choice of the teacher/leader.

How, then, does such a group begin to discover needs? First, they must determine whose needs are being assessed and whose needs will be fulfilled if such a program is instituted. These questions must be asked continually in order that:

> Teachers or leaders will not satisfy only their own biases;

> Parents' opinions and needs will not be assessed for political reasons but rather as co-partners in developing the program;

> Administrators of church, school, agency and their respective boards or committees will not be by-passed at critical stages of planning, in order that they might fully understand the

methodologies and objectives of the program and support the program at critical times.[14]

Once the human dynamics of needs assessment are addressed, how does a planning group assess the needs? Following are a number of methods for consideration:

—Direct interviews or questionnaires with those to be served;
—Surveys or questionnaires of all concerned: administrators, teachers, parents, trustees, board of directors, community-at-large, students;
—Hearings or meetings with representatives from key community factions;
—Research into national statistics combined with information-gathering in the local setting.

Another important factor in any such project is meeting the needs, and the teacher in an educational setting is the most important element in successfully fulfilling this objective.

THE ROLE OF THE SEX EDUCATOR

The history of concern for better training of sex educators parallels concern for introducing public sex education programs. However, the need for better-trained sex educators has never seemed greater than it is now. As our understanding of the complexity of human sexuality grows, we recognize more and more the important role performed by the teacher/leader. The traditional concerns of parents regarding sex education programs—how much information at each age level, the correlation between information and experimentation, the presentation of values, the role of the parent and the school—can be satisfied more easily if the right person is found to do this important job. The teacher is the key to effective sex education with any age group. The sex educator profile that follows reflects his/her importance to a program. A good sex educator

Has achieved a healthy attitude toward his/her own sexuality;

Has the quality of empathy (sensitive to the attitudes, values and feelings of other persons);

Can understand clearly material about human personality which comes from a variety of fields and utilize this information in teaching;

Can communicate warmly and effectively;

207

Has an inherent respect and concern for other persons, regardless of age, race or socioeconomic status;

Finds life satisfying and rewarding, particularly when contributing to the well-being of others;

Is able to safeguard, with strict confidentiality, private and personal material communicated to him/her.

Is able to relate to students in an open and trusting manner while maintaining an appropriate professional attitude;

Can create a supportive climate in the classroom, enabling students to express their true feelings and honest opinions;

Has the ability and willingness to cooperate fully and easily with professional colleagues.[15]

Many in the sex education field feel strongly that the time has come to recognize sex education as a professional specialty. This can only happen when clearly defined standards for the training of sex educators have been established and embodied in programs offered through colleges and universities. Adequate professional standards are a critical concern for all of us if we are to truly educate, correct some of the results of miseducating our young people, and provide for their well-being.

Once in the classroom, a teacher/leader may find it helpful to consider the practical suggestions offered by Burt Saxon, which reflect his five-year experience in New Haven, Connecticut.

Start small and on safe grounds, beginning with basic sex information;

Involve students and parents in planning the course;

Don't force students to participate;

Get administrators to support (or, hopefully, to continue to support) your efforts;

Have a consultant to help with difficult questions from students (you will never know all the answers);

Get in touch with your own sexual values and feelings. The more aware you are, the more you can help students clarify their own values;

Give some thought about how much of yourself you will share with your students (the integration of your presentation of objective information, attitudes and the expression of your own biases and feelings).[16]

Saxon indicates that students will respect a teacher who can offer a definite position without being autocratic. He reminds teachers that they can expect no more openness from their students than they are willing to demonstrate themselves. He also suggests that the use of a team approach to teaching sex education can provide diversity in value systems, alleviate teacher anxiety, check personal biases, and multiply professional strengths in content and communication skills.

CHOOSING APPROPRIATE RESOURCES

Although the educator is the key to a successful program, resources can serve as an important supplement. Considerations previously mentioned with regard to definition and scope of sexuality and educational objectives inform resources appropriate for a particular program. But instructional materials are tangible: they can be seen and read; they can be distorted and misinterpreted. Sex educators need well-developed rationales to justify the use of instructional materials that contain explicit photographs and language. These rationales should be developed before such materials are chosen, in concert with established objectives. This is the point at which the planning group can play an important role and when the involvement of parents and youth is necessary. There are no hard, fast rules for choosing materials, given the uniqueness of each community. A sex education program can be compromised before it has even started due to confrontation over sex education materials.

In order to avoid such conflicts, consider the questions set forth by Derek L. Burleson for reviewing materials:

Have objectives been clearly stated before the selection of sex education materials to help implement those objectives? Are the course objectives to provide information, clarify values, improve communication skills? How are particular resources helpful or not helpful?

Are the materials appropriate for the physical, intellectual and social maturity of their intended audience?

Do the materials present accurate, complete and up-to-date information?

Do the materials reflect a bias toward any single point of view? (It's impossible for any writer to be unbiased, however. Be aware of the biases you are presenting.)

Do the materials reflect the equality of the sexes, and avoid rigid sex stereotyping?

Do the instructional materials have supportive resources in the form of teacher's manuals, discussion guides or bibliographies?

Does the final selection process involve the input of both parents and youth?[17]

MEETING THE NEEDS OF THE WHOLE PERSON

Up until now needs assessment has only been made in terms of educational needs. However, any program of this kind should anticipate other types of support services. All too often these services develop independently of one another. For instance, until recently, the family planning and sex education movements were developing separately. Family planning meant contraception, while sex education meant teaching information about sexuality but avoiding the subject of contraception. Efforts are being made to integrate the two.

A 1970 report, which was supported by the Forum on Family Planning and Family Economics of the White House Conference for Children, offers these reasons for integrating family planning and sex education programs:

Increased recognition and understanding of the complex physical, psychological and social dimensions of human sexuality;

Development of sex education models which include an understanding of family planning within a context of responsible behavior;

The realization that availability of contraception alone does not ensure utilization, especially where pregnancy planning

210

is most crucial. Family planning has been realized in its broadest sense only where linked to an understanding of particular people's life priorities and mediated through an appropriate education system;

The sexual climate in which concepts related to actual behavior can be expressed openly and reflected in education services and/or law.[18]

A study conducted from October 1974 through February 1975 in Los Angeles-area family planning clinics revealed that

four out of ten family planning patients have sexual problems with which they would like help. Clinic staff underestimate by half the degree of sexual dysfunction among patients, and tend mistakenly to believe that younger, Latin, unmarried and less educated women have more problems, while underestimating the sexual problems among non-Latin white and black women. Two fifths of staff members do not routinely ask patients questions relating to sex, largely because of time pressures. Yet, many sexual problems of patients can be handled just by providing correct information. Addressing issues of sexuality directly is important for family planners since sexual confusion often results in contraceptive failure.[19]

Community planning groups for sex education will find that individuals are in need of additional help, such as:
—crisis intervention—a need to work out an immediate problem where a decision or course of action is necessary for the individual immediately;
—support through personal discussion with another or with a group, in order to sort out feelings or confusion;
—referral to professional help, whether it be medical or some sort of individual counseling.
Meeting these needs requires that those who are involved in community sex education programs be in liaison with other community services and agencies. Creative new kinds of approaches have developed in some communities to coordinate or fill these needs in part. They may include:
Peer-group sex information and education programs or service delivered to students by students.—A student drop-in center may offer sex information and materials and a referral book containing names, locations, telephone numbers, contact person, fee schedule, and other information about agencies and institutions

offering the kinds of medical and/or counseling services related to student needs. Such programs are usually created with the help of trained advisors through public schools or other institutions accessible to young people.

College- or high-school-based sexual health care services.— These services are critical for college-age students, since most are in their prime child-bearing years, almost all have reached the age of majority, and most will become sexually active before they graduate. A survey of the particular student body would reveal the services most needed in a community. These may include contraceptive counseling and prescription; pregnancy testing and/or counseling; sex-related counseling and/or therapy; printed materials providing basic facts about sexuality; seminars or courses in human sexuality; abortion and sterilization services or referrals; hotlines or crisis intervention; gynecological examination; VD diagnosis and treatment.

Programs that serve the needs of those who wish to be anonymous, such as family planning, abortion clinics, private referrals supported through Planned Parenthood, private and public hospitals, or government agencies. Sex still seems to be a sin or at least an embarrassing and controversial reality for all of us at times. For those of us who cannot seek help openly, with the care and support of friends, services of this type need to be made *available* and *affordable.*

The development of sex education opportunities in public schools and communities has not only begun to better prepare young people for lives as responsible, sexual adults, but it also serves as a somewhat unique model in public education. The heated debate over sex education continues in a number of places, but there are as many other communities that have created vital forums for sharing, appreciating, collaborating, and responding, ultimately to the benefit of all. The issue involves personal experience and conviction, social responsibility and theological belief. Few other subjects can arouse so many people's attention. Thus, the multiplicity and depth of experience and belief in any given community on the issue of human sexuality becomes apparent in a discussion on sex education. Our educational institutions are frequently criticized for presenting single-minded approaches to history or literature unrepresentative of the diverse and rich heritage of a number of Americans (including members of religious, ethnic, and racial minorities). Too often these challenges are not addressed.

But during the last two decades many have learned the lesson well that we cannot attempt to present a homogeneous approach to sex education. And we shouldn't, since the experience of learning to understand and appreciate one another's differences instead of destroying them and working toward some common understanding of responsibility and shared values is a truly exciting and uniquely American experience in community building. In no other discussions concerning public education do we find such a vital mixture of involvement on the part of parents, professionals, students, and community leaders. Few other agendas have enabled people to recognize and appreciate the interrelatedness of personal growth and responsible citizenship, the rights of the individual and the role of the state, religious belief and social responsibility—in other words, how democracy functions in a pluralistic community working to meet the educational needs of its members. If we were to attempt such dialogue and mutual interaction in some other areas of education (e.g., in the instruction of our young people about the history, language, traditions, and economics of these very same communities), we would hopefully experience less conflict than most have during the painful development of a pluralistic approach to sex education, accompanied by more wisdom concerning the strength of our diversity and possibilities for common bonds.

CHAPTER 7

The Community of Faith and Human Sexuality

Several teenagers and church education executives met to talk about improving education in the church. One youth said, "Let's face it! The only curriculum young people have is the life of their local congregation." That congregational life, for most of us, is the setting in which we learn what the gospel means, how to understand the Bible, what worship is, and what the guidelines for Christian living are.

Earlier in this report sexuality was defined as having emotional, physical, cognitive, value-laden, spiritual, personal, and social dimensions. In those terms and in most of those dimensions each congregation is a faith community that relates to human sexuality. Consider: The congregation is composed of males and females. Persons of various ages, shapes, sizes, backgrounds, and genders relate to one another as caring persons. The church is strongly concerned with relationships. Language and understandings about persons and their sexuality are part of the church's life in worship, education, fellowship, counseling, group activities, and missionary expression.

The church is a moral community dealing vitally with guidelines for human conduct and moving toward convictions of the good, the fitting, the norm, the ought. Spirituality is the special domain of the community of faith, as persons seek to understand the mystery, awe, and wonder of human experience and to build linkages to other human beings and to the holy God whom the church worships and serves.

The church understands in special ways the social dimension of sexuality, for we believe in a God who sustains people in day-to-day life, who enters history, and who calls us to be disciples of peace, justice, and love. Our vocation is to work to achieve the full humanity of persons. Christians are called to shape a holy commonwealth, a civic community in which justice and human well-being prevail. Our calling is to stand in solidarity with the oppressed, including the sexually oppressed as well.

The church is a community of grace, receiving not only its message but its very life from God. Thus, we participate in a community of gift-giving and gift-receiving. Somehow when the church lives up to its full promise, our diverse gifts as persons are able to be given and received by the whole community of faith.

SOME UNITED CHURCH OF CHRIST YEARNINGS

The inquiry process that undergirded this study was not sufficient in scope to gain a full sense of the concerns, hopes, and dreams of members of the United Church of Christ as they approached sexuality issues. Some data has been gathered that is direction-pointing. The United Church Board of Homeland Ministries has developed significant understandings of the composition and representative concerns of United Church of Christ active members through administration of a Church Membership Inventory instrument. This project is part of the board's Area Mission Strategy research. In a given participating congregation, persons are asked to complete the questionnaire in the setting of a Sunday morning service. A tabulation is furnished the church to help it plan its future ministries. One question asks persons to identify help they seek from their church: "I want my church to help me to . . ."

Results from questionnaires completed by nearly 66,000 church attenders in close to 1,000 United Church of Christ congregations in ten conferences[1] reveal that roughly three fourths of the active members are seeking help from their church in the following areas:
—building good moral foundations for their personal life
—finding meaning for personal existence
—raising their children properly
—working for justice in the community and the world
—meeting personal problems of anxiety and conflict
—being aware of the needs of others in the community

One section in the same questionnaire provides an opportunity for members to answer an evaluation question for their particular congregation. "How helpful has your church actually been to you in the following areas of your life?" In the six areas mentioned above, the gap between expectation and delivery was significant. The desire for help in these areas was 14 to 27 percent higher than the church's performance.

None of the help areas was identified as having an explicit sexuality dimension. But it seems obvious that in each category the meeting of our expectations touches our lives as sexual persons: In the face of the changing times in which we live, we want help in moral understanding and action. We want to be persons of worth and to help others to understand themselves as persons of worth. We want guidance in raising our children. Our own fears, anxieties, and conflicts touch many areas of our life, not the least of which is the sexual. We want to increase our awareness of others, to care about their well-being, and to seek justice for them.

The church's resources—Lord, life, faith, calling, people— provide rich possibilities in the area of human sexuality. There is no way a congregation can avoid dealing with sexuality. It is, after all, a community of persons who are sexual. The key question is "How will we, in our congregation, deal with the nature and meaning of our sexuality?"

THE BIBLE AND OUR COMMON LIFE

We are a community that cares about the Bible. The forms of our life as a people emerge from experience with the church's book. Our contemporary experiences as the people of God are informed by the book and its life. In turn, our experiences shape the ways we receive the Bible's life and message. In the community of faith we meet God, the creator and redeemer of human experience and of history. We learn of a God who has created us male and female and who loves us. Such grace is unique in our experience, and we struggle to find words that convey the richness of that experiencing. In moments of doubt and darkness we are aware of others in the Bible and in Christian experience who find a loving God in the midst of their sexuality, and their experience carries us for a while.

As we seek to convey our Christian experience sometimes our vocabulary betrays us. If we limit our metaphors of God only to words such as father, he, and king, we lose the richness and insights of nongender metaphors—creator, redeemer, friend, holy, love, grace, peace, light, hope, truth, wonder, power, and shalom. The use of masculine-associated metaphors denies the fullness of the biblical tradition with more feminine-oriented images, such as womb, bosom, mother, daughter, midwife, wisdom, seamstress, housekeeper, and nurse. If the church is to be true to the full promise of the Bible, we need to recover for all persons the richness in meaning of female and nongender as well as male images for divine reality.

The Bible is a book about love of ourselves, our neighbor, and God. It provides insights into the meaning of being in a community of fidelity, intimacy, and covenant. It deals with marriage

216

and divorce, with chastity and adultery, with fornication and self-denial, with heterosexual and homosexual acts. Somehow the Bible is our story, with all its ambiguity. In the community of faith each of us can find ourselves and share that autobiography.

And what a cast the book has: Adam and Eve and their children, Abraham and Sarah, Moses and the people of Israel, Jeremiah, the nameless lovers of Song of Songs, the woman taken in adultery and her accusers, Deborah and the Judge, Mary and Elizabeth, Peter and Paul, Mary Magdalene. The book of faith is so full of the stuff of our life—what richness for Bible study, for teaching and learning, for liturgy and preaching.

There is, the good book says,

a time to be born, and a time to die;
a time to plant and a time to uproot . . .
a time to weep and a time to laugh;
a time for mourning and a time for dancing . . .
a time to embrace and a time to refrain from embracing . . .
a time to love and a time to hate . . .

—Eccelesiastes 3:2-8, NEB

In a word, a time to be sexual and to use our sexuality as God's gift.

THE CHURCH—THE BODY
How remarkable it is to think that we are called the *body of Christ*. Jesus is called "the Word made flesh." For ancient Hebrews or for modern Christians, to speak of ourselves as Jesus' body is startling but invigorating! We are to embody the being of Jesus. That says two things: We need to understand the person of Jesus and we need to learn embodiment.

John A.T. Robinson, a New Testament scholar, is fascinated with Paul's use of the image of the body. Paul is struck by the nature of human boundedness. "Who will deliver me from this body of death?" Paul asks, in Romans 7:24. Robinson contends that "Paul saw that the Christian gospel . . . [is] very different. For the body is not simply evil: it is made by God and for God. Solidarity is the divinely ordained structure in which personal life is to be lived."[2]

Robinson sees the body as the central concept in Paul's thought about God and humanity. The great themes of the letters are bound together through the use of the body motif:

It is from the body of sin and death that we are delivered; it is from the body of Christ on the Cross that we are saved; it is into His body the Church that we are incorporated; it is by His body the Eucharist that this Community is sustained; it is in our body that its new life has to be manifested; it is to the resurrection of this body to the likeness of His glorious body that we are destined.[3]

And Jesus is for real—fully human, fully God, the creeds say. Docetism (from the Greek word meaning to seem) is the heresy which in effect said that Jesus was play-acting—that he·didn't need to eat or sleep because he was superhuman. On the contrary, the incarnation means that the Word did become flesh, fully human with desires and hopes and physical needs. What is it to say that Jesus was fully man? What was the nature of his sexuality? Did he get his feelings hurt? Did he wonder about the changes in his body? Did he fight with his parents? What is it to *be* his body?

The scripture gives us some clues. Jesus seemed at ease with both men and women. He cut through the stereotypes, barriers, and conventions that separated people. There was in his life—as the gospels share it—neither bond nor free, male nor female, for all were one in him. He was the genial guest at a wedding feast. It was he who interceded for an adulterer and prevented harm or possibly death to her.

James Nelson reflects on the meaning of the humanity of Jesus:

Can you see the truth of your sexuality and your embodiment vindicated in Christ? He is no sexless, docetic apparition, but the enfleshment of God in a man. Can you also see that the gracious word of acceptance frequently comes through the hidden Christ, the Christ incognito? It may be in the ecstasy and playfulness of sexual communion with your beloved. It may be in such a simple act as the spontaneous hand placed on your arm by a friend, but in that moment you were aware of healing—and hasn't the church long known that healing often comes with "the laying on of hands?" And it may not be heresy, either theological or moral, to suggest that grace may be expressed and reunion discovered in the loving touch of your own body.[4]

The whole life of the congregation is judged by the ideal of the Word made flesh. How do we embody the truth of the gospel that in Christ we are all one? How do we demonstrate that we are members one of another? How does the foot know that it has any relationship to the elbow or the knee of Christ's body? How does the body work when some of its members are missing? How is bread broken and life shared in ways that all persons—regardless of orientation, marital status, or life-style—feel they belong? How are the gifts of each person's uniqueness given and received in such a way that we, though many, become one?

THE COVENANTING PEOPLE

Central to biblical understanding and to the experience of the people of God is the reality of covenanting. The biblical notion of covenant is used primarily to describe a state of being and commitment between God and the people of God. It conveys fidelity, mutuality, and uniqueness, being together for common purposes. The chosenness of the people of Israel is not for special privilege but, rather, to be a means to express God's righteousness, justice, and concern for the whole human community.

Walter Brueggemann identifies the elements included in the biblical idea of covenant: "All important relations are covenantal, which means they are a) based on vows, b) open to renegotiation, c) concerned with mutual decisions, d) affecting all parties involved, e) addressing life and death issues and f) open to various internal and external sanctions."[5]

In churches of the Congregational tradition the covenant is understood to be at the heart of the church's life. The church by definition is the people of the covenant. In this tradition new persons received into membership agree to "own" the covenant. The gist of the vow is, It is my covenant, freely made. By this act I enter into this covenant people, their life and mission.

The notion of covenant is a central motif in the Reformed tradition as well. William Parsons, an expert on German Reformed history, tells of the covenant notion of marriage during the eighteenth century. Husband and wife worked as a team in the fields and shared a covenantal notion of marriage that shocked their neighbors because of its uniqueness.[6]

The United Church of Christ Statement of Faith reminds us that God "bestows upon us the Holy Spirit, creating and renewing the church of Jesus Christ, binding in covenant faithful people of all ages, tongues, and races."

The covenant is not static. It represents, rather, the sinews of common life of an active people in touch with an active God, with holy purposes for deepening common life and realizing a new order of justice, community, love, and human wholeness.

Covenant is a central motif in human relationships. The church begins with a new covenant in Christ's blood as bread is broken, wine is shared, promises are remembered, and hope is rekindled. Covenants are made between pastor, elders or deacons, and the congregation they serve, between fellow members of a congregation, and between members and parents in baptismal vows.

The United Church of Christ Order for Marriage identifies marriage as "a sacred and joyous covenant" through which husband and wife "give to each other companionship, help, and comfort both in prosperity and adversity." Walter Brueggemann describes the biblical notion of covenant as applied to the marriage relationship:

> A covenantal understanding of marriage affirms that the central issue in the relationship is not control or possession but *fidelity*: "The Lord was witness to the covenant between you and the wife of your youth, to whom you have been faithless, though she is your companion and your wife by covenant" (Malachi 2:14). The purpose of marriage is not primarily to secure property though that is a factor. Nor is it primarily to have children, though in the culture of the ancient world it is much desired. Nor is it pleasure in any primary way, though marriage is surely presented as pleasurable. . . . But rather than any of these emphases, marriage is for the exercise of faithfulness, for the enduring honoring of vows whereby every dimension of humanness is enhanced. Marriage is not based primarily on erotic or romantic feelings though they are not unrecognized, but on the readiness to take the covenant partner in abiding seriousness. "Love" thus is recharacterized in the Bible as *loyalty to promises made*.[7]

We need to enlarge the notion of covenant in our common life—members of the youth group covenanting with one another to serve common purposes; covenants to take common action; the congregation celebrating covenantally key passages of our lives and the commitments we make to one another.

So much cultural pressure is on the side of conformity to what is, to socialization to the status quo. But Christians are collaborators in a new creation. As covenant partners we are called to the creation of new possibilities in human relationship. A dynamic covenant sustains partners through myriad challenges to fidelity and creativity. A covenant people model out the meaning of mutuality.

A COMMUNITY OF LOVE
As we saw in Chapter 3, "Faith, Ethics, and Sexuality," the Christian experience of love has three dimensions: *eros*—sensual,

earthly delight celebrated in the Song of Songs; *philia*—the deep friendship of a Jonathan and David or a Jesus and Mary Magdalene, brotherly and sisterly love; *agápe*—the self-giving love characterized by empathy and the powerful images of 1 Corinthians 13. These dimensions of love are not zones or compartments of human experience but are blending components of our interaction with one another and with God. Love is the metaphor of divine self-giving.

There is mystery and gift in the notion of divine self-giving. In what ways is our sexuality expressive of the nature of God? How is it that words like communion, faithfulness, trust, beauty, passion, wonder, self-giving, ecstasy, and intimacy describe our experience with one we love as well as our response in faith to the holy God? The love of God and of neighbor and self (detailed in Chapter 3) is interdependent and interwoven. "See how these Christians love one another," was the compliment paid the early church. It is an ideal for all of us now.

Such loving is inclusive. God loves everyone and we are called to do the same. Love doesn't begin with categorizing persons by sexual orientation, age, or marital status. The Bible is a good model for us. In its pages we meet people in their full personhood and not as types or examples.

Such loving is directed toward the left-out, the one most in need. The Bible has a bias toward the poor, the victim, the excluded. The one wounded on the Jericho road is our neighbor. The one sheep lost is the special object of our caring. There are always those among us whose special needs cry out for attention: this one faces an unwanted pregnancy; another's marriage is on the skids; a third has deep anxieties about personal worth; another faces discrimination on the job because of gender or orientation. We are called to love each person as ourselves, as well as to learn to love those who are different from ourselves.

RITE AND SACRAMENT

We humans love a party. Something there is in us that wants to be in touch with the power of God and the presence of valued people to bless our special times of hope, of birth, of death, of tragedy, of moving on, of new relationship. We are a community of sacrament and celebration.

Common things—bread, wine, water, the touch of hands—become the means by which grace touches us. The central act of worship honors—no, shares—a body: broken, shared, and made whole. The common stuff, bread, nourishes us in body and faith. We bring our bodies to communion and we share Christ's body.

Similarly, in the new covenant we are in touch with blood, not merely juice—but blood. Christ died that others may live. Love is costly. The blood reminds us of the coursing, pulsating dynamic of life; of the pain of our distance and separation from one another; of the hurt we give and receive; of the ebb and flow of our bodies with life. Somehow our life forces are transformed into something holy.

Baptism puts us in touch with the body of Christ everywhere and through all time. Yet, it is about this tiny infant named by the community of faith, valued for his or her uniqueness, and dependent upon us—our faith, our caring, our presence. We remember how such a life begins. And the mystery of our womanhood and our manhood and our unity is celebrated.

Or the one who kneels there is a youth who faces life with its precariousness. So much life has gone before. He or she knows so much—so much more than we know he or she knows. It is an act of faith. "I believe, help my unbelief." It is an adult thing, this rite of passage.

Or the one who stands before the water awaiting the touch of anointing is an adult. It is a new passage. Some calling of a thousand forces sends us to this altar to share this act, to enter the dying and rising of the holy one.

In each case the community of faith participates, celebrates, stands by as those who care. Through the use of rite and celebration the church blesses stages and relationships, is an instrument of grace, and lifts up before neighbor and God the central meanings of human existence: marriage and loving; birth and new being; death and brokenness; confirmation and community; hope and resurrection.

Liturgy means literally "the work of the people." When it reaches its fullness, liturgy and life are interchangeable. Time after time the people gather in their uniqueness from their several places, seeking to be known and to know in that uniqueness. We yearn to bring the things that matter most to the gathered community and to the altar. We bring, too, the persons we are and the sexuality that is part of our personhood. We seek forgiveness and affirmation and promise.

The church is spoken of as the body of Christ, but often our life-style as a congregation seems to be sitting and listening to the choir or to the preacher. Yet, we call it corporate worship (in Latin the word means literally "to shape into a body"). So, let our liturgy be full of body. The choir embodies the words and the melody. The preacher embodies the Word in his or her personhood. From the Black experience let us develop the pattern of oral response to testimony and preaching. From the New England tradition let us stand for the reading of the scripture, the hearing of the word. Or, as is part of Christian practice in some places, let us sit with the palms of our hands upturned for the reading of the scripture, as a channel for the flowing of life: inward; outward. Let us move to the chancel to receive communion. Let us bring our offering to the place of dedication.

And there is the kiss of peace. Paul says it: "Greet one another with the kiss of peace." (See 1 Corinthians 16:20.) That admonition is thought to have come from a communion rite in the life of the early church—the kiss: the holy kiss. Perhaps if we knew better how to share holy kisses in the life of the community of faith, our world would have fewer unholy ones.

Rite and sacrament relate to stages and passages. John Westerhoff has been developing an approach to faith, education, life passage, and liturgy that is integrative. He speaks of *life crisis rites*: "My personal preference is: baptism for children at birth; first communion around first or second grade, a new "covenanting" ritual in early adolescence . . . ; ordination to Christian vocations (for all) in mid-adulthood . . . ; and last rites at death."[8]

Westerhoff speaks of such crisis rites as marriage, divorce, going away to school, a new home, a new job, retirement. But whether or not we agree with his specifics, his thesis is instructive. A *life crisis rite*, he suggests, has three related phases:

(1) a separation phase marked by a ceremonial withdrawal of persons from their previous status, role, or state in the community; (2) a transition phase which prepares persons, through ceremonial events, training, and often ordeals for their new status, role, or state in the community; and (3) a reentry phase which, by a ceremony, establishes persons in their new status, role, or state, and reincorporates them in the community.[9]

The marriage service is, of course, a central example of such a rite. Because it is a legal and civil act, the church is freed from carrying all the freight. It is not the keeper of the secular keys. People can be married legally without the church. So we are free to determine when and how we will celebrate commitments. This man and this woman are joined in *holy* wedlock because the central motif of their commitment is one of covenant between persons, with God and within the covenant community. The marital rite seems to reach to the foundations of human life, to the creation as male and female, to the becoming of one flesh, to the possibility of fidelity and the nurturing of love.

223

We know how to celebrate a marriage, and most weddings are joyous, good occasions in the life of the community of faith. Yet, we need to use our imaginations about ways to sustain marriage in the life of the community of faith. Counseling and marriage enrichment programs help. Rites to celebrate significant anniversaries can be important as well. Without excluding the nonmarried, the church can be the nurturing community through which vows of marital fidelity are celebrated and sustained. At the same time, there is another commitment that yearns for blessing: a couple cannot marry, for reasons they consider valid, and yet their commitment to each other is loving, long term, monogamous, covenantal. A gay couple enters into what they believe is a holy union. How shall the community of faith engage in corporate worship to value such persons, to honor their commitment, and to pray for their well-being? We need to learn from one another how to do this.

The United Methodist Church has developed a liturgy for divorced persons. Jeanne Audrey Powers, who prepared the service, says:

> At precisely the time when individuals are most lonely and need to establish links of communications with others, members of the Christian community know least how to respond, and the person is usually met with silence, embarrassment and whispered conversations that end abruptly when the person enters a room.
>
> Partly because it is assumed that the divorcing couple wish to keep their private affairs to themselves, partly because the breakdown of a marriage in a close circle of intimates is an immediate threat to those marriages which are still alive, partly because the church has too seldom known how to deal with sin except to pronounce judgment upon it . . . the church . . . has been excluded from offering the gift of Christian community to those who are most in need of it.[10]

THE CIVIL COVENANT

Standing with the oppressed; passionately seeking for justice in our common life; sharing visions of the meaning of community, fidelity, wholeness; acting to change sex-role stereotypes; opposing sexual violence; being Christians who love one another at work in the life of the world—this is us, the church, addressing issues of sexuality.

Our agenda is long, because life is complex and our life is

long. It may be fostering the kind of sex education that chapter 6, "Some Perspectives on Sex Education," envisions in the public school. It may involve putting pressure on local television stations to provide better programming that does not glorify violence, misuse sex, or exploit images of women. It may involve support of the victims of sexual violence both in preventive and in therapeutic ways.

Or it may involve supporting public officials who are willing to stick their necks out to eliminate discriminatory enforcement of statutes. Or it may involve providing alternative institutions. After all, for a long time it was clergy who provided an abortion counseling service to help women in need secure safe medical treatment. That form of civil disobedience honors these convictions: the belief in a will higher than the civil covenant, which must take precedence, the desire to transform the common life, and the calling to minister to persons in need.

Churches that care about the quality of life must learn to care about the quality of life in the public sector. Our calling is two-fold: to support those ventures, laws, and persons through which our fullest humanity is enhanced; to oppose those forces, laws, and structures that dehumanize and oppress. An ethics of sexuality involves serious attention to the common good.

CONGREGATIONAL LIFE-STYLE
We demonstrate our real views of sexuality in the life-style we forge together in our congregation. Inevitably, we deal with human beings who have had sexual dimensions all of their lives. We need to think carefully together about how best to nurture persons and to shape a faith community.

We must be intentional about it. For example, we might say something like this: "In this congregation we intend to deal with sexuality in specific ways. We will use diverse images about God. We will offer diverse role models. We will seek to deal with sexual development in both our education and counseling programs. We will make sustained efforts to prevent relational breakdown as well as to develop therapeutic ministries for those in trouble. We will seek to introduce persons in this congregation to men and women of faith who express diverse life-styles and who are committed to overcome the effects of sexism and racism. We will seek to address specific instances of sexual abuse, sexist practice, or sexual deprivation of handicapped persons in order to stand with victims and build a more humane society."

Being intentional involves trying to help people anticipate the critical situations they may meet in their own lives. Seminars about issues that may now seem only hypothetical may help people to face choices in birth control or in dealing with issues of physical violence, child-rearing, or marital discord.

Being intentional involves giving special attention to ways persons are or feel excluded from the life of the church. So much, exclusion comes subtly and implicitly rather than directly. No church would say that it wants to exclude single people or that it doesn't care about youth or that the needs of older adults are unimportant. Yet, persons often feel excluded. For example, a group of United Methodist single persons issued a "Singles Manifesto" in April 1976:

Singles call upon the church to be aware of the many single persons who are in the church and community, together with the varieties of singleness (never married, divorced, widowed) . . . and:

To recognize singleness as a legitimate life style and an acceptable status.

To affirm persons who are single through choice or circumstance by structuring church activities and programs to be inclusive rather than exclusive (not family or age oriented only).

To develop within the life of the church support structures uniquely designed to meet the needs of single persons and/ or one parent families.

To be aware that single persons need to FEEL and BE a part of the whole church's struggle to become a family.

To be aware that single persons are ready to share their gifts and talents as part of the total ministry of the church.

To recognize the injustice and inequities that single persons experience in economic, social, political areas of life and become involved as an agent of change. . . .

To develop a theology which deals with divorce as a fact of life and recognizes divorced persons and one-parent families resulting from divorce as acceptable persons who need love and support.

To become aware of cultural stereotypes which tend to assume marriage as the only acceptable life style.[11]

Being intentional involves watching our language. We have seen how our language about God can limit our perception about the fullness of God as well as our sense of worth. But the language in stained glass and in common discourse may discriminate or turn people off. A stained-glass window with a text like, "Except one be born again *he* cannot enter the kingdom . . ." may say to a young woman that she can't receive faith's benefits. If all the pictures in the parlor of past clergy are male, it will be hard for men as well as for women to understand that women have been ordained in the United Church of Christ tradition for nearly a century and a quarter.

Letty Russell reminds us of the relation of language and social patterns: "language and social structures are reciprocal in relationship. Language not only shapes given concepts of reality and ways of acting, it is also shaped by changes in concepts and social behavior."[12]

We probably can't change the stained-glass windows even if we thought it was a good idea, but much can be done with environment through the use of banners, paintings, sculpture, drama, and dance. This requires an intentionality: "we will deal with the meaning of sexuality. We will seek to compensate for the effects of racism and sexism."

For example, Michelangelo's "David" is a superb portrayal of the biblical character. It conveys the naturalness of the naked body—strong, yet gentle—and in its own way is an ode by the artist to the creator. Picasso's painting of a nursing child is a superb statement of nurture and communion between persons. Or one could use some of Kathe Kollwitz' remarkable portraits of women, which convey their strength, diversity, poignancy, and joy.

How long has it been since the Bible study in your church examined Song of Songs, the book of Ruth, or Genesis 2—3? These rich parts of our tradition help us to understand more fully our creation as male and female.

EDUCATION

Education in the church has two dimensions—the implicit and the explicit. We are often teaching when we don't know we're doing so, and we often teach what we don't intend. This is sometimes called "the hidden curriculum" and refers to the subtle ways in which meaning is conveyed. For example, a toy store window display shows people-at-work figures. The persons are both male and female, and their skin color represents varied racial backgrounds. However, the women are all portrayed in traditional roles: housewife in apron, nurse, stewardess. The implicit message is strong for both boys and girls, whose play shapes today's world and their image of tomorrow's possibility.

We usually refer to education as planned activity, explicit presentation of ideas and content. Even here, some of it is still subtle. If, for example, to teach sex education we bring into our church "experts," clear with parents everything that will be done, and put on a different emotional tone, we may have given unintended messages. We have conveyed the unnaturalness, difficulty, inaccessibility of sexuality to ordinary human beings.

Approaches to sex education, of course, need to be competently done. Chapter 6, which focuses on sex education, describes approaches in public education, many of which could be applied to family and church settings as well.

Peggy Way, who has been doing sexual counseling for fifteen years, wrote a memorandum as part of this sexuality study to share her experience. She emphasizes the importance of clergy being equipped for counseling situations they are likely to face. She is clear

> that ministries in the area of human sexuality demand an order of self-awareness and self-acceptance of one's own sexuality that is too seldom developed in theological education or ongoing education. I find this especially true in a permissive cultural scene, when the burden is sometimes placed upon the person who is *not* sexually active or has what has become to be thought of as "conservative" sexual preferences.[13]

The point is that one should be at ease with oneself and one's own choices in the area of sexuality. One can be most helpful to another in standing firm on one's own convictions based on experience. It is not necessary to know everything, to be able to be of help. Knowing one's limitations and when to refer counselees for more experienced help is a mark of mature helpfulness.

Eleanor Morrison, along with the Michigan Conference task force on sexuality, has been doing sex education with church groups for some time. She identifies some elements in her own experience under the rubric *"What I Have Learned in Working with Church People in the Area of Human Sexuality—some essential ingredients and design considerations that seem to help*

people get in touch with their own sexuality."[14] She describes
the ingredients:

—An atmosphere that allows people to be who they are and who
they have been without judgment—positive or negative—but
simply accepts their uniqueness and humanity.
—A group setting in which such stereotypical labeling as deviant,
abnormal, free, hung up, liberated, repressed, weird is off
limits in describing oneself or others.
—A learning situation that invites people to—
  • look carefully at their own past messages, fantasies, feelings,
    and experiences about human sexuality
  • listen reflectively to others' perceptions of their past
  • engage in activities (in a group atmosphere of the type de-
    scribed above) that encourage them to think directly about
    their present style of sexuality, with the opportunity to ex-
    press to others present attitudes, beliefs, and values that
    motivate their present behavior (without revealing the
    private behaviors), and to hear, in a nonjudgmental climate,
    viewpoints that coincide with or diverge from their own. (A
    recognition of the diversity within any given church group
    often comes as a surprise to many.)
  • review a range of options of attitude and be given permission
    to think seriously about each of them, without fear of
    ostracism, perversion, or immorality. (The theological im-
    portance of choices responsibly arrived at is an important
    resource here.)
  • express to others their fears, ambivalences, convictions, or
    delights in an exploratory manner that leaves them free to
    change but permits response from others
  • "speak the truth in love" about themselves and others,
    practicing some arts of two-way communication, which are at
    the heart of functional interpersonal sexuality
  • understand the difference between appropriate and inap-
    propriate self-disclosure and to make choices for themselves
    about maintaining their personal style of communication
    and the importance of privacy
  • interact with peers of both sexes (in a group small enough
    to allow individual "air time" but large enough to allow
    "freedom to pass") about a wide range of sexuality content,
    utilizing methods that permit people to be fully *themselves*,
    without roles or facades, experiencing themselves and others
    in fresh ways
  • reclaim an ethical and theological perspective that encom-

passes carnality, body pleasure, fantasies, and feelings as legitimate human experiences—and that enables people to move beyond specific sexual acts as inherently sinful or good to examine the relational dimensions that tend to exploit, alienate, and demean—or enhance, enliven, and refresh persons.

The opportunity to talk freely about matters long tabooed or restricted can be a liberating experience for many people. Such an opportunity needs to be provided with the minimal threat and maximal protection of people's fears, reticence, and hesitancy ("modeling" by leadership is especially important in this regard).

While specific courses and approaches to sex education are desirable, attention should be given to ways of dealing with sexuality in ongoing educational ventures, such as adult education groups, youth ministry, church school, and confirmation preparation. Let's take confirmation as an example.

The issues of sexuality bear on confirmation in several ways: First, youth who participate in confirmation programs and rites bring their sexuality with them. It's part of who they are and what they have been for a long time. Second, dealing with biblical and ethical material or with samples of human experience can shed light on the meanings of adolescent sexuality. Third, explicit content can help youth understand that the church is serious about affirming personhood and addressing tough social issues.

LEADERSHIP
Whatever the style, there is a reciprocity in leadership: those who lead and those who are led interact in interdependent ways. In a church situation we usually know one another well. We need to find comfortable, affirming ways to work and serve together that acknowledge our sexuality without being hurtful or invading another's privacy.

A congregation that seeks to express its concern about sexuality needs to give special thought to its pastor and his or her family. The pastor's sexual expression ought to be her or his own business save as trouble develops in that area for which help is sought or in the quite rare event of sexual misconduct. The pastoral ministry is a lonely vigil for many clergy and those they love. A caring church will be empathetic but liberating.

If the pastor is a single person his or her relationship with a congregation may be especially difficult. Often pastoral search committees reject out of hand candidates who are not married.

When a pastor's marital situation changes, the congregation often finds it difficult to accept and to be present in nurturing ways.

The ministry is a goldfish bowl. Parishioners want to be able to look up to their pastor as a moral example. At the same time, pastors are human beings with a full dose of sexuality. For some parishioners it is hard to relate to their pastor as a sexual being; for others, it is difficult *not* to do so. The healthy community of faith is one in which members are glad that God has made them male and female and find nurturing ways to be present to one another.

Since leadership is reciprocal, pastors should respect the integrity of their congregations and should take great care in their own sexual practices. They should seek to model a leadership style that affirms others but also respects their own uniqueness.

Studies show that clergy and doctors are the persons most frequently consulted in regard to sexual problems. Clergy and congregations should equip themselves to be effective in this area. A congregation can be a therapeutic community, accepting persons as lovable no matter what kind of trouble they're in or need they have.

Peggy Way's memo provides the wise comment that "the overarching context is the ministerial imperative that we have no choice but to prepare ourselves to work with all people and all possible situations, regardless of our positions on them!"[15]

The church, too, at all levels of its life needs to give sustained attention to the nature of church leadership in congregation and society and to its relationship to life-style, marital status, or sexual preference. We deal with covenants and callings. Those who will covenant together to walk in the Lord's ways are God's people—a mixture of saints and sinners.

Those whom we ordain are not finally "ours" to ordain. God calls to ministry. We share in that calling, honor it in another and in ourselves, and celebrate it in acts of ordination.

In the final analysis the church is both gift and the bearer of gift. All that we are, including our sexuality, is a gift of God. God loves the world in a way that is fleshly, loving, faithful—forever and ever. In Jesus we are participants in a new covenant of life, of hope, of love, of justice.

We as sexual creatures are created free to use the gifts of life and of sexuality in ways that ennoble and endear—or betray and demean. That freedom is a gift to have, to hold, to express, to share.

We as sexual creatures are made for relationship, for com-

Appendix:
United Church of Christ Background

The United Church of Christ, a denomination of almost two million members, was formed in 1957 by the union of the Congregational Christian Churches and the Evangelical and Reformed Church. The broadly representative governing body of the denomination is called the General Synod, which meets biennally. As noted in the preface, the 1975 synod called for such a study.

In 1975 the Tenth General Synod gave first priority status to Women in Church and Society. The report of the Task Force on Women in Church and Society, whose work during 1971-75 prepared the foundation for that priority, called for a study of human sexuality. That report said in part:

> When we do not affirm our embodiedness, we are afraid to know and value our own bodies and experience fear, shame and guilt about our being. This causes us to hide our feelings and to project them on others, often making the other a sex object. This objectifying of the other is an underlying factor in both racism and sexism. Until we clarify our attitudes regarding our sexuality, we tend to feel guilty about our sexual feelings and are often uncertain in our working relationships with persons of the opposite sex. Only when women and men come to terms with their sexuality can we stop relating to each other totally from a ground of unconscious sex, and treat each other as professional peers. This is particularly important in areas of the ministry where interaction between men and women often involves extremely personal, intimate sharing and interaction.
>
> We also need to understand the base from which we often project our fantasies on groups whom we believe do not reflect our sexual inhibitions. This has been instrumental in our stereotypes of woman as sex object and temptress, of minorities, particularly Blacks, as being overactive sexually, and also of the tendency of heterosexuals to project a greater degree of sexual activity and promiscuity on homosexuals than upon those engaged in heterosexual activity. Until we come to terms with our own sexuality our interactions with members of the same sex, the opposite sex, and other racial groups will be fraught with sexual stereotypes and unrealistic behavior expectations.

233

Other actions of previous synods have identified concerns for family life and for sexual ethics. The Fifth General Synod in 1965 expressed, through its Long Range Planning Committee, concerns for ethical issues in medical and scientific areas and for social ethics.

The Eighth General Synod (1971) adopted a position on "Freedom of Choice Concerning Abortion." The position statement began:

> Standing in the Hebrew-Christian tradition, we affirm God as the Source of life—our life, all life, life to the full. God has called us to share the work of creation . . . giving us the privileges and responsibilities of fellowship in the family and in the wider unities of society. Thus we affirm the freedom with which God endowed men and women, but we affirm and receive this as freedom bound to responsibility. At its best our Western legal tradition, too, has served the dual purpose of protecting human freedom and helping human beings to discharge their responsibilities to one another.

The 1971 synod committed itself to support a position of freedom of choice in abortion and called upon the United Church of Christ to develop programs of counseling, sex education, family planning, and leadership development to address issues of human sexuality. The Executive Council of the United Church of Christ took the following action in October 1973:

> The Executive Council, recognizing that Associations have final responsibility for ordination and standing and acknowledging that such responsibility must be exercised within the context of a clear understanding of the theology of ordination,
>
> A. Recommends that congregations, Associations and Conferences initiate programs of study and dialogue with regard to the implications (meanings) of human sexuality, in all its mystery, at its broadest and deepest levels in the theological context.
>
> B. Directs the Council for Church and Ministry and its successor body to continue its study of the relationship between ordination and human sexuality in consultation with congregations, Associations and Conferences for the purpose of developing resources for the study of human sexuality and developing a process for decision making that may be utilized by Associations in the matter of ordaining affirmed homosexuals.
>
> C. Recommends to Associations that as they continue to clarify their understanding of the theology of ordination they give serious consideration to the position of the Council for Church and Ministry in the matter of human sexuality: "In the instance of considering a stated homosexual's candidacy for ordination, the issue should not be his or her homosexuality as such, but rather, the candidate's total view of human sexuality and his or her understanding of the morality of its (expression)."

D. Directs the Council for Church and Ministry and its successor body to make progress reports and possible recommendations to the Executive Council during the present biennium.

The Ninth and Tenth synods faced issues related to particular expressions of sexuality by gay and bisexual persons, and the latter synod called for a comprehensive approach to "the dynamics of human sexuality." The 1975 synod, in a pronouncement (broad policy statement), affirmed the civil rights of gay persons and in related actions sought to provide counseling resources for persons of gay or bisexual orientation and for clergy counseling them. The text of the pronouncement is as follows:

The purpose of this pronouncement is to make a statement on civil liberties. It is not within the province of this pronouncement to make an ethical judgment about same-gender relationships. However, this pronouncement may well serve to further dialogue that will clarify the ethical issues involved in human sexuality.

There is, in the United States, a significant minority of persons whose civil liberties, and whose right to equal protection under the law, are systematically and routinely violated. Discrimination related to affectional or sexual preference in employment, housing, public accommodations, and other civil liberties, has inflicted an incalculable burden of fear into the lives of persons in society and in the church whose affectional or sexual preference is toward persons of the same gender.

Most directly affected are the 10% of the population whose affectional or sexual preference, according to the research of Alfred Kinsey, is predominantly toward persons of the same gender. Also affected is the one-third of the American population which Kinsey found to have had at one time or another an adult same-gender sexual experience. Public revelation of even a single experience often results in the presumption that a person is same-gender-oriented and thus subject to social sanctions including violations of her or his civil liberties. Even the civil liberties of persons whose affectional or sexual preference is a well-guarded secret are vulnerable. Inquiry by private investigatory agencies into the personal life of the individual is often a pre-requisite for employment. Draft records, insurance investigations, arrest records (even when charges have been dismissed or the defendant acquitted), and investigations instigated on the basis of anonymous accusation or rumor, all provide an employer, landlord, and other persons information used to justify discrimination.

Discrimination Causes Suffering

A constant fear of losing one's job and home, and the economic and social consequences of such a loss, creates suffering in human life.

Living as presumed heterosexuals, same-gender-oriented women and men, are intimidated into silence, forced into lives of duplicity and deception, by the hostility of the majority society. Such duplicity and deception, and their current alienation, sometimes evolving to isolation and depression and culminating in suicide, are necessarily detrimental to the growth of the individual and to the growth of interpersonal relationships. Today, same-gender-oriented persons, our sisters and brothers in human community and in Christian community, are struggling to free themselves from the fear which the reality of discrimination, particularly in employment and in housing, has inflicted upon them. Such persons are taking a moral stance against discrimination and the violence that it does to human dignity. They seek to secure protection for their full civil liberties and equal protection under the law. The church must bear a measure of responsibility for the suffering visited upon same-gender-oriented persons since often the traditional Judeo-Christian attitude toward same-gender relationship has been used as a primary justification for denial and violation of civil liberties and the perpetuation of discrimination against such persons.

The Religious Perspective

Christian love for God and our neighbor in God impels us to cherish the life and liberty of all women and men. We proclaim a unity under God which transcends our division, and find in Christ our measure for being human.

As Christians, we seek to personify the liberating Gospel of Jesus the Christ and to follow his example in our relationships with others. This means that we try to have love and respect for each other—for individual well-being, quality of life, personality, dignity, and self-actualisation.

The Christian churches have a long tradition of concern for human justice and civil liberties. From the days of the Hebrew prophets, we have been charged to pursue justice for all who are oppressed. In its most faithful moments the church has been recalled to the words of Amos: "I hate, I despise your feasts, and I take no delight in your solemn assemblies. . . . But let justice roll down like the waters, and righteousness like a mighty stream" (Amos 5:21, 24). Insofar as the church has been concerned for social justice, it also necessarily has been concerned for civil liberties. Historically, branches of the Protestant churches have been the most significant single influence in the rise of concern for basic civil rights in the Western world. The tradition of the United Church of Christ is a particularly rich heritage of such concern. First suffering the denial of liberty at the hands of both civil and ecclesiastical authorities in the Old World, our ancestors claimed these rights for themselves in the New World. Realizing that the rights of none were secure until the rights of all were secure, our ancestors-in-faith gradually extended their civil liberty concern to the whole of society.

In faithfulness to that biblical and historic mandate, we hold that, as a child of God, every person is endowed with worth and dignity that human judgment cannot set aside. Denial and violation of the civil liberties of the individual and her or his right to equal protection under the law defames that worth and dignity and is, therefore, morally wrong. Our Christian faith requires that we respond to the injustice in our society manifested in the denial and violation of the civil liberties of persons whose affectional or sexual preference is toward persons of the same gender.

Affirmation of Civil Liberties

Therefore, without considering in this document the rightness or wrongness of same-gender relationships, but recognizing that a person's affectional or sexual preference is not legitimate grounds on which to deny her or his civil liberties, the Tenth General Synod of the United Church of Christ proclaims the Christian conviction that all persons are entitled to full civil liberties and equal protection under the law.

Further, the Tenth General Synod declares its support for the enactment of legislation at the federal, state, and local levels of government that would guarantee the liberties of all persons without discrimination related to affectional or sexual preferences.

Further, the Tenth General Synod calls upon the congregations, Associations, Conferences, and Instrumentalities of the United Church of Christ to work for the enactment of such legislation at the federal, state, and local levels of government, and authorizes the Secretary of the United Church of Christ to commend this Pronouncement to the Conferences for distribution by them to their respective state legislators and representatives in the Congress of the United States.

The 1977 General Synod took the following action:
RESOLVED, That the 11th General Synod of the United Church of Christ:

1. Receives the report, "Human Sexuality: A Preliminary Study" with appreciation, and commends it to the congregations, associations, conferences, and instrumentalities of the United Church of Christ for study and response.
2. Reaffirms the present important ministries throughout the United Church of Christ and recommends the development of new liturgies, theology, and counseling services which enable the full participation and sharing of gifts of all persons: children, youth, older persons, nuclear families, those who live alone, or chose other lifestyles.
3. Calls upon the United Church Board for Homeland Ministries to continue to provide leadership in developing resources concerning human sexuality for appropriate use by various age groups in local churches and to provide consultative services and training for conferences, associations and congregations who wish

to sponsor programs concerned with human sexuality and family life.

4. Requests the UCC-related seminaries, conferences, and instrumentalities to continue developing courses and resources through which clergy, seminary students, and laity may be prepared to minister in the area of human sexuality and to address related public policy issues.

5. Urges pastors, members, congregations, conferences and instrumentalities to support programs in which information about human sexuality can be made available through such major American institutions as elementary and secondary education, adult education, social welfare agencies, medical services, and the communication media.

6. Encourages the congregations of the United Church of Christ, assisted by conferences and instrumentalities, to study and experiment with liturgical rites to celebrate important events and passages in human experience (transitions, anniversaries, separations, and reunions) and relationships of commitment between persons. The Office for Church Life and Leadership and the Board for Homeland Ministries are asked to facilitate the sharing of such liturgical experience.

7. Calls upon the Board for Homeland Ministries, the Commission for Racial Justice, the Office of Communication, and the conferences to develop and share model programs that can help local churches minister to and educate their communities about the components of sexual violence, including rape, marital violence, child abuse, abusive medical practices, and domination and submission images in the media of relationships between women and men portrayed as exclusive expressions of human interaction.

8. Calls upon pastors, congregations, conferences and instrumentalities to address, in their own programs and in those of public and private agencies, the concerns for sexuality and lifestyle of persons who have physical or emotional handicaps, or who are retarded, elderly, or terminally ill.

Because of its faithful ministry through care of the young, handicapped, retarded and aged, we urge the Council for Health and Welfare Services to encourage administrators and staff of member institutions to respect the needs for intimacy of adult persons served, and protect the right of sexual expression as important to self-worth, affirmation of life, and avoidance of isolation.

9. Urges the Board for Homeland Ministries, the Commission for Racial Justice, and the Office for Church in Society to work for the protection of persons threatened by coercive use of sterilization, medical treatment, experimental research, or the withholding of medical information, and to fully inform these persons of their rights under the law.

10. Calls upon pastors, members, congregations, conferences and in-
    strumentalities to encourage the extension of contraceptive in-
    formation and services by both public and private agencies for
    all youth and adults as instrumental to preventing undesirable
    pregnancies and fostering responsible family planning.

11. Affirms the right of women to freedom of choice with regard to
    pregnancy expressed by the Eighth General Synod and inter-
    preted as a constitutional right in the January 22, 1973 decisions
    of the Supreme Court which remove the legal restrictions on
    medical termination of pregnancy through the second trimester.
    Pastors, members, congregations, conferences, instrumentalities
    and agencies are urged to resist in local communities or in legisla-
    tive halls attempts to erode or negate the 1973 decisions of the
    court and to respect and protect the First Amendment rights to
    differences of opinion and freedom from intimidation concern-
    ing the issue of abortion.

    Deplores the June 20, 1977 decision of the US Supreme Court
    and recent actions of the US Congress that effactually deprive the
    poor of their Constitutional rights of choice to end or com-
    plete a pregnancy, while leaving the well-to-do in the full enjoy-
    ment of such rights.

    Calls upon UCC members, congregations, associations, con-
    ferences and instrumentalities to assure that publicly supported
    hospitals provide medical services to women within their usual
    service area to exercise their Constitutional right to end or
    complete pregnancies; and to petition their State legislatures
    and the US Congress to assure that poor will be provided with
    medical services to exercise their Constitutional rights to end or
    complete pregnancies.

12. Calls upon instrumentalities to address the economic structures
    which victimize women (and men) and explore such strategies
    as compensation for housework and child care, Social Security
    for homemakers, programs for displaced homemakers, insurance
    benefits for pregnancies, and quality day care.

13. Affirms the wide public attention being given to issues related to
    sexuality and sex roles, particularly as they affect women, but
    expresses concern regarding the need to explore such issues as
    they affect men. The 11th General Synod urges the Board for
    Homeland Ministries, the Office for Church Life and Leader-
    ship, conferences, associations, and congregations to develop
    programs which take into account the needs, experiences and
    viewpoints of both males and females, and which encourage
    further understanding of sexual identity; the effects of sex role
    stereotyping and present economic, legal, political and other
    societal conditions based upon gender.

14. Recommends to all instrumentalities, agencies, conferences,
    associations, and congregations that language they use reflect
    both feminine and masculine metaphor about God, and draw

upon the diverse metaphor of God represented in the Bible, in the Christian tradition and in contemporary experience.

15. Recognizes that diversity exists within the UCC about the meaning of ordination, the criteria for effective ministry, and the relevance of marital status, affectional or sexual preference or lifestyle to ordination and performance of ministry. It requests the congregations, associations, and conferences to address these issues seeking more full and common understanding of their implications.

   It requests the Office for Church Life and Leadership to develop resources to facilitate such understanding.

16. Urges congregations, associations, conferences, and instrumentalities to work for the decriminalization of private sexual acts between consenting adults.

17. Urges that States legislatively recognize that traditional marriage is not the only stable living unit which is entitled to legal protection in regards to socio-economic rights and responsibilities.

18. Deplores and condemns the dehumanizing portrayals of women and men, the abuse of children, and the exploitation of sex in printed and electronic media of communication, recognizes the rights of adults to access to sexually explicit materials, and affirms that efforts toward change must recognize First Amendment principles.

A segment of synod delegates who had voted against the eighteen recommendations submitted the following minority statement:

Whereas 34% of the delegates to the Eleventh General Synod voted negatively on "Recommendations in Regard To Human Sexuality Study"; and

Whereas "Human Sexuality: A Preliminary Study," the foundation for these Recommendations, was preliminary in nature; and

Whereas the Executive Council sent the Study to the Eleventh General Synod without recommendation, and sent it to delegates too late for sufficient time for study; and

Whereas we feel it is important that local churches have opportunity to examine, discuss, and respond to the Study; and

Whereas it appears there is a limited theological, biblical, and ethical viewpoint reflected in the Study which does not characterize the diverse perspectives of the United Church of Christ; and

Whereas there is a diversity of sociological and psychological perspectives not reflected in the Study; and

Whereas we appreciate the opportunity to engage in significant theological and ethical discussion; and appreciate the work done by those involved in preparing the Study to open this dialogue;

Therefore be it resolved that:

   (1) We call upon the local churches, Associations, and Conferences of the United Church of Christ to examine and discuss

the Study and, prior to the Twelfth General Synod, respond to the Study through their Conference structures;

(2) We call upon the local churches, Associations, and Conferences to seek study materials on the subject reflecting biblical, theological, and ethical perspectives not reflected in the Study;

(3) The minority resolution be included in the study guide prepared by the United Church Board For Homeland Ministries and wherever the eighteen recommendations of the Eleventh General Synod are reported.

In another action the 1977 synod voted:

Whereas, gay and bisexual persons have become victims of violence, including murder, allegedly as a result of fanatical prejudice kindled recently by those who publicly espouse and exploit irrational fear; and

Whereas, the recent referendum in Dade County, Florida, represents a new reactionary movement which may eventually erode the civil liberties of all; and

Whereas, the United Church of Christ in its heritage and in its theology has a commitment to compassion for, and liberation of, oppressed minorities.

Resolved, that this Eleventh General Synod:

1. Reaffirms the action of the 10th General Synod in its Pronouncement on Civil Liberties Without Discrimination Relating to Sexual or Affectional Preference;

2. Deplores the use of scripture to generate hatred, and the violation of civil rights of gay and bisexual persons; and

3. Calls upon individual members, local churches, associations, conferences and instrumentalities to continue to work for the enactment of civil rights legislation at the federal, state and local levels of government.

The Executive Council of the United Church of Christ on July 7, 1977 acted as follows:

WHEREAS the Eleventh General Synod of the United Church of Christ meeting in Washington, D.C. on July 1-5, 1977, specifically identified the need for continued, thoughtful and faithful study of all aspects of human sexuality as a shared concern of all delegates to the General Synod by adopting both a majority action and a minority resolution on "Recommendations in regard to Human Sexuality," and

WHEREAS both such actions of General Synod "shall be utilized in the same manner" as required by the General Synod Standing Rules, and

WHEREAS the General Synod specifically identified "HUMAN SEXUALITY: A Preliminary Study" as a needed resource in that continuing study which we hope will be constructive,

THEREFORE, the Executive Council commits itself to utilize

241

"HUMAN SEXUALITY: A Preliminary Study" in addressing this issue and urges local churches and other gatherings of faithful people to use it for study and response as we continue to grow as a people. The Executive Council commends the United Church Board for Homeland Ministries and the Study Team for their hard work in preparing a report which breaks new ground as it seeks to address a profound human issue from a biblical perspective.

Notes

TOWARD A DEFINITION OF SEXUALITY

1. Eleanor S. Morrison and Vera Borosage, eds., *Human Sexuality: Contemporary Perspectives* (Palo Alto, Calif.: Mayfield Publishing Co., 1973), pp. ixf.

2. The Boston Women's Health Collective, *Our Bodies, Ourselves* (Rev. ed.; New York: Simon & Schuster, 1976), p. 38.

CHAPTER 1: A COLLAGE— SOME FACTS AND PERSPECTIVES

1. Yoshio Fukuyama, "The Church, the Family, and the Sexual Revolution." Unpublished paper, January 1977.

2. Edmund S. Morgan, ed., *The Puritan Family: Religion and Domestic Relations in Seventeenth-Century New England* (New York: Harper & Row, 1966).

3. Yoshio Fukuyama, "A Sociological Perspective on the Church and Human Sexuality." Unpublished paper, February 1977.

4. Robert J. and Amy Levin, "Sexual Pleasure: The Surprising Preference of 100,000 Women," *Redbook*, September 1975, p. 52.

5. There were no regulations regarding abortion or birth control until well into the nineteenth century. In fact, abortion on request and the dissemination of contraceptive and abortion-related knowledge were legal until the passage of the Comstock laws in 1872.

6. Terri Schulz, "Though Legal, Abortions Are Not Always Available," *The New York Times*, "News of the Week in Review," July 2, 1977. Copyright © 1977 by The New York Times Company. Reprinted by permission.

7. Ibid.

8. *Education and Treatment in Human Sexuality: The Training of Health Professionals*, WHO Technical Report Series, No. 572 (Geneva: World Health Organization, 1975), p. 6. Used by permission.

9. Daniel Callahan, *11 Million Teenagers: What Can Be Done About the Epidemic of Adolescent Pregnancies in the United States*, (New York: Alan Guttmacher Institute, 1976), p. 17.

10. Quoted with permission from ibid.

11. Yoshio Fukuyama, "Religion and Sexuality: A Sociological Perspective." Unpublished paper, July 1976, p. 7.

12. Marvin B. Sussman, "Family Sociology," in *Current Research in Sociology*, ed. Margaret S. Archer (The Hague: Mouton, 1974).

13. These data are gathered as part of the Area Mission Strategy research project of the United Church Board for Homeland Ministries through the Church Membership Inventory. Participating conferences are Central Atlantic, Florida, Illinois, Kansas-Oklahoma, Massachusetts, Minnesota, Nebraska, Ohio, Penn Central, and South Central.

14. Robert Staples, "Research on Black Sexuality: Its Implications for Family Life, Sex Education and Public Policy," *The Family Coordinator*, April 1972.

15. Robert Staples, "Human Sexuality: The Minority Perspective." Unpublished paper, January 1977, p. 2.

16. Harold Jow, Report of the PAAM Commission on Human Sexuality, February 19, 1977.

17. Yoshio Fukuyama, "A Memorandum on Asian Americans and Human Sexuality." Unpublished paper, January 1977, p. 2.

18. Samuel Acosta, Convocation Report, April 1977, translated from Spanish.

CHAPTER 2: BIBLICAL FOUNDATIONS

1. Quoted by T. H. L. Parker in *Karl Barth* (Grand Rapids, Mich.: William B. Eerdmans, 1970), p. 25.

2. Phyllis Bird, "Images of Women in the Old Testament," *Religion and Sexism,* ed. Rosemary Radford Ruether (New York: Simon & Schuster, 1974), p. 46. Copyright © 1974 by Rosemary Radford Ruether. Used by permission of Simon & Schuster, Inc. The material in the following sections on the legal codes, wisdom literature, historical writings, as well as the summary at the end, is heavily dependent upon this article.

3. Ibid., pp. 60f.

4. Ibid., pp. 64f.

5. Ibid., p. 46.

6. Ibid., p. 71.

7. Phyllis Trible, "Depatriarchalizing in Biblical Interpretation," *Journal of the American Academy of Religion*, Vol. 41 (1973), p. 31. The material in the following section on human images of Yahweh follows closely this article.

8. The following exegesis of the book of Ruth is largely a condensation of an article by Phyllis Trible, "Two Women in a Man's World," *Soundings*, Fall 1976, pp. 251-79.

9. The following exegesis of the Jeremiah passages follows closely an article by William L. Holladay, "Jeremiah and Women's Liberation," *Andover Newton Quarterly*, Vol. 12, No. 4 (March 1972), pp. 213-23.

10. See ibid., p. 219.

11. See *inter alia*, Kate Millett, *Sexual Politics* (New York: Doubleday, 1970), pp. 51-54; Eva Figes, *Patriarchal Attitudes* (Greenwich, Conn.: Fawcett, 1970), pp. 38f; Mary Daly, "The Courage to See," *The Christian*

Century, September 22, 1971, p. 1110; Sheila D. Collins, "Toward a Feminist Theology," *The Christian Century,* August 2, 1972, p. 798; Lilly Rivlin, "Lilith: The First Woman," *Ms.,* December 1972, pp. 93, 114.

12. The following section is a reprint of an article by Phyllis Trible, "Eve and Adam: Genesis 2—3 Reread," *Andover Newton Quarterly,* Vol. 13, No. 4 (March 1973), pp. 251-58. Used by permission.

13. Cf. E. Jacob, *Theology of the Old Testament* (New York: Harper & Bros., 1958), pp. 172f; S. H. Hooke, "Genesis," *Peake's Commentary on the Bible* (London: Thomas Nelson, 1962), p. 179.

14. E.g., Elizabeth Cady Stanton observed that Genesis 1:26-28 "dignifies woman as an important factor in the creation, equal in power and glory with man," while Genesis 2 "makes her a mere afterthought" (*The Woman's Bible,* Part I [New York: European Publishing Company, 1895], p. 20). See also Elsie Adams and Mary Louise Briscoe, *Up Against the Wall, Mother . . .* (Beverly Hills: Glencoe Press, 1971), p. 4.

15. Cf. Eugene H. Maly, "Genesis," *The Jerome Biblical Commentary* (Englewood Cliffs, N.J.: Prentice Hall, 1968), p. 12: "But woman's existence, psychologically and in the social order, is dependent on man."

16. See John L. McKenzie, "The Literary Characteristics of Gen. 2—3," *Theological Studies,* Vol. 15 (1954), p. 559; John A. Bailey, "Initiation and the Primal Woman in Gilgamesh and Genesis 2—3," *Journal of Biblical Literature,* June 1970, p. 143. Bailey writes emphatically of the remarkable importance and position of the woman in Genesis 2—3, "all the more extraordinary when one realizes that this is the only account of the creation of woman as such in ancient Near Eastern literature." He hedges, however, in seeing the themes of helper and naming (Genesis 2:18-23) as indicative of a "certain subordination" of woman to man. These reservations are unnecessary; see below. Cf. also Claus Westermann, *Genesis, Biblischer Kommentar* 1/4 (Neukerchener-Vluyn: Newkirchener Verlag, 1970), p. 312.

17. James Muilenburg, "Form Criticism and Beyond," *Journal of Biblical Literature,* March 1969, pp. 9f; Mitchell Dahood, "Psalm I," *The Anchor Bible* (New York: Doubleday, 1966), *passim* and esp. p. 5.

18. See 1 Chronicles 4:4; 12:9; Nehemiah 3:19.

19. See Psalm 121:2; 124:8; 146:5; 33:20; 115:9-11; Exodus 18:4; Deuteronomy 33:7, 26, 29.

20. L. Koehler and W. Baumgartner, *Lexicon in Veteris Testamenti Libros* (Leiden: E. J. Brill, 1958), pp. 591f.

21. The verb *bnh* (to build) suggests considerable labor. It is used of towns, towers, altars, and fortifications, as well as of the primeval woman (Koehler-Baumgartner, op. cit., p. 134). In Genesis 2:22 it may mean the fashioning of clay around the rib (Ruth Amiran, "Myths of the Creation of Man and the Jericho Statues," *BASOR,* No. 167 (October 1962), p. 24.

22. See Walter Brueggemann, "Of the Same Flesh and Bone (Gen. 2:23a)," *Catholic Biblical Quarterly,* October 1970, pp. 532-42.

23. In proposing as primary an androgynous interpretation of *'adham,*

I find virtually no support from (male) biblical scholars. But my view stands as documented from the text, and I take refuge among a remnant of ancient (male) rabbis (see George Foot Moore, *Judaism* [Cambridge, Mass.: Harvard University Press, 1927]), I, 453; also Joseph Campbell, *The Hero with a Thousand Faces* (Meridian Books, The World Publishing Company, 1970), pp. 152ff., 279f.

24. See e.g., G. von Rad, *Genesis* (Philadelphia: Westminster Press, 1961), pp. 80-82; John H. Marks, "Genesis," *The Interpreter's One-Volume Commentary on the Bible* (Nashville: Abingdon Press, 1971), p. 5; Bailey, op. cit., p. 143.

25. Cf. Westermann, op. cit., pp. 316ff.

26. Verse 24 probably mirrors a matriarchal society (so von Rad, op. cit., p. 83). If the myth were designed to support patriarchy, it is difficult to explain how this verse survived without proper alteration. Westermann contends, however, that an emphasis on matriarchy misunderstands the point of the verse, which is the total communion of woman and man (ibid., p. 317).

27. U. Cassuto, *A Commentary on the Book of Genesis*, Part I (Jerusalem: Magnes Press, n.d.), pp. 142f.

28. Von Rad, op. cit., pp. 87f.

29. Ricoeur departs from the traditional interpretation of the woman when he writes: *"Eve n'est donc pas la femme en tant que 'deuxieme sexe'; toute femme et tout homme sont Adam; tout homme et toute sont Eve."* But the fourth clause of his sentence obscures this complete identity of Adam and Eve: *"toute femme peche 'en Adam, tout homme est seduit 'en Eve."* By switching from an active to a passive verb, Ricoeur makes only the woman directly responsible for both sinning and seducing. (Paul Ricoeur, Finitude et Culpabilite, II. *La Symbolique du Mal*, Aubier, Editions Montaigne [Paris: 1960]. Cf. Paul Ricoeur, *The Symbolism of Evil* [Boston: Beacon Press, 1969], p. 255).

30. McKenzie, op. cit., p. 570.

31. See Bailey, op. cit., p. 148.

32. See Westermann, op. cit., p. 340.

33. For a discussion of the serpent, see Ricoeur, *The Symbolism of Evil*, op. cit., pp. 255-60.

34. Cf. Edwin M. Good, *Irony in the Old Testament* (Philadelphia: Westminster Press, 1965), p. 84, note 4: "Is it not surprising that, in a culture where the subordination of woman to man was a virtually unquestioned social principle, the etiology of the subordination should be in the context of man's primal sin? Perhaps woman's subordination was not unquestioned in Israel." Cf. also Henricus Renckens, *Israel's Concept of the Beginning* (New York: Herder & Herder, 1964), pp. 127f.

35. *Contra* Westermann, op. cit., p. 357.

36. Von Rad, op. cit., pp. 94, 148.

37. The exegesis of the Song of Songs closely follows the article by Phyllis Trible, "Depatriarchalizing in Biblical Interpretation," *Journal of the American Academy of Religion*, Vol. 41 (1973), pp. 42–47.

38. Ibid., p. 44.

39. John J. McNeill, *The Church and the Homosexual* (Mission, Kans.: Sheed Andrews & McMeel, 1976), p. 50. The exegesis of the Sodom and Gomorrah story in this report depends largely on the research done by McNeill and was found by the Sexuality Study team to have considerable merit as a challenge to the traditional interpretation of that portion of scripture.

40. For a sensitive treatment of this difficult and important subject, see R. Lofton Hudson, *'Til Divorce Do Us Part* (New York: Thomas Nelson, 1974).

41. Guenther Bornkamm, *Paul* (New York: Harper & Row, 1971), p. 111. In this statement and in the context in which it appears, Bornkamm represents the findings and views of many modern scholars; cf. also Victor P. Furnish, *Theology and Ethics in Paul* (Nashville, Tenn.: Abingdon Press, 1968), especially pp. 113–35.

42. Robbin Scroggs, "Paul and the Eschatological Woman," *Journal of the American Academy of Religion*, Vol. 40 (September 1972), pp. 283–303, recovers the apocalyptic and eschatological view of Paul and relates it to the contemporary work of Brown and Marcuse.

43. Ibid. See also the more popular treatment of the same subject "Paul: Chauvinist or Liberationist?" *The Christian Century*, Vol. 89 (1972), pp. 307–9, and his further discussion of the subject "Paul and the Eschatological Woman: Revisited," *Journal of the American Academy of Religion*, Vol. 42 (September 1974), pp. 532–37.

44. Elaine H. Pagels, "Paul and Women: A Response to Recent Discussion," *Journal of the American Academy of Religion*, Vol. 42 (September 1974), pp. 538–49.

45. Ibid., p. 547.

46. For a sensitive and accurate treatment of this subject, see McNeill, *The Church and the Homosexual*, op. cit. Compare also W. Norman Pittenger, *Time for Consent* (London: SCM Press, 1970).

47. For an example of the role of critical theology from a particular viewpoint, see Elizabeth S. Fiorenza, "Feminist Theology as a Critical Theology of Liberation," *Theological Studies,* Vol. 36 (December 1975), pp. 605–26.

48. In one dimension of its "canon within the canon," the Western Protestant churches have emphasized a "sin and grace" motif at the expense of other facets of the gospel that need a renewed emphasis. In this connection see Krister Stendahl, "The Apostle Paul and the Introspective Conscience of the West," *The Writings of St. Paul,* ed. Wayne A. Meeks (New York: W. W. Norton, 1972), pp. 422–34.

49. Some guidelines for the meaning of covenantal community as applied to family life are found in an article by Walter Brueggemann, "The Covenanted Family: A Zone for Humanness," *Journal of Current Social Issues*, Winter 1977.

CHAPTER 4: PSYCHOSEXUAL DEVELOPMENT

1. Herant A. Katchadourian and Donald T. Lunde, *Fundamentals of Human Sexuality* (New York: Holt, Rinehart & Winston, 1972), p. 173.

2. Helen S. Kaplan, *The New Sex Therapy: Active Treatment of Sexual Dysfunctions* (New York: Brunner-Mazel, 1974), p. 2.

3. John H. Gagnon and William Simon, *Sexual Conduct: The Social Sources of Human Sexuality* (Chicago: Aldine Publishing Co., 1973), p. 127. Used by permission.

4. A.C. Kinsey, W.B. Pomeroy, and C.R. Martin, *Sexual Behavior in the Human Male* (Philadelphia: W.B. Saunders Co., 1948), p. vii.

5. Sigmund Freud, *The Basic Writings of Sigmund Freud* (New York: Modern Library, 1965), p. 583.

6. Ibid., p. 597.

7. Anne P. Copeland, "Attitudes Towards Sex-Role Socialization in Mentally Retarded Children." Excerpts from an unpublished masters thesis, p. 3. American University, Department of Psychology.

8. Gagnon and Simon, op. cit., p. 9.

9. Ibid., p. 20.

10. Joseph H. Pleck, "The Psychology of Sex Roles: Traditional and New Views," in Libby A. Cater and Anne F. Scott, eds., *Women and Men: Changing Roles, Relationships, and Perceptions* (Palo Alto, Calif.: Aspen Institute for Humanistic Studies, 1976), pp. 183f. Used by permission of The Aspen Institute and Mrs. Libby Cater.

11. Ibid., p. 184.

12. Ibid., p. 185.

13. Marcia Millman, "Observations on Sex Role Research," *Journal of Marriage and the Family*, November 1971, p. 772. Copyright 1971 by the National Council on Family Relations. Reprinted by permission.

14. Ibid., pp. 772f.

15. Ibid., p. 773.

16. Pleck, op. cit., p. 186.

17. Eleanor S. Morrison, "Psychosexual Development: An Outline of Some Major Considerations." Unpublished paper, January 1977, p. 8.

18. John Money and Anke Ehrhardt, *Man and Woman, Boy and Girl* (Baltimore: Johns Hopkins Press, 1973), pp. 2f.

19. Morrison, op. cit., p. 11.

20. Pleck, op. cit., p. 190.

21. James Harrison, "A Critical Evaluation of Research on Masculinity/Femininity and a Proposal for an Alternative Paradigm for Research on Psychological Differences and Similarities Between the Sexes." Unpublished doctoral thesis for the Department of Psychology, New York University, 1975, p. 216. Used by permission of the author.

22. Ibid., pp. 223, 226.

23. Ibid., p. 229.

24. Pleck, op. cit., pp. 187f.

25. Eleanor E. Maccoby and Carol N. Jacklin, "What We Know and Don't Know About Sex Differences," *Psychology Today*, December 1974.

26. Lisa A. Serbin and K. Daniel O'Leary, "How Nursery Schools Teach Girls to Shut Up," *Psychology Today*, December 1975, p. 57.

27. Ibid., p. 58.

28. Ibid., p. 102.

29. I.K. Broverman, D.M. Broverman, F.E. Clarkson, P.S. Rosenkrantz, and S.R. Vogel, "Sex Role Stereotypes and Clinical Judgments of Mental Health," *Journal of Consulting and Clinical Psychology*, Vol. 34 (1970), pp. 6f. Copyright 1970 by the American Psychological Association. Reprinted by permission.

30. Philip Goldberg, "Are Women Prejudiced Against Women?" *Transition*, Vol. 5 (1968), p. 30.

31. Sandra Lipsitz Bem, "Androgyny vs. the Tight Little Lives of Fluffy Women and Chesty Men," *Psychology Today*, September 1975, p. 60. Used by permission.

32. Ibid.

33. Pleck, op. cit., pp. 191f.

34. Bem, op. cit., p. 62.

35. Pleck, op. cit., p. 195.

36. Edmund Bergler, *Homosexuality: Disease or Way of Life?* (New York: Collier, 1956), pp. 1–10.

37. Judd Marmur, "Homosexuality" in *Sexuality and Human Values*, ed. Mary S. Calderone (New York: Association Press, 1975), p. 32.

38. Elizabeth Ogg, "Homosexuality in Our Society," *Public Affairs Pamphlet No. 484* (Public Affairs Committee, Inc., 1972), p. 7.

39. Mark Freedman, "Homosexuals May Be Healthier Than Straights," *Psychology Today*, March 1975, p. 30.

40. Wainwright Churchill, *Homosexual Behavior Among Males* (New York: Hawthorne, 1967), p. 105.

41. Freedman, op. cit., p. 30.

CHAPTER 5: SEXUALITY AND PUBLIC POLICY— AN OVERVIEW

1. John Stuart Mill, *On Liberty* (New York: Macmillan, 1926), chap.1.

2. Patrick Devlin, *The Enforcement of Morals* (London: Oxford University Press, 1965), pp. 9, 11.

3. 405 U.S. 438 (1972).

4. 410 U.S. 113 (1973).

5. Christopher Tietze and Sara Lewit, "Legal Abortion," *Scientific American*, Vol. 236 (January 1977), p. 21.

6. Norman Bernstein and Caroline Tinkham, "Group Therapy Following Abortion," *Journal of Nervous and Mental Illness*, Vol. 152 (May 1971), pp. 303-15.

7. Theodore Lidz, *The Person: His and Her Development Through the Life Cycle* (New York: Basic Books, 1968), p. 350.

8. Barbara Ehrenreich and Deirdre English, *Complaints and Disorders: The Sexual Politics of Sickness* (Old Westbury N.Y.: Feminist Press, 1974), p. 84.

9. *Relf v. Weinberger*, 372 F. Supp. 1196 (1974).

10. Cedric W. Porter, Jr. and Jaroslav F. Hulka, "Female Sterilization in Current Clinical Practice," *Family Planning Perspectives*, Vol. 6 (Winter 1974), p. 37.

11. 274 U.S. 200 (1927).

12. Les Payne, "Sterilization: Abuses by Doctors, Neglect by the U.S.," *Newsday* (n.d., 1974), p. 15A.

13. William J. Bremner and David M. DeKretser, "The Prospects for New, Reversible Male Contraceptives," *New England Journal of Medicine*, Vol. 295 (November 11, 1976), p. 1111.

14. Gail Sheehy, *Hustling* (New York: Dell Publishing Co., 1974), p. 12.

15. 413 U.S. 15 (1973).

16. David A. J. Richard, "Free Speech and Obscenity Law: Toward a Moral Theory of the First Amendment," *University of Pennsylvania Law Review*, Vol. 123 (1974), p. 63.

17. Al Katz, "Free Discussion v. Final Decision: Moral and Artistic Content and the 'Tropic of Cancer' Trials," *Yale Law Journal*, Vol. 209 (1970), p. 216.

18. Michael Goldstein and Harold Kant, with John J. Hartman, *Pornography and Social Deviance* (Berkeley: University of California Press, 1973), p. 146.

19. From *Censorship: For and Against*, ed. Harold H. Hart, copyright 1971 Hart Publishing Company, Inc., p. 91. Used by permission.

20. James Phillips, "Crackdown on Porn," *Newsweek*, Vol. 89 (February 28, 1977), p. 21.

21. *Paris Adult Theatre 1 v. Slaton*, 413 U.S. 49, 63 (1973).

22. Massey, "A Marketing Analysis of Sex-Oriented Materials," *Technical Report of the Commission on Obscenity and Pornography*, Vol. 4, p. 55.

23. Del Martin, *Battered Wives* (San Francisco: Glide Publications, 1976), p. 12.

24. Morton Bard and Katharine Ellison, "Crisis Intervention and Investigation of Forcible Rape," *The Police Chief*, May 1974, pp. 68-74. Used by permission.

25. Memorandum from Donna Schaper, January 1977.

26. Ibid.

27. "Really Socking It to Women," *Time*, February 7, 1977.

28. Molly Haskell, "Rape Fantasy: The 2,000-year-old Misunderstanding," *Ms.*, November 1976.

29. Lisa Brodyagar, Margaret Gates, Susan Singer, Marna Tucker, Richardson White, *Rape and Its Victims: A Report for Citizens, Health Facilities and Criminal Justice Agencies*, National Institute of Law Enforcement Assistance Administration, U.S. Department of Justice, November 1975, p. vii. Used by permission.

30. Ibid.

31. Ibid., p. xi.

32. Brief *Amici Curiae*, in the Supreme Court of the United States, October Term, 1975, No. 75-5444, p. 6.

33. Ibid., p. 11.

34. Martin, op. cit., p. 176.

35. Ibid., p. 11; based on Letty Cottin Pogrebin, "Do Women Make Men Violent," *Ms.*, November 1974, p. 55.

36. Ibid., p. 11; based on Raymond Parnas, "The Police Response to Domestic Disturbances," *Wisconsin Law Review* (1967), p. 914, n. 2.

37. Ibid., p. 11; based on Raymond Parnas, "Police Discretion and Diversion of Incidents of Intra-Family Violence," *Law and Contemporary Problems*, Vol. 36, No. 4 (Autumn 1971), p. 54, n. 1.

38. Ibid., p. 11; based on Northeast Patrol Division Task Force, Kansas City Police Department, "Conflict Management: Analysis/ Resolution." Taken from first draft, p. 58.

39. Ibid., p. 11; based on Commander James D. Bannon, from a speech delivered before a conference of the American Bar Association in Montreal, 1975.

40. Ibid., p. 11; based on J.C. Barden, "Wife Beaters: Few of Them Ever Appear Before a Court of Law," *The New York Times*, October 21, 1974, Sec. 2, p. 38.

41. Ibid., p. 12; based on Laura White, "Women Organize to Protect Wives from Abusive Husbands," *Boston Herald-American*, Sunday edition, June (22 or 29), 1975.

42. Ibid., p. 12; based on Betsy Warrior, "Battered Lives," *Houseworker's Handbook*, Spring 1975, p. 25.

43. Ibid., p. 12; based on Warrior, op. cit., p. 25.

44. Ibid., p. 12; based on Lois Yankowski, "Battered Women: A Study of the Situation in the District of Columbia." Unpublished (1975), pp. 2-3.

45. Ibid., pp. 12-13; based on Sue Eisenberg and Patricia Micklow, "The Assaulted Wife: 'Catch 22' Revisited." Unpublished, University of Michigan, Ann Arbor, 1974, p. 18.

46. Ibid., p. 13; based on Morton Bard, *Training Police as Specialists in Family Crisis Intervention* (Washington: U.S. Government Printing Office, 1970), p. 1.

47. Ibid., p. 13; based on Barden, op. cit., p. 38.

48. Ibid., p. 13; based on Yankowski, op. cit., p. 3.

49. Ibid., p. 13; based on Eisenberg and Micklow, op. cit., p. 16.

50. Ibid., p. 13; based on Montgomery County Council, Maryland, "A Report by the Task Force to Study a Haven for Physically Abused Persons" (1975), p. 17.

51. Ibid., p. 13.

52. Ibid., p. 19; based on Joyce Brothers, "A Quiz on Crime," *San Francisco Sunday Examiner and Chronicle*, June 22, 1975, Sunday Scene, p. 6.

53. Ibid., based on Bill Peterson, "System Frustrates Battered Wives," *Washington Post*, November 2, 1974, p. 18.

54. Memorandum from Beverly Wildung Harrison, January 1977.

55. William H. Masters and Virginia E. Johnson, *Human Sexual Inadequacy* (Boston: Little, Brown & Co., 1970), p. 11.

56. Beverly Harrison, op. cit.

57. Goldstein and Kant, op. cit., p. 149.

58. B.M. Gudridge, "Sex Education in Schools," *Technical Report of the Commission on Obscenity and Pornography*, Vol. 5, p. 29.

59. Quoted with permission from Daniel Callahan, *11 Million Teenagers: What Can Be done About the Epidemic of Adolescent Pregnancies in the United States*, published by The Alan Guttmacher Institute, New York, 1976, pp. 57f.

60. *Carey v. Population Services International*, No. 75-443 (June 9, 1977).

61. Callahan, op. cit., p. 45.

62. Ibid., p. 58.

63. C. Henry Kempe and Ray E. Helfer, eds., *Helping the Battered Child and His Family* (Philadelphia: J.B. Lippincott Co., 1972), p. xiii.

64. *Human Sexuality* (Chicago: American Medical Association, 1972), p. 135.

65. Alex Comfort, "Sexuality and Aging," quoted by permission from the *SIECUS Report*, Vol. 4, No. 6, July 1976. Copyright © Sex Information and Education Council of the U.S., Inc. Hempstead, N.Y.

66. Judith Wax, "It's Like Your Own Home," *The New York Times Magazine*, November 21, 1976.

67. *Doe v. Commonwealth's Attorney for City of Richmond*, 403 F. Supp. 1199 (1975).

68. See page 173 of the text for an explanation of the Eisenstadt decision.

69. Information on employment derived principally from E. Carrington Boggan, et al., *The Rights of Gay People* (New York: Avon, 1975).

70. *McConnell v. Anderson*, 451 F. 2d 193 (8th Cir., 1971).

71. *Boutilier v. Immigration and Naturalization Service*, 387 U.S. 118 (1967).

72. *Baker v. Nelson*, 291 Minn. 310, 191 N.W. 2d 185 (1971).

73. *Jones v. Hallahan*, 501 S.W. 2d 588 (Ky. App. 1973).

74. *Isaacson v. Isaacson*, No. D. 36867, Supr. Ct. Washington for King County (Dec. 22, 1972).

75. *A. v. A.*, 514 P. 2d 358 (Ore. App. 1973).

76. Marilyn Riley, "The Lesbian Mother," *San Diego Law Review*, Vol. 12 (July 1975).

77. Frederick E. Bidgood, "Sexuality and the Handicapped," quoted by permission from the *SIECUS Report*, 1976 Special Issue on the Handicapped. Copyright © Sex Information and Education Council of the U.S., Inc. Hempstead, N.Y.

78. "How to End Sex Problems in Our Prisons," *Ebony*, November 1976, p. 87.

79. Richard G. Singer and William P. Statsky, *Rights of the Imprisoned* (Indianapolis: Bobbs-Merrill Co., 1974), p. 566.

80. Patricia Wald in Bruce J. Ennis and Paul R. Friedman, eds., *The Mentally Retarded Citizen and the Law* (New York: Practicing Law Institute, 1973), II, 1045-46. Used by permission of Patricia M. Wald.

81. Robert Farmer, *The Rights of the Mentally Ill* (New York: Arco, 1967), p. 58.

82. Personal communication with David F. Addlestone, litigation director of the National Discharge Review Project at the Georgetown University Law Center.

83. Susan Brownmiller, *Against Our Will: Men, Women and Rape* (New York: Simon & Schuster, 1975), p. 104.

84. Ibid., p. 25.

85. *In Order to Establish Justice*, 1975. Available from Office of Church Life and Leadership, Box 179, St. Louis, Missouri 63166.

86. Rose K. Goldsen, "Toys and the Imagination of Children," *Human Behavior*, December 1976, p. 19.

87. Dr. Leon Kass, "Babies by Means of In Vitro Fertilization: Unethical Experiments on the Unborn," *New England Journal of Medicine*, Vol. 285 (1971), p. 1175.

88. George Annas and Aubrey Milunsky, *Genetics and the Law* (New York: Plenum Publishing Corp., 1976), pp. 366-67.

89. Robert Edwards in Richard Restak, *Premeditated Man: Bioethics and the Control of Future Human Life* (New York: Viking Press, 1975), p. 59.

90. Jones F. Bonner in Paul Ramsey, *Fabricated Man: The Ethics of Genetic Control* (New Haven: Yale University Press, 1970), p. 65.

91. Bernard Häring, *Manipulation: Ethical Boundaries of Medical, Behavioral and Genetic Manipulation* (Middlegreen, Slough [U.K.]: St. Paul Publications, 1975), p. 64.

92. Herman J. Muller, *Man's Future Birthright* (Albany: State University of New York Press, 1973), p. 135.

93. "Mixed Singles," *New Times*, October 1, 1976, p. 41.

94. *B. v. B.*, 78 Misc. 2d 112; 355 N.Y.S. 2d 712 (1974).

95. Harry Benjamin in Boggan, op. cit., p. 152.

96. Paul Bohannan, ed., *Divorce and After* (Garden City: Doubleday, 1971), p. 25.

CHAPTER 6: SOME PERSPECTIVES ON SEX EDUCATION

1. Patricia Schiller, *Creative Approach to Sex Education and Counseling* (New York: Association Press, 1973), p. 22. Used by permission.

2. Sol Gordon, *Let's Make Sex a Household Word: A Guide for Parents and Teachers* (New York: John Day Company, 1975), p. 153.

3. Thomas F. Stanton, "Sex Education for Adolescents" in *Understanding Adolescence*, ed. James F. Adams (Boston: Allyn and Bacon, Inc., 1968), p. 267. Copyright © 1968 by Allyn and Bacon, Inc. and used by permission.

4. Bruno Bettelheim in Gordon, op. cit., p. 160.

5. William Simon, "Sex," *Psychology Today*, 1969, p. 25.

6. From *Values in Sexuality: A New Approach to Sex Education* by Eleanor S. Morrison and Mila Underhill Price, copyright 1974 Hart Publishing Company, Inc., p. 10. Used by permission.

7. Sex Education Committee: New York State Coalition for Family Planning, *Sex Education: A Critical Concern* (Planned Parenthood of New York City, Inc., 1975), p. 3.

8. Ibid., p. 4.

9. Ibid.

10. Sylvia Jacobson, "Sex Education: A Community Project," *Journal of Research and Development in Education*, Vol. 10, No. 1 (Fall 1976), p. 24. Used by permission.

11. Burt Saxon, "Our First Five Years: Sex Education at Lee High School," *Journal of Research and Development in Education*, Vol. 10, No. 1 (Fall 1976), p. 31. Used by permission.

12. Lester A. Kirkendall, *Sex Education as Human Relations* (New York: Inor Publishing Co., 1950), p. 159.

13. Morrison and Price, op. cit., p. 9.

14. Sex Education Committee: New York State Coalition for Family Planning, op. cit., p. 33.

15. Schiller, op. cit., p. 222f.

16. Saxon, op. cit., p. 33.

17. Derek L. Burleson, "Guidelines for Selecting Instructional Materials in Sex Education," *Journal of Research and Development in Education*, Vol. 10, No. 1 (Fall 1976), pp. 80f. Used by permission.

18. Schiller, op. cit., p. 26.

19. Joshua S. Golden, Margaret Golden, Susan Price, and Anna Heinich, "The Sexual Problems of Family Planning Clinic Patients as Viewed by the Patients and Staff," *Family Planning Perspectives*, Vol. 9, No. 1 (January/February 1977), p. 26.

CHAPTER 7: THE COMMUNITY OF FAITH AND HUMAN SEXUALITY

1. Included in these statistics are congregations in the Central Atlantic, Florida, Illinois, Kansas-Oklahoma, Massachusetts, Minnesota, Nebraska, Ohio, Penn Central, and South Central conferences of the United Church of Christ.

2. From *The Body, A Study in Pauline Theology* by John A.T. Robinson (London: SCM Press, 1952), pp. 8f. Distributed in the USA by Alec R. Allenson, Inc., Naperville, Illinois. Used by permission.

3. Ibid., p. 9.

4. James B. Nelson, "Reconciliation: The Body of Christ and the Human Body," *Theological Markings*, Spring 1974, p. 25. Used by permission.

5. Walter E. Brueggemann, "The Covenanted Family: A Zone for Humanness," *Journal of Current Social Issues*, Winter 1977, p. 18. Used by permission.

6. William T. Parsons, oral presentation at consultation on United Church of Christ history sponsored by the United Church Board for Homeland Ministries, January 1975, Philadelphia, Pa.

7. Brueggemann, op. cit., p. 20.

8. From *Will Our Children Have Faith?* by John H. Westerhoff III,

pp. 59f. Copyright © 1976 by The Seabury Press, Inc. Used by permission of the publisher.

9. Ibid., pp. 58f.

10. Jeanne Audrey Powers in article by Karen Peterson, Van Nuys, California *Valley News*, April 28, 1977.

11. United Methodist Church, Northern California/Nevada Single Adult Task Force. Used by permission.

12. Letty M. Russell, ed., *The Liberating Word: A Guide to Non-sexist Interpretation of the Bible* (Philadephia: Westminster Press, 1976), p. 16.

13. Peggy Way, Memorandum for Sexuality Study, January 1977.

14. Eleanor Morrison, memorandum for Sexuality Study, July 1976.

15. Way, op. cit.

Bibliography

About Your Sexuality. Unitarian Universalist Association, 25 Beacon Street, Boston, Massachusetts 02108, 1971. Extensive, expensive, comprehensive, explicit book-filmstrip program. Offers no Christian guidance. Lovingly frank. Needs good leader (s) . Real help for youth but really loaded.

Charles Birch and Paul Albrecht, eds., *Genetics and the Quality of Life*. Elmsford, N.Y.: Pergamon Press, 1976. 232 pages (paper) . Developed from World Council of Churches analysis of ethical issues related to genetic experimentation. Review of the issues and literature.

The Boston Women's Health Collective, *Our Bodies, Ourselves*. New

York: Simon & Schuster, 2d ed., 1976. 383 pages (paper). Remark-able review of health issues from a feminist perspective. Sections on anatomy, sexuality, relationships, abortion, pregnancy, and birth provide vital self-understanding and basic information and under-standing.

Susan Brownmiller, *Against Our Will: Men, Women and Rape*. New York: Simon & Schuster, 1975. 472 pages (paper). Major study of the history of rape. The thesis is that rape is less an isolated "sex" crime than a social institution, a political and social crime against women as such.

Christians and the Meaning of Sexuality, packet for senior-highs and their parents, prepared by Board of Discipleship, United Methodist Church, Nashville, Tennessee 37202, 1971. Available from Cokesbury Bookstores. Several booklets intended for group study with a student's book (*Youth Views Sexuality* by Ellis B. Johnson) for individual use. Solid Christian perspective. Not as explicit, comprehensive, or as expensive as *About Your Sexuality*.

Alex Comfort, *The Joy of Sex: A Gourmet Guide to Love Making*. New York: Simon & Schuster, 1972. 253 pages (paper). Explicit, tender, comprehensive guide to sexual expression. The drawings are intimate, affirming, revealing, encouraging. Emphasis upon technique, with a concern for mutuality.

Sally Gearhart and William R. Johnson, eds., *Loving Women—Loving Men: Gay Liberation and the Church*. San Francisco: Glide Publica-tions, 1974. 165 pages (paper). A lesbian and a gay man reflect upon their experiences with the church. The book conveys the dynamic of the gay liberation movement and introduces gay perspectives on the life of the church and on biblical understanding.

Bruce Henderson, *Human Sexuality: An Age of Ambiguity*, ed. John Gagnon. Boston: Little, Brown & Co., 1975. 65 pages (paper). Gagnon was part of the Kinsey Institute, and the booklet reviews cultural and research findings that provide a perspective on contemporary under-standings of sexuality, sexual expression, and orientation.

Richard Hettlinger, *Sex Isn't That Simple: The New Sexuality on Campus*. New York: Seabury Press, 1974. 185 pages (paper). Written by a college chaplain. Insightful analysis of changing sexual values and the complexity of sexual decisions. Has useful appendixes that contain information on birth control, abortion, and venereal disease.

Shere Hite, *The Hite Report: A Nationwide Study on Female Sexuality*. New York: Macmillan, 1976. 638 pages (paper). Analysis of 3,000 women and their sexual experiences. Hite gives a number of quota-tions that indicate women's perceptions and approaches to sexual expression. Somewhat sensational. Does not represent a scientific sample.

Human Sexuality: New Directions in American Catholic Thought. New York: Paulist Press, 1977. 322 pages. Report of a study commissioned by the Catholic Theological Society of America and given no official standing by the Roman Catholic Church. Reviews biblical, historical, theological, and empirical material but places heavy emphasis upon the pastoral dimensions of sexuality.

Herant A. Katchadourian and Donald T. Lunde, *Fundamentals of Human Sexuality*. New York: Holt, Rinehart & Winston, 1972. 514 pages (paper). Prepared as a textbook for college classes. Has comprehensive sections on biology, anatomy, sexual behavior, and cultural expressions of the erotic. Brief treatment of legal and moral issues.

Eleanor E. Maccoby and Carol N. Jacklin, *The Psychology of Sex Differences*. Stanford, Calif.: Stanford University Press, 1974. 634 pages. Definitive survey of research findings on sex roles and sex differentiation. Maccoby pioneered in this field. Concluding chapter is a succinct summary of the findings.

David R. Mace, *The Christian Response to the Sexual Revolution*. Nashville: Abingdon Press, 1970. 142 pages (paper). Readable but brief review of the treatment of sex in the Bible and in the Christian tradition. Includes some proposals for a Christian response to contemporary trends in sexuality.

John J. McNeill, *The Church and the Homosexual*. Mission, Kans.: Sheed Andrews & McMeel, 1976. 211 pages. McNeill, a Jesuit, struggled for several years before these writings could be published with an imprimatur. Positive view of homosexuality that summarizes biblical, theological, and psychological studies of homosexuality.

Del Martin, *Battered Wives*. San Francisco: Glide Publications, 1976. 269 pages (paper). Provides perspective and documentation on the mistreatment and brutality directed against women by their spouses. Something of a tract, it is a pioneering vista on a phenomenon of growing consequence in American life.

Rollo May, *Love and Will*. New York: W. W. Norton, 1969. 352 pages (paper). Analysis of the nature of love and the place of will in loving. Has major sections on sexuality and sexual love. Reflects May's extensive psychiatric practice and his Christian insights.

John Money and Anke A. Ehrhardt. *Man and Woman, Boy and Girl*. Baltimore: Johns Hopkins Press, 1973. 325 pages (paper). A pioneering work in the effort to develop a theory of psychosexual development based upon research in chromosomal and hormonal changes. The book is somewhat technical and concentrates on somewhat abnormal illustrations. Money is the ranking expert in the field.

Edmund S. Morgan, ed., *The Puritan Family: Religion and Domestic Relations in Seventeenth-Century New England*. New York: Harper & Row, 1966. 196 pages (paper). A historical statement of the development and character of the Puritan family.

Eleanor S. Morrison and Vera Borosage, eds., *Human Sexuality: Contemporary Perspectives*. Palo Alto, Calif.: Mayfield Publishing Co., 2d ed., 1977. 504 pages (paper). A thorough review of the territory. Prepared for use in college courses. Three dozen essays by different authors.

W. Dwight Oberholtzer, ed., *Is Gay Good: Ethics, Theology, and Homosexuality*. Philadelphia: Westminster Press, 1971. 288 pages (paper). A series of essays on various perspectives related to homosexuality.

Joseph H. Pleck and Jack Sawyer, eds., *Men and Masculinity*. Englewood Cliffs, N.J.: Prentice-Hall, 1974. 184 pages (paper). A series of essays that analyze growing up male. Examines the relationships of men with women, children, and one another as well as with work and society. Has a concluding section on the men's liberation agenda. A variety of authors present material, often with a highly existential flavor.

W. Norman Pittenger, *Making Sexuality Human*. Philadelphia: United Church Press, 1970. 96 pages. Highly readable theological-ethical statement on human sexuality by a British theologian who has given a great deal of attention to the subject. A helpful overview.

Rosemary Radford Ruether, *New Woman—New Earth: Sexist Ideologies and Human Liberation*. New York: Seabury Press, 1975. 221 pages. Provides a vigorous historical and theological analysis of woman as viewed in Christian history. Carefully documented. Suggests new possibilities for being woman and being woman in relation to man if sexist ideologies are confronted and overcome.

Letty M. Russell, ed., *The Liberating Word: A Guide to Non-sexist Interpretation of the Bible*. Philadelphia: Westminster Press, 1976. 121 pages (paper). Prepared to help persons understand sexism in biblical text and translation, the book provides important insights into the patriarchal nature of biblical religion and offers alternative understandings.

Thomas A. Shannon, ed., *Readings in Bioethics: Basic Writings on the Key Ethical Questions That Surround the Major, Modern Biological Possibilities and Problems*. New York: Paulist-Newman Press, 1976. 513 pages (paper). A series of essays by different authors on ethical issues in the field of biology and related sciences. The perspective is predominantly Roman Catholic but extremely progressive. The sections on abortion, research and human experimentation, and genetic engineering have the most relevance to the sexuality study.

June Singer, *Androgyny: Toward a New Theory of Sexuality*. Garden City, N.Y.: Anchor Press/Doubleday, 1976. 375 pages. The author develops an understanding of androgyny with extensive insights from Western and Eastern religion and literature. She seeks to construct a theory of the meaning of androgyny as an approach to life and the future.

Lewis B. Smedes, *Sex for Christians*. Grand Rapids, Mich.: William B. Eerdmans, 1976. 250 pages (paper). A positive approach to sexuality written in popular form by a conservative Christian theologian.

Ralph W. Weltge, ed., *The Same Sex: An Appraisal of Homosexuality*. Philadelphia: United Church Press, 1969. 164 pages (paper). The book was a landmark when published in 1969, partly because it presented views of the homophile community by gay persons themselves. A series of essays that deal with the phenomenon of homosexuality and that provide ethical and legal perspectives on it and on gay persons.